Hand, Head and Heart

Samuel Carter Hall and *The Art Journal*

We are wearied, hand, head and heart, . . .
A more irksome task than that of criticism . . .
can hardly be undertaken by a writer of generous
sentiments, emotions and sympathies.

SAMUEL CARTER HALL
in The Art Union, June 1845

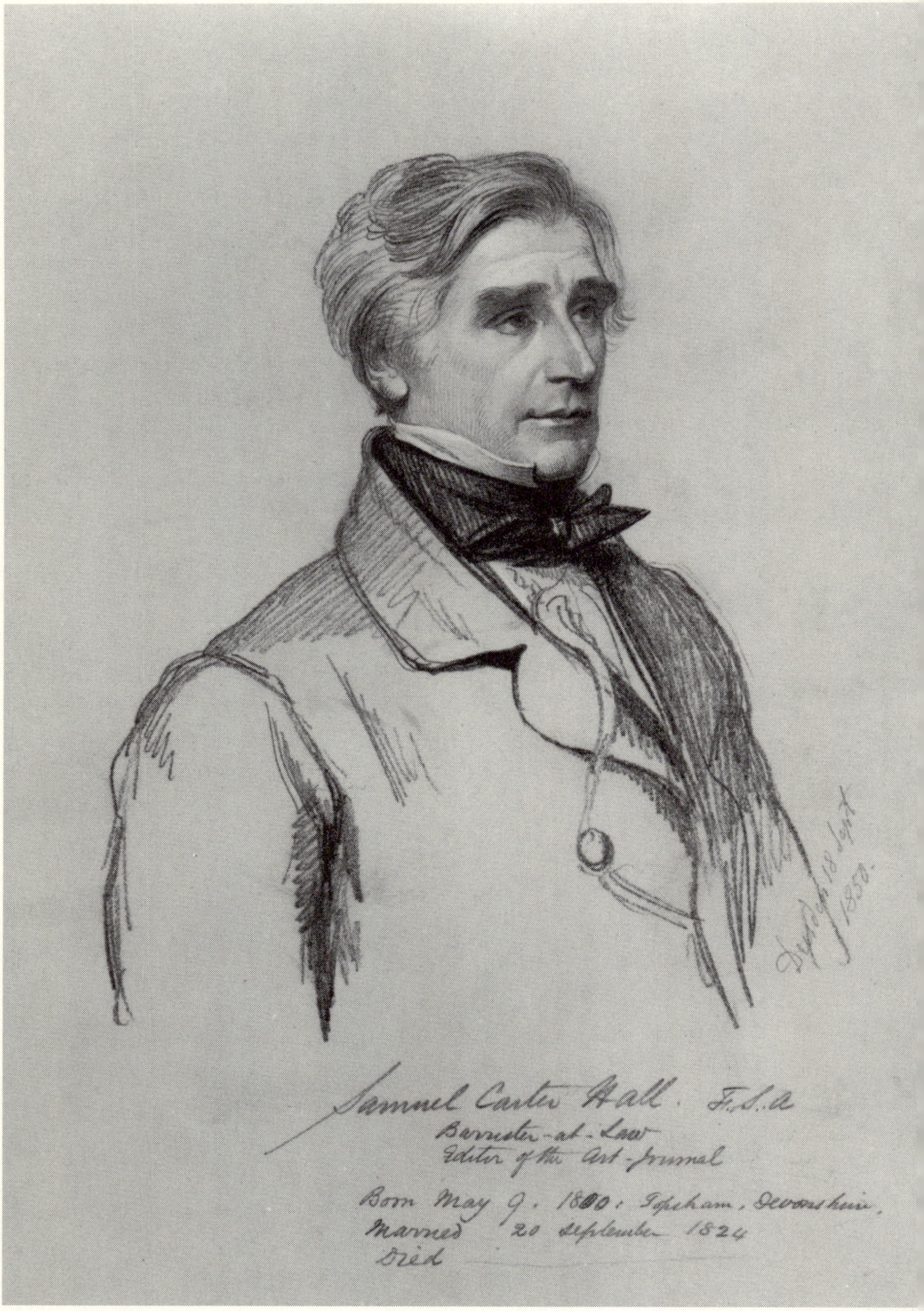

Carl Christian Vogel von Vogelstein, *Samuel Carter Hall*

Hand, Head and Heart

Samuel Carter Hall and *The Art Journal*

HAZEL MORRIS

MICHAEL RUSSELL

First published in Great Britain 2002
by Michael Russell (Publishing) Ltd
Wilby Hall, Wilby, Norwich NR16 2JP

Typeset in Sabon by Waveney Typesetters
Wymondham, Norfolk
Printed and bound in Great Britain
by Biddles Ltd, Guildford and King's Lynn

ISBN 0 85955 273 X

Contents

List of Illustrations

BETWEEN PAGES 160 & 161

Acknowledgements

I should like to express my thanks to the following for their help during the course of my research: the Archivist of the Royal Academy of Arts; the staff of the Boston Public Library Rare Books Department; of the Boole Library, University College, Cork; of Cork City Library; of the Department of Special Collections, Glasgow University; of the Archives Department, Hertfordshire County Council; of the University of Iowa Libraries; of the National Library of Ireland; and, in particular, to the staff of Cambridge University Library for their help over a number of years.

I am grateful to the State Art Gallery, Dresden for the reproduction of the drawing of S. C. Hall by Carl Christian Vogel von Vogelstein; to the photographic department of Cambridge University Library for the photographs from books in the Library collection; to the Department of Libraries and Theatres, Manchester Central Library for the photograph of the Art Treasures Exhibition; to Chertsey Museum, Surrey for the photograph of the watercolour of Anna Maria Hall, and to Mme Barrère for her kindness in allowing me to take photographs of West Stow Hall.

Acknowledgements

1

England's First Journal of Art

'I had to create a public for art,' Samuel Carter Hall wrote in his memoir in 1883.[1] Few people would have made the claim, and with such aplomb, but Hall was a man very conscious of his achievements. He was writing about the foundation of *The Art Union* (later to become *The Art Journal*), a publication that today is such a valuable source of information about the art world of the nineteenth century. A public for art there undoubtedly was by the 1880s, as could be seen in the crowded rooms of new private galleries, and from Whistler's complaint that 'art was upon the town' and was becoming 'a sort of common topic for the tea-table'. How far Hall was justified in making his claim, the following chapters will I hope make clear.

During a dinner party at the house of Richard Hodgson (of the print publishers Hodgson and Graves), Charles Landseer, elder brother of Edwin Landseer, expressed a regret that there was no periodical publication representing the arts in England nor, for that matter, in Europe. There were some periodicals in Paris, but they included acting, music and dance. Hodgson was enthusiastic about the idea and offered to put up the capital for a journal of art if Hall would edit it. Hall consented, on condition that the proprietors would not interfere in any way with his duties as editor, and never require him to publish a single line of which he did not approve. Hall was always to have complete confidence that he was publishing all shades of public opinion and taste in art. He allowed no interference in the editing of *The Art Journal*, nor in the other periodicals which he conducted during his life. We find him writing in 1878 to a would-be contributor to *Social Notes* (the periodical that involved him in three lawsuits): 'Lord Townshend [Marquess Townshend, the proprietor] is not the Editor ... I must be the judge of what ought to be, and must be done, in the conduct of the publication for which I am responsible.'

The first number of *The Art Union* appeared on 15 February 1839. It consisted of eighteen pages and was priced 8d. In the introduction the editor remarked on the fact that nearly every profession except the artist's had an organ by which it might be justly represented. The object of the journal, he went on, was 'to supply to artists accurate and useful information upon all subjects in which they are interested, and to the public the means of justly ascertaining and estimating the Progress of Art both at Home and Abroad'.

The issue of 13 August had an article on 'The Present State of the Fine Arts in Great Britain' which seems to bear the stamp of Hall's authorship. It stated that during the French Revolution when property was insecure 'many works of art were clandestinely exported from Italy, Holland and Spain to agents in this country which, in a short time, created a class of dealers whose interest it was to decry everything English and enhance, by every means of description, the importations of foreign art'. Hall's championship of British art had begun.

The partnership with Hodgson did not last long. At the end of the first year Hall objected that while he was away a review of David Roberts's collection of drawings in the Holy Land and Egypt, which had been approved by him, had been removed and another inserted in its place. Hall paid Hodgson £200 (for Hall a substantial sum) and became the sole proprietor and editor of *The Art Union*.

The prospects were not encouraging: British art was at low ebb. Constable was more appreciated on the Continent than he was in England, Sir David Wilkie was growing old and William Etty's sensual and glowing nudes upset many Victorians who could only accept such freedom in old masters. The Classical Revival was not to take place until the 1860s; John Ruskin had not yet sprung to Turner's defence and the exposition of his art in *Modern Painters*. Ten years were to elapse before Rossetti was to add 'P.R.B.' to his signature. Even established artists found only subsistence for their art, and many survived by giving lessons. Sculptors were even worse off.

The Royal Academy had its annual exhibition in the east wing of the recently completed National Gallery in Trafalgar Square. There had been admission charges since the first exhibition in the old rooms, not only for financial reasons, but as its first President said, 'to prevent the room being filled by improper persons, to the entire exclusion of those for whom the Exhibition is apparently intended'.[2] The Watercolour Society held its first exhibition in April 1805 with an admission fee of one shilling, catalogue included. In the same year the British Institution held its first exhibition 'for the sale of the production of British artists, to excite the emulation and exertion of young artists by premiums'. In 1842 the premiums ceased. The Society of British Artists held its first exhibition in Suffolk Street in 1824. Its members were warned 'to go hand in hand with the Royal Academy'.

These exhibitions were frequented by the educated and well-to-do middle classes, but not by the masses of people who knew little about the subject of art and who, anyway, could not afford the admission fee. Hall, like many Victorians, probably had a sense of mission where education was concerned. His first object was to conduct a journal which would awake an interest in art in all classes of society. His second object was to help British artists, and many an unknown artist was grateful for the promotion of his work in *The Art Journal*. In the first number he wrote:

> Our estimate of British art is, indeed, high; too high perhaps, for those who overrate ancient productions, and value a picture, as they do wine, in proportion to its age. We take it to be indisputable that the artists of Great Britain greatly surpass the existing artists of any nation.

Hall, however, was also a sound business man, and never allowed his personal opinions to interfere with the editing of the journal. The market was flooded with periodicals (though there were few writers on art). Hall had edited other journals, and knew only too well how seemingly popular ones could lose their appeal.

Not surprisingly, the first numbers of *The Art Union* were sparsely illustrated, for Hall had very little capital. Prints were becoming more and more popular. The process of mezzotinting and engraving on steel had been invented in 1823, and Turner and Constable welcomed the medium as suitable for their works. Some artists tried publishing their own plates, but by the 1840s print publishers were in control and played an important part in the world of art. Engraving rights often exceeded the value of the picture itself.

In 1834 Thomas Kibble Hervey published *Illustrations of Modern Sculpture*, a series of engravings accompanied by descriptive prose and illustrative poetry. Hervey was a poet and editor whose poem 'Australia' and other poems like it had a considerable vogue. He was a voracious reader of everything except, it seems, the law, which he went to Cambridge to read but left the university after two years without a degree. He became editor of *The Athenaeum* in 1846, and was respected as a sound, if sometimes caustic, critic of art and literature.[3] *Illustrations of Modern Sculpture* was not a success. The plates are engravings of the works, among others, of such sculptors as Canova, Westmacott, Chantry and Baily.

In 1843 Hall bought Hervey's plates and ventured on the issue of them in *The Art Union*. 'I had numerous warnings that I was ruining the publication; and not once, but several times, a plate of semi-nude figures torn through, was sent to me by post, with protest against such attempts to introduce "indecencies" into families.'[4] The first engraving, *The Dancing Girl Reposing* by Canova, was published in *The Art Union* in February 1847 with *Maternal Love* by E. H. Baily, *Resignation* by Francis Chantry, *Prometheus* by Samuel Manning the Younger, *The Sleeping Children* by Chantry, and *The Distressed Mother* by Richard Westmacott appearing in the following months. The other plates in Hervey's work were afterwards published as *The Sculpture Gallery: a series of 81 Engravings accompanied with Descriptive Prose and Illustrative Poetry by S. C. Hall, T. K. Hervey Esq and other living authors, 1849–54*. There is a historical and critical essay on sculpture, a description of each piece of sculpture and details of where the original sculpture was exhibited. In some cases the then whereabouts of the sculpture is given.

Hall was careful in his choice of the first sculpture plates. Who could be offended by the subject of innocent children and exemplary mothers? E. H. Baily had a large practice in portrait studies, busts and monuments, but he preferred domestic to classical subjects and *Maternal Love* was typical of what he was producing. Chantry's *Resignation* shows the artist's love of simple broad lines. Hall also produced an engraving of Chantry's *Sleeping Children* which had been immensely popular when it was exhibited at the Royal Academy in 1817.[5] The treatment is naturalistic, and the children appear relaxed in sleep rather than cold in death (one holding a bunch of snowdrops was thought to be very poetic). *The Distressed Mother* by Richard Westmacott was a slightly different version of the theme of motherhood. It was an attempt by Westmacott at a modern approach. The mother sits by a roadside cradling her child in her arms. This is not a fallen woman, such as the Pre-Raphaelite painters were later to portray, but a virtuous mother fallen on hard times. Her bare feet and breast are both a concession to the antique and an indication of her poverty. Westmacott, in a letter to T. K. Hervey, said it was designed to represent an exhausted female sitting with her infant in her arms and pack at her feet on a wearisome journey, and that this was a reference to the benevolent disposition and character of Mrs Warren (widow of the Bishop of Bangor) in whose memory the monument was erected. The connection between the woman, however virtuous, and Mrs Warren is a little obscure.[6]

The ten years from 1839 to 1849 were very difficult ones for Hall. He was working on his three volumes of *Ireland: Its Scenery, Character, etc.* which necessitated five tours over there, followed by his architectural work *The Baronial Halls and Picturesque Edifices of England*. *The Art Union*, meanwhile, was not covering its expenses. Torn between his desire for independence and a realistic view of the finances of the journal, Hall decided to sell his share to George Virtue, the man whom Henry Curwen regarded as 'the first Art Publisher of his time'.[7] *The Art Union* became *The Art Journal* in 1849 with Virtue as its proprietor and publisher and, in 1851, with Samuel Carter Hall as its editor on an annual salary of £600. This, however, was all in the future.

2

The Athens of Ireland

Samuel Carter Hall says in his *Retrospect of a Long Life* that he was born at Geneva Barracks, County Waterford on 9 May 1800.[1] The Halls were a Devonshire family and his father, Colonel Robert Hall, lived in the Manor House at Topsham. He married Ann Kent, who came from Ottery St Mary, on 6 April 1790. Colonel Hall raised a regiment in 1794 for service within Great Britain and Ireland – the Devon and Cornwall Fencibles – and soon was ordered to Ireland. It was while Colonel Hall was quartered at Geneva Barracks that Samuel Carter was born.

New Geneva was on a site of about twelve acres, enclosed by a high stone wall with flanking towers at the angles, intended for a colony of watchmakers and intellectuals from Geneva.[2] The enterprise was not a success; the colonists demanded too many privileges which it was not thought suitable to grant and in May 1784 they returned home. In the following year, in place of the university that would attract scholars from all over Europe, an army barracks was built. Geneva Barracks, as it was called, acquired some notoriety for its use as a prison during the 1798 rebellion, housing men for transfer to a guardship at nearby Passage East. Little remains today except the surrounding walls and a farmhouse which may possibly have been part of the barracks. The regiment was recalled to England in 1802 and disbanded after the Treaty of Amiens.

Robert Hall had twelve children, the three youngest being born in Ireland. These three were William Sandford, Robert Revis and Samuel Carter. William Sandford, who was born in Cork in 1795, later established a mechanics institute in the city. Robert Revis had a colourful career. He fought with the Greeks against the Turks, was a leader in the Mexican War of Independence and finally died off the Cape of Good Hope where it was thought that he fell overboard and was eaten by a shark.

Having such a large family to support, it seems that Colonel

Robert Hall decided he could best do this by returning to Ireland. Between 1815 and 1820 he invested money in mines in County Kerry and West Cork. Of the thirteen mines that he opened, the most important was on Ross Island, Lough Leane, Killarney, from which copper was obtained to the value of £100,000, but which ended in disaster when the mine was flooded. His efforts to lease a cobalt mine from Colonel Herbert at Muckross, Killarney, were initially thwarted by the Colonel's objection that the mine was in sight of the house, but finally the lease was granted. Cobalt was a costly mineral, and after a time a cheaper substitute was discovered and came into general use, except for the finer and more expensive pieces of Staffordshire ware. The mine at Muckross ceased to be worth working.

Samuel Carter (or Carter as his friends called him, and the name which will be used in the following chapters) was strangely reticent about his boyhood in Ireland, though he wrote and talked about the country all through his adult life. He says that they lived in Glandore on the coast of Cork, but later they seem to have moved to Cork City. Carter's mother must have found it necessary to supplement the family income, for he says in his memoirs that she ran a business in Cork.[3] Unfortunately he does not specify what sort of business; it is unlikely to have been very big and there is no further mention of it.

Samuel Carter spent the formative years of his life in a city of intellectual and cultural renown. The prosperity of Cork had increased during the Napoleonic Wars, and its citizens were strong protagonists of the 1800 Act of Union, hoping that free trade with England would bring further wealth. A library was established, and the year 1807 saw the foundation of the Royal Cork Institute, the focus of the city's intellectual life, itself a galaxy of talent. In 1816 a Society for Promoting the Fine Arts was formed, and in 1818 the city was presented with casts of famous antique sculptures, originally presented by Pope Pius II to George IV and now given to Cork at the instigation of Lord Ennismore, a distinguished patron of the arts whose collection of paintings at Convamore, between Fermoy and Mallow, was famous.[4]

The literary life of this 'Athens of Ireland', as the city was called, centred on Bolster's Bookshop in Patrick Street where famous visitors, such as Sir Walter Scott, were brought.[5] Here Samuel Carter would have met his friends, men who were to achieve artistic and literary fame. Writing about the people of Cork Thackeray said:

> A stranger too must remark the extraordinary degree of literary taste and talent amongst them, and the wit and vivacity of their conversation. The love for literature seems to an Englishman doubly curious, the citizens are the most book-loving men I ever met ... I think in walking the streets every Englishman must remark that the superiority in intelligence is here, and not with us.[6]

Among them were Daniel Maclise, who later made some charming drawings of Carter's wife; John Hogan the sculptor; the poets Jeremiah Callanan and John Augustus Shea; Francis Mahony, to become famous in *Fraser's Magazine* for his monthly series 'The Works of Father Prout'; William Maginn; and Thomas Crofton Croker who published *The Fairy Legends and Traditions of the South of Ireland* anonymously in 1825. The last two were to play important parts in Carter's life.

William Maginn was born in Cork in 1793 where his father was an eminent headmaster of a private school. He graduated from Trinity College, Dublin in 1811 and obtained an LLB from that University in 1819. Under the name of Crossman, he began to write articles on the classics for the *Literary Gazette*, a paper very much esteemed in Cork, and to send literary contributions to *Blackwood's Magazine*, some in his own name. William Jerdan, the editor of the *Gazette* described him as 'romanticist, parodist, politician, satirist, linguist, poet, critic, scholar – pre-eminent in all and in the last all but universal'.[7] E. V. Kenealy, his biographer, in a letter to Carter, said: 'He was I really think our greatest literary man since Swift.'[8] He could entertain on any number of topics and thought that conversation should be useful rather than gaudy. He described himself as 'a randy, bandy, brandy, no Dandy, rollicking jig of an Irishman'.[9]

The Cork Philosophical Society, which was founded in 1813, met once a week during one season of the year and also held debates. Maginn was never a speaker (he had a slight impediment), but helped in the debates. Carter belonged to a rival similar society and its members, whom Maginn dubbed 'the Prigs', became targets for Maginn's jibes in *Blackwood's* and the *Literary Gazette*. According to Carter, a paper war continued for some time until, in 1820, he wrote *The Talents* (the name he gave to Maginn and his friends), attacking them in what in old age he called a 'poetical folly'.[10]

The Talents, a dramatic sketch, is set in Best's Hotel, Patrick Street, where the members of the Philosophical and Literary Society spent many convivial evenings. The Dramatis Personae, eight in number, are the real members with their names thinly disguised, with Maginn and a surgeon named Gosnell the main characters. Maginn opens the scene with the lines:

> Again I tread upon Dissention's ground,
> And still the wheel of Sisyphus turns round:
> Still must a Hydra head be lopt,
> Still must another Ass's ear be cropt.

The poem continues in this vein with Maginn welcoming and describing each friend, and bidding the company 'Come fill your bowls and we will have a toast, "Perdition catch the Prigs".' Some of the footnotes are very near the bone and no doubt these rather than the satirical jingle itself (which ends with the friends staggering home at daybreak) gave rise to the hostility which Carter encountered. He had made many friends, but enemies too. It was time to go and, like so many young men of talent, he decided to leave Ireland and make his way to London.

Before he finally went to England, Carter spent some time in Dublin. Though the Act of Union of 1800 was to be a matter of political controversy during the whole of the nineteenth century, ostensibly the immediate changes resulting from the Union appeared small. The Union did not emancipate the Catholics, and the Protestant Ascendancy, looking to the Union as a protection, continued. All his life Carter was to preach the benefits derived from the Union. The re-telling of history with widely divergent interpretations was a feature of intellectual life. Despite the Union, Dublin was still a prosperous city, though with great differences between rich and poor. Social life reflected that of London, with entertaining in the splendid eighteenth-century houses and 'drawing rooms' at the Castle during the Season, which took place before the London

Season. It was in this society that Carter was to be entertained by Sydney, Lady Morgan.

Sydney Owenson (as she was born) says in her memoirs that she was the great-granddaughter of Sir Maltby Crofton of Longford House, County Sligo.[11] Her father, Robert, who became an actor, was the son of a *mésalliance* of her grandmother with a feckless local farmer. Sydney Owenson's literary success dates from 1806 when she wrote *The Wild Irish Girl*. It pleaded against the wrongs which she passionately believed the people were subjected to, and gave detailed descriptions of Celtic dress and ancient Irish customs which she wrapped up in a vivid romantic story set in a mouldering castle. The character of Glorvina, the Princess of the Castle, was always identified with Lady Morgan herself.

The Marquess and Marchioness of Abercorn were charmed by Sydney Owenson and proposed that she should spend part of the year with them in Ireland at Barons Court or in England at Stanmore Priory, and it was through the Abercorns that she met, and married, their family physician, Charles Morgan (later knighted). Lady Morgan soon became a leader in the literary society of Dublin and gave weekly parties in her house in Kildare Street. To one of these parties, just before he went to London, Carter was invited, and in later life he was to express some gratitude to Lady Morgan. When he left her house he had in his pocket a letter of introduction to Henry Colburn, one of the foremost literary publishers in London.

3
The Magazines

To Anthony Trollope, a young man leaving Ireland and arriving in London with high aspirations was a familiar figure and the one he portrays in his novel *Phineas Finn*. Carter's circumstances were very similar to those of Phineas, although set some forty years earlier. Phineas, aged twenty-two, came to read law and, like Carter, had a small allowance from his father. He belonged (as Carter had) to debating clubs in Ireland. Like Phineas, Carter had 'already done a little for the magazines'.

Thomas Crofton Croker was always ready to help promising young men arriving from Ireland. He himself, on his arrival in London, had obtained a clerkship in the Admiralty through the influence of John Wilson Croker.[1] He married Marianne, the daughter of the watercolourist Francis Nicholson. He was a keen antiquarian and an adequate painter, and was now preparing his *Fairy Legends and Traditions of the South of Ireland*. Carter evidently received much kindness and advice from Croker, and met many of the distinguished writers and artists of the day at his house. Meanwhile Lady Morgan's letter of introduction to Henry Colburn resulted in Carter's contributing to the *New Monthly Magazine* and other periodicals. Nevertheless, Carter often found himself short of money, and once even turned to Croker for help.

Friday morning, April 4th 1823

My dear Sir,

If it will not inconvenience you I should feel much obliged by your lending me two or three pounds for a few weeks, as the non publication of my essays in last weeks Musem [?] (which however are to appear in this) has put me out of my reckoning. Your leaving a note for me tomorrow morning with your servant enclosing the above, will materially oblige me; but I must entreat your pardon for this trespassing on your kindness.

In a postscript he adds, 'I have written to my father about the mines.'

The answer (enclosing two pounds) was immediate, if not enthusiastic.[2] This borrowing of money from an old Cork friend may seem surprising, but it should be remembered how vulnerable people in the professions were in the early part of the nineteenth century, and the number of bankruptcies that were reported in the newspapers of the time. Victoria Glendinning points out in her biography of Anthony Trollope that the Trollopes themselves accepted handouts when they had to.

At the end of 1822 Carter was introduced to the Italian patriot and poet Ugo Foscolo, and became his literary secretary. Foscolo had left Italy, embittered by the cession of Venice to Austria, and finally settled in England in 1816. He contributed to the *Edinburgh Review* and the *Quarterly Review*. According to Carter, Foscolo built 'Digamma Cottage' in Regent's Park, which he decorated and furnished on borrowed money that he had little hope of repaying. He lived grandly, and was waited on by three handsome young women, who were allowed to receive attentions only from him. (A secretary who followed Carter and breached this convention was challenged by Foscolo to a duel.) There was little work to do, and Carter did not remain long in this bizarre household.

In 1823 Carter became a parliamentary reporter in the old House of Commons with its cramped and ill-ventilated chamber. In 1824 he became a law student. His decision to settle to a profession (though he never actually practised after being called to the bar in 1841) was probably influenced by the fact of his marriage to Anna Maria Fielding on 20 September 1824.

Anna Maria, the daughter of Sarah and William Fielding, was born in Anne Street, Dublin on 6 January 1800. Sarah Fielding's mother, Anna Maria Earls, married George Carr of Bannow after Earls died. George Carr's mother was Frances, daughter of Nathaniel Boyse, and it was through her that Carr inherited the estate at Graige near Bannow, County Wexford. Carter says that his wife's grandmother, Anna Maria Earls, belonged to a Huguenot family that came to England and established a silk factory at Spitalfields. He went on to say that her father was killed in the Gordon Riots. He says that they were very proud of this ancestry and their name, the spelling of which he was unsure, was De Jaout of Renz en Champagne.[3]

Anna Maria Fielding was taken by her mother to live at Graige with the latter's stepfather, George Carr, when she was a few weeks old. Her childhood was spent in this Irish country house, visiting other houses of the local gentry, driving to church at Bannow, walking down to play at Ballyteige Bay and being taught by the local schoolmaster, whom she wrote about afterwards in her Irish sketches. There is scarcely anything left of Graige today except the remains of the large walled garden facing the bay, and a holy well surmounted by an ancient stone.[4] Bannow church is a ruin; it faces what was Bannow Island before the estuary silted up. The monument in the church to Anna Maria (died 1815) and George Carr (died 1824), restored by 'M. Carr and Anna Maria, wife of Mr S. C. Hall', can still be seen (though the inscription is barely legible). Carr died intestate, so although the young Anna Maria had been looked on as George Carr's adopted daughter and heiress, all the property went to Carr's nephew, Richard Boyse. Sarah and Anna Maria Fielding left Graige in 1815 after the death of Sarah's mother and went to live in London.

After their marriage, Carter and Anna Maria settled down in London, Carter as a member of the Inner Temple and dependent on contributions to various periodicals. Sarah Fielding, who by all accounts was a charming and accomplished woman, and to whom Carter was devoted, lived with them at 27, Ashley Place, Victoria. There was the disappointment over the expected inheritance from George Carr, who had died the year of their marriage, but Anna Maria soon started on a literary career of her own and they were both extremely hard-working. Her first recorded work, a sketch about her old Irish schoolmaster 'Master Benn', was published in the *Spirit and Manners of the Age* (which was edited by Carter) in January 1829. It was followed by a book of sketches in the same year, with a second series in 1831, and revised as *Popular Tales of Irish Life and Character* in 1842. These tales were immensely popular in England, but not in Ireland. They are romantic stories, peopled by a benevolent landlord class and a contented, sometimes comical, lower order of society, but told with affection and nostalgia for a much-loved country. Anna Maria prided herself on her unbiased opinions, but in her attempt not to offend either Protestant or Roman Catholic, she pleased neither. There is a long letter from her to Thomas Crofton Croker, attacking his review in the *Literary Gazette* of Charlotte Elizabeth Tonna's writing, in which Anna Maria considers that he should have singled her out as an impartial observer of Irish life.[5]

> I must say that you have forgotten that some Irish writers at all events have not fostered prejudices, and you have swept us all away ... I think I have some claims to be mentioned among Irish writers and it would do me a great injury to be left amongst those who have entered either the political or religious lists.[6]

In 1826 Carter founded and edited *The Amulet or Christian and Literary Remembrancer*. The preface to the annual shows how very wordy Carter could be, even by Victorian standards. More impressive was his commissioning of illustrations from established artists such as J. Ward, H. W. Pickersgill and Landseer. *The Amulet* lasted eleven years and then the publishers, Westly and Davies, went bankrupt. Carter, having benefited from the profits, found himself answerable for the debts.

Carter was editor of the *Morning Journal* from 1829 to 1830, and in the same year he wrote a history of France for Colburn's Juvenile Library. In 1836 he edited *The Book of Gems: The Poets and Artists of Great Britain*. In the fashion of the time, the older poems are written in their original orthography rather than in their modern transcriptions. There is one specimen of each poet and painter, with contemporary commissioned engravings. Facsimiles of autographs of famous people, so prized at the time, are included at the end of the book.[7] *The Book of Gems* is a good example of the taste in art and literature in the early part of the nineteenth century, and of the catalogue of artists most of the names survive today. The demand in England was for paintings of familiar scenes, certain aspects of history and illustrations to widely read authors.[8] In this context it is worth noting that Keats went out of fashion soon after his death in 1821, Milton was not in vogue, and Goldsmith and many of his eighteenth-century contemporaries were seldom seen as sources of inspiration in the Royal Academy exhibitions.

William Drummond's poem 'The Instability of Mortal Glory' is illustrated by Augustus Wall Callcott with his *Ruins on the Nile*. Callcott's studio, with his bright and highly finished paintings, was as fashionable as his semi-invalid wife's drawing room, filled with exotic plants. The illustration to Phineas Fletcher's poem 'The Purple Island' is by W. Collins, father of the novelist Wilkie Collins. His paintings were immensely popular, with their pleasingly fluid technique and fresh colouring – colouring which has not lasted well today because of his experiments with pigments. His importance here lies in his having established the tradition of picturesque rustic landscape favoured by Carter and many other topographical writers of the time.

Though Carter had worked with artists in the production of *The Amulet* and *The Book of Gems*, his work up till now had been almost entirely literary, apart from a few pieces of art criticism in the magazines. The prestigious periodicals of the time were the *Edinburgh Review*, followed by *Blackwood's* – the Tory answer to it – and the *Quarterly Review*. The *Edinburgh Review* introduced a far higher tone of discussion in its pages than was usual in other periodicals. In its early years it did not take a strong political line, but under its editor Francis Jeffrey (afterwards Lord Jeffrey) it became progressively more Whig. William Hazlitt wrote of it: 'It was not the principles of the *Edinburgh Review*, but the spirit that was looked at with jealousy and alarm. The principles were by no means decidedly hostile to existing institutions, but the spirit was that of fair and free discussion; a field was open to argument and wit.' Of the *Quarterly Review*, edited by J. G. Lockhart, he said: 'Nothing is required but the political creed or external circumstances of the writer.'[9]

Hazlitt obviously disliked the *Quarterly Review*; he wrote instead for the *Edinburgh Review*, though its politics were uncongenial to him and he only contributed literary articles. In fact he despised the Whigs and loathed the Tories. The *Quarterly Review*, unlike the *Edinburgh Review*, had an article on the fine arts in nearly every number. In *Blackwood's Edinburgh Magazine* (originally *Edinburgh Monthly Magazine*) politics and literature were intermingled with witty, impudent sketches of personalities; it was satirical and fearless. (It was in *Blackwood's*, it may be remembered, that William Maginn had attacked Carter and the 'Prigs'.) These periodicals had considerable influence with the educated public in the first half of the century.

The periodicals that Carter had edited fell far short of these highly regarded competitors. It was time for him to consider where his future lay – whether it was in the world of literature or fine art. He undoubtedly had a great love of art, yet one wonders where he acquired enough knowledge to conduct such a journal as *The Art Union*, as he was soon to do. It could not all stem from reading in the extensive library of Richard Sainthill, a wealthy merchant of Cork, studying the Canova casts in the Cork Institute, or exchanging ideas with the painters and sculptors there who were his friends. Nevertheless, Carter was astute. There were few writers on art at the time, and he saw how popular they could become, particularly among the new patrons of art, the owners of the mills and factories of the North and Midlands.

In the meantime Henry Colburn offered Carter the sub-editorship of the *New Monthly Magazine*, and on the retirement of Thomas Campbell he became editor, though it seems that he reverted to being sub-editor under Lytton Bulwer. The Halls and Bulwer became friends (though Anna Maria never got on with Rosina, Bulwer's temperamental Irish wife), visiting each other and discussing literature. Bulwer Lytton (as he came to be known) is now regarded as having been an influential critic of prose fiction in the early part of the century, and Anna Maria constantly asked his advice about her work.[10] But the *New Monthly* soon came under attack from a quarter which must have brought back disquieting memories to Carter, for the instigator was Dr William Maginn.

Fraser's Magazine for Town and Country was established by William Maginn and his bohemian friend Hugh Fraser, with the publisher and bookseller James Fraser in 1830. The first few numbers were almost entirely written by Maginn and Fraser and, though they contained some serious matter, they were principally satirical articles attacking all and sundry with caustic wit. The magazine was ultra-Tory in its views. This was at the zenith of Maginn's career, when he was courted in literary society and sought after by publishers. *Fraser's Magazine* attracted much literary ability, and its contributors frequently met in the back room of the premises at

215, Regent Street for convivial evenings. Such a gathering was recorded by Daniel Maclise in his drawing of the Frasians. The success of *Fraser's Magazine* was assured when a series of articles was launched entitled 'The Gallery of Literary Portraits', the text by Maginn with drawings by Maclise.

Lytton Bulwer's novels, on account of their philosophical pretensions, tended to invite ridicule, and the 'Epistle to the Literati' which *Fraser's* published in December 1831, addressed to E. L. Bulwer, had all the sting and nimble attack on 'Puff' in which Maginn delighted. 'The Epistle' brushed aside any merit in producing novels on high society (such a one, it claimed, could be dished out with a preparation of five weeks) and maintained that Bulwer would be mistaken if he thought that he was qualified extempore to edit a magazine. 'The Epistle' continued:

> Whatever it may become hereafter, [it] has hitherto been the most namby-pamby production in the world, the most potent political article in which would not have the power of influencing the opinion of a lady's lap-dog. As for other articles they are trash; the sonnet to the King is of the same style of servility as that which pervaded the satire of the Siamese Twins. Puff King, Puff Ministers, Puff Chancellor ... this is the independence of Listin Bulwer.[11]

Against Carter's advice, Bulwer replied calling *Fraser's* 'a coarse, illiterate periodical', and complaining of its uttering falsehoods respecting him and the *New Monthly*. He insisted that before the November 1831 number he had had no connection with the publication.[12] The circulation of the *New Monthly* began to decline and by 1833 Bulwer and Colburn parted, and Carter resumed the editorship until 1836. Carter, with his views on temperance and his strong domestic ties, could never have become an habitué of the back room of *Fraser's*, but his continued antipathy to *Fraser's Magazine* obviously stemmed from his clashes with Maginn and, perhaps, from a latent jealousy of Maginn's scholarship and brilliance. Maginn died in poverty in Walton-on-Thames in August 1842. E. V. Kenealy wrote to Carter after Maginn's death asking for information as to Maginn's contributions to the *New Monthly Magazine* or other publications.[13] Carter replied rather stiffly, saying that he could not help. 'During my Editorship of the *New Monthly Magazine*, Dr. Maginn never wrote for it.'[14]

Carter himself said that *The Book of British Ballads*, which he published in two volumes in 1842–44, was more important for the illustrations than for the text. The ballads were largely drawn from *Reliques of Ancient English Poetry*, collected and edited by Thomas Percy, later Bishop of Dromore, in 1765. Carter's ballads are illustrated by wood engravings from designs by contemporary British artists. The annuals of the 1820s and 1830s, with decorated steel engravings, were becoming less popular. At the same time, with the advance in the technology of printing, wood-engravings were increasingly used for illustrations of literature, and artists like Mulready, Horsley and Maclise were producing delicate designs, which in some cases were valued as highly as the text.[15]

Rudolph Ackermann's publication, in 1817, of coloured lithographs after Dürer's designs for the Prayer Book of Maximilian I influenced the style of illustrating literary works in both Germany and England. Instead of being part of the letterpress, the illustrations now surrounded or stood beside the text and became important in their own right. This is the style adopted in Carter's *Book of British Ballads* and their separation from the text by a ruled line further emphasises their importance. The second volume is dedicated to Louis of Bavaria in recognition of the work of German artists.

Carter had hoped that Richard Dadd would illustrate several of the ballads, but as it turned out he only did the designs for one, 'Robin Good-Fellow'. With the text is included a copy of a woodcut from a work of 1628 in the library of Sir Francis Egerton. This shows a hairy savage dancing in the centre of a ring of pygmies. Robin in the ballad is a mischievous fellow, up to all sorts of tricks, yet capable of acts of benevolence such as spinning thread and sweeping the hearth for maidens while they sleep. Dadd's paintings, on the whole, are claustrophobic, so filled are they with the discordant facets of his highly developed imagination. In his illustrations to the ballad, Dadd's Robin (or Puck) is more like the malicious Phooka of Ireland, and his mischievousness, though apparently innocent, is tinged with evil. In 1834 Dadd returned from a visit to the East with a disorder of the brain, and shortly after killed his father. The rest of his life was spent first in St Mary of Bethlehem

Hospital and later in Broadmoor, where he painted many of his masterpieces.

The second volume of the *Ballads* was illustrated by a group of artists who worked in the German style. They included F. R. Pickersgill, J. N. Paton, J. Gilbert and J. Tenniel. Joseph Noel Paton is best known for his fairy paintings which, on the whole, are his most original. Fairy pictures satisfied the Victorian appetite for and fascination with the subconscious. They were romantic and an antidote to the drab materialism of the time; many of them had a latent sexual content. Paton's illustrations to 'Elfinland Wud' in the *Ballads* are a foretaste of his fairy pictures of Oberon and Titania which were to make him so popular. The clear outlines of the romantic female with the harp and the supernatural hag at the end are in the German style of painting.

Frederick Richard Pickersgill in his early paintings was particularly influenced by the German painter Moritz Retzsch. Retzsch aimed at the English market with his illustrations of Shakespeare, and the appeal of his paintings seems to have been in their narrative style and economy of line. Pickersgill's illustrations for the ballad 'Hengist and Mey' have the cold, hard outlines so favoured by Retzsch.

Whether or not *The Book of British Ballads* was a financial success, it certainly placed Carter in the forefront of editors publishing illustrated works. He was now becoming a respected writer on art, and an influential promoter of modern British art.

4
Ireland Revisited

Since 1825 the Halls had been touring Ireland indefatigably to research an extensive work which they called *Ireland: Its Scenery, Character, etc.* They made five journeys, visiting each county in turn and talking endlessly to country people. Sometimes they hired a car for ten shillings a day (the expenses of a man and horse included) or they used Bianconi's 'long cars', vehicles where passengers sat on the sides, back to back, with no covering. Bianconi, an Italian, bought up horses cheaply after Waterloo and, by 1846, had made enough money to buy an estate called Longfield at Goolds Cross, County Tipperary. His daughter married a nephew of Daniel O'Connell. The land around the late-eighteenth-century house is now used for a stud

The first edition of *Ireland* was produced in twenty separate parts. Each part contained engravings on steel and some on wood, with landscapes from paintings by such artists as J. Brierly, Thomas Crofton Croker, A. Nicholl, T. S. Prout, Daniel Maclise and Thomas Creswick. The texts were about forty-eight pages long and each part was priced at half-a-crown. *Ireland* in three volumes was published between 1841 and 1843. The work was written mainly by Carter, using sources such as Lewis's *Topographical Dictionary of Ireland*, Lodge's *The Peerage of Ireland*, Dr O'Hallahan's *Introduction to the History and Antiquities of Ireland*, translations of the Four Masters, and County Histories. The Halls visited and fully described places of interest mentioned briefly by county historians. For instance, Carter considered that the county historians had neglected the three Druidal stone circles near Lough Gur, County Limerick and the wedge tomb nearby. This was a communal grave built by people living near the lake in about 2,500 BC. Archaeologists excavating the tomb in 1938 found the bones of at least eight adults and four children, together with some cremated bones. The large stones, or megaliths, which still remain today, were originally covered by a mound of smaller stones. No doubt Carter would be pleased to know that a board next to the restored tomb now gives the following information: 'Samuel Carter Hall who visited the tomb in the 19th century wrote that it was covered by a mound of stones, that an old woman lived in it for many years. After her death the mound was destroyed by money diggers.'

Perhaps Anna Maria and Carter stayed a few miles away with the Croker family at Ballynagarde, Ballyneety, a late-eighteenth-century house that now stands gaunt and derelict near the Limerick road. They certainly went to Graige when in Wexford, for they refer to the 'now decaying walls of Graige'.[1]

The Halls appear to have believed that everything was improving in Ireland. Carter wrote to Lytton Bulwer, 'I assure you I returned from Ireland much more liberal in opinion as to the government policy in regard to that country. I saw so much improvement ... I certainly cannot speak and write as I have done against the Irish executive.'[2] And the advertisement to the first edition stated, 'Of late years a decided improvement has taken place among classes throughout Ireland – referable to causes upon which it will be the authors' duty to comment. The country is on the eve of a new era.' Ironically, this was just before the famine.

The Times, on 12 October 1841, said of *Ireland* that it was written 'in a spirit of great moderation although not entirely free from bias'. 'The work evinces throughout a desire to exhibit things as they really are, and to extend equal-handed justice to all parties and all sects.' And the *Morning Chronicle*, on 10 November, thought: 'For its impartiality and truthfulness the two editors have been more than once complimented by persons of every party. Partisans may differ from the conclusions at which Mr and Mrs Hall have arrived, but no one will venture to say that either the lady or her husband have stated or misrepresented anything.'

The Halls would have been very upset by any accusations of misrepresentation. Nevertheless, from the very fact that Anna Maria was so anxious, as she points out, to avoid giving any political or religious offence, she hardly presents a true picture of Ireland at the time.[3] Later Irish writers were inclined to believe that the majority of Victorian travellers in Ireland were innocents, taken in by the plausible natives whose eloquence fell on sympathetic ears. Anna

Maria scarcely comes into this category. Reared in the countryside by George Carr and Sarah Fielding, she was perfectly aware of the tendency of the Irish peasant to sacrifice accuracy in the telling of a good story and, above all, in the desire to please. There was, too, the temptation to exploit the comical side offered by the Irish to the traveller, likely to go down well with an English readership. W. B. Yeats wrote in his Introduction to *Fairy and Folk Tales of the Irish Peasantry*:

> Croker and Lover, full of the ideas of harum-scarum Irish gentility, saw everything humorised. The impulse of the Irish literature of their time came from a class that did not – mainly from political reasons – take the populace seriously, and imagined the country as a humorist's Arcadia: its passions, its gloom, its tragedy, they knew nothing of. What they did was not wholly false; they merely magnified an irresponsible type, found oftenest among boatmen, carmen and gentlemen's servants, into the type of a whole nation, and created the stage Irishman.

There is a good deal of truth in this; but the writings of Croker and Lover, whether treating the Irish as comic or heroic figures, were all part of the nineteenth-century Romantic Movement. Lady Morgan's readers were fascinated by the plethora of ancient customs and 'antiquities' in *The Wild Irish Girl*, her romantic tale of a Celtic princess. The thinly veiled political propaganda was of secondary account. Thomas Moore saw in the Irish 'the tone of defiance, succeeded by the languor of despondency – a burst of turbulence dying away into softness – the sorrows of one moment, lost in the levity of the next'.[4] His romanticism and patriotism were for the drawing room, his *Irish Melodies* for the rich and the educated – for 'those who can afford to have their national zeal a little stimulated without exciting much dread of the excesses into which it may hurry them ... ' Later in the century Lady Gregory, encouraged by Yeats, learnt Irish and went tirelessly from house to house taking down stories in order to enlarge their knowledge of idioms in the local dialect.

The part played by the Halls in this literary movement is rather more complex. *Ireland: Its Scenery, Character, etc.* has two authors.

The volumes were written to attract English people to come and judge Ireland for themselves and in this one senses that Carter had a feeling of mission. Both the Halls undoubtedly wrote about Ireland as they saw it, but the *Quarterly Review* complained that there was too much Irish eloquence, 'luxuriant lakes' and 'sparkling billows', 'which tend to dim the beautiful realities'.[5]

As a boy, Carter had acquired a love of archaeology, architecture and history, and these carefully researched aspects are still of interest today. But all the pervasive input – story-telling and Irish dialogue (presumably Anna Maria's) – seldom amuses, and most of her stories (sometimes tragic) have a moral slant. These were superfluous in a topographical work which already had romantic legends and antiquarian interests. Carter himself, as an Englishman, may have been unaware of the pressures on the Irish which sometimes caused them to present themselves in a comical light. He had a romantic belief in the approach of a golden era in Ireland where all classes would benefit from the advantages of the Union with England.

The Halls were economical with their literary output, but made full use of their researches. In 1843 they published *A Week in Killarney*, which is more of a travel guide than a literary work. Based on the material that they had gathered for *Ireland*, it was informative and extremely popular. It highlights how the advent of steam and the extension of the railways had reduced the travelling time from London via Dublin or Cork. Carter gave the cost from London to Killarney as £6 first class and £5 second class. Most inns, he said, charged one shilling and sixpence for a bed, the same for breakfast and about £2 for dinner. Details are given as to how to travel in the country, either by public or by private car. Posting by poste-chaise cost one shilling per mile, and sixpence a mile per person by car. The book went into three editions, and was followed in 1853 by *Handbooks for Ireland*: *Dublin and Wicklow*; *The North and Giant's Causeway*; *The South and Killarney*; and *The West and Connemara.*

In 1842, after the first volume of *Ireland: Its Scenery, Character, etc.* was published, Carter was made a Fellow of the Society of Antiquaries.

5
Copy or Fake?

In the first issue of *The Art Union*, Carter had complained that their interest in importing foreign art was causing some dealers to belittle that of the British School. Ever since the French Revolution the number of imported paintings had been rising. Many of them were fakes, a profitable market in an era when prospective purchasers had none of the scientific aids of today to help them detect forgeries. In 1826 the duty on imported pictures had been reduced, and Carter maintained that the Government should have foreseen the harmful effect that the change would have on British art. The result, he wrote in *The Art Union* of 1839, was 'an influx of worthless and injurious copies, which besides preventing sales of works by our own artists, cannot but have impaired the public taste'. He now set about warning the public in *The Art Union* of the sales of spurious 'old masters' at impossibly low prices.

The number of pictures imported into the country between 1833 and 1838 (inclusive) was 45,642, according to *The Art Union* of 1839. Carter knew some of the Commissioners of Customs (almost certainly W. Dickinson in the Controller's office) and he was supplied with the numbers of imports, which he published monthly. During 1843 the number was about twenty per cent less than during the previous years – a significant decline. *The Art Union* quickly earned a reputation for its fight against dishonest dealers and its exposures of fakes, and letters flooded into the editor's office. A letter from a 'Constant Reader' in Sheffield, quoting the title page of a sale catalogue as 'The Private Gallery of First Class Paintings, the property of a distinguished collector' (where most of the paintings were ridiculously cheap and obvious forgeries), caused Carter to comment, 'If people will be cheated with their eyes open, we must say that they deserve no sympathy ... Such cases as this to which our correspondent refers are of weekly occurrence.'[1]

Carter was not always prudent, but for the time being he did not actually name dealers he believed to be selling fakes. Though by now he was receiving threatening letters, he was not to be deterred in his campaign against imported fakes; but he was prudent enough – at least for the time being – not to cite offending dealers by name. By 1850, when *The Athenaeum* promised to enter the war against fakes, Carter could assure the editor that there were now few instances of fraud practised against Manchester cotton-spinners buying bogus 'old masters'. 'The whole process and practice,' he claimed, 'from beginning to end, we have successfully exposed ... On the other hand, we have frequently shown the wisdom of purchasing works by British artists.'[2]

By 1854 Carter was satisfied that prices were finding their level. Fakes with fancy attributions were still being offered at sales, but they would now generally only cost a few shillings. In *The Art Union* of that year, Carter reported that Mr G. Robinson of Bond Street was holding regular sales of guaranteed works of modern art. He felt sure that the public, in time, would prefer to pay reasonable prices for pictures in good condition with bright colours, rather than trifling sums for dirty and decaying canvases of doubtful authenticity.

Carter disapproved of the lack of surveillance over artists copying pictures in the National Gallery and the British Institute. He thought that the honest student of art gained little, as his efforts were unsupervised, and that more often than not the copyist had fraudulent intentions. The pictures most frequently copied, he said, were by Canaletto and W. van de Velde, whose works were in great demand. Even more serious was the fact that the forgery of painting did not come under the statutory law of forgery, and could only be made a matter of inquiry at common law. There was much controversy as to the question of what were words of warranty or contract, and what were words of description. It seemed, said Carter, that merely putting down the name of an old master in a catalogue as the painter of a particular picture was not an actionable warranty.[3] Quoting several cases, *The Art Journal* advised buyers to insist on a written warranty before putting down their money.

British art was, without question, indebted to Carter for his crusade against the fraudulent dealings in old masters. Why, indeed, buy dark, sometimes cracked paintings, likely to be fakes, when a picture by a living artist could easily be verified or, better still, when pictures could be commissioned straight from the easel? For the discerning, there were plenty of examples of the work of young aspiring artists in *The Art Journal*. By the 1850s there was a growing demand for modern British art (particularly in the North) and by 1863, according to Tom Taylor, the patronage of living art had increased tenfold since the beginning of the century.[4] Dishonest dealers began to turn their attention to modern art, particularly of the British School, and these Carter pursued relentlessly.

A sale took place in Birmingham on 31 August and 1 September 1854, at the sale room of a firm called Ludlow and Robinson, of the pictures of a dealer called Hart. The catalogue published fairly stringent conditions of sale. Buyers had to pay a deposit of five shillings in the pound (if required) immediately on the close of bidding – 'The lots to be at the risk of the purchaser from the fall of the hammer, and to be removed with all faults and errors of description at the end of each day's sale.' Lots not paid for one day after the sale would be resold, and the purchaser would lose the deposit and be liable for the expenses of the resale. But what roused Carter to make a bitter attack on Hart and the auctioneers was, first, the additional note saying that customers doubting the genuineness of any of the paintings of living artists (guaranteed at the time of offering) might, previous to payment, submit them to the artists for verification and, secondly, the low prices of the pictures. How could anyone, he wrote, get a picture to the artist on the day of the sale, and why was Hart asking about one sixth of the current value of works of such artists? 'Moses Hart', as Carter mistakenly called him, was well known for his nefarious dealings in the art market, and now the people of the provinces were to be tricked with his 'cart load of rubbish'. But Carter had gone too far. He had only, as he admitted later, seen the catalogue with the prices, not the actual pictures; also, he knew nothing of the auctioneers. When letters arrived defending the honesty of Ludlow and Robinson, Carter printed them together with what amounted to an apology in *The Art Journal*.

Hart instituted a case for libel against Carter and the case, Hart v Hall, was heard at Warwick Assizes on 28 March 1855. The counsel for the plaintiff maintained that Hall had written his article in *The*

Art Journal based on the priced catalogue and, not having seen the pictures, on mere surmise. He claimed that Hall had sneered at Hart, misnaming him 'Moses'. Hart did not appear. Several people gave evidence as to his previous fraudulent dealings and said that he was known as a 'picture pickler' (one who employed an inferior artist to get up a picture in the style of a well-known artist). The judge discouraged the counsel for the defence from recalling previous dubious sales in which Hart had been involved, but involuntarily exclaimed, on being shown an earlier catalogue of a sale at Preston, 'Why they have put in *The Three Marys* by Ludovico Carracci which is at Lord Carlisle's!' The jury returned a verdict for the plaintiff with damages of 40 shillings.

After the trial Carter wrote a long article in *The Art Journal* accepting the verdict, but justifying his actions in the case. If Hart's lawyer had only asked for a retraction with reference to the Birmingham sale, Carter said, he would have granted his request, but Hart also demanded what was tantamount to belief in the integrity of the dealer and the *bona fides* of his previous sales. To this Carter could not agree. He admitted that most of the pictures at Birmingham were authentic, but could not resist listing a number of paintings at Hart's other sales that were fakes. He resented the fact that most of the artists whose pictures had been copied had been reluctant to appear for the defence. He quoted *The Times*'s report of the trial.

> The learned judge, summing up, spoke with severity of the offence of publishing in newspapers imputations upon the characters of individuals without ample sufficient grounds, and expressed his opinion that, if people would assume to themselves functions which nobody expected them to discharge and, under a sense of what they chose to call duty, inflict serious injury upon others, they ought to be compelled to make a full compensation for the wrong so inflicted.[5]

Carter did not have to publish the judge's summing up, and was evidently quite unabashed by it. He maintained it was his duty to protect the public and British artists from the machinations of dishonest dealers. *The Art Journal,* to him, was the bulwark against fraud and the debasement of art, the propagator of good taste and the champion of British art.

Carter reported a rather different case in 1855. In 1851 E.M.Ward had painted *James II Receiving the Intelligence of the Landing of the Prince of Orange*, which was bought by Jacob Bell of Langham Place. Bell gave Ward permission to make an artist's copy of the picture which was subsequently sold to dealers called Melton and Clarke who, in turn, sold it to a man in Preston. Ward had now discovered that a faked copy was on the market and, seeking redress, he engaged a solicitor named Darville. Darville made an application to a magistrate of the Marlborough Street Court for assistance or, failing that, advice. The pecuniary injury to Ward, he explained, was slight; it was his reputation that would suffer. Ward might apply to Chancery for an injunction against the holder of the faked copy to restrain to sell it as an original, but there might be several copies in existence. The magistrate admitted that, as the law stood, such dangers were a serious matter for artists, and in his opinion they were not sufficiently protected, but that he was powerless to help. Ward had at least publicised the artists' cause. Carter complained that for years he had been fighting alone against fraudulent dealers. He demanded that artists 'as a body' rouse themselves into action and demand protection from the legislature.

> If a publisher desires to engrave a painting by an artist of note, he must first pay him a considerable sum for the right to do so, although the engraving may, and generally does, extend the fame of the painter; but artists are content oftentimes to see their pictures imitated, and their own professional characters thereby endangered, without remonstrance, or at least without a movement to hinder such iniquitous proceedings.[6]

Having burnt his fingers in the Birmingham case, Carter was quick to report that Isaacs, the Liverpool dealer who had bought the faked copy, was a man of integrity and never implicated in fraud.

In July 1855 a complaint came from a member of the very body of artists that Carter claimed he was protecting. Francis Danby objected that an engraving called *The Enchanted Island – Sunset* in the March *Art Journal* was not the real subject that he had painted in 1852 under the name *An Enchanted Island*. 'The possessor of the original picture is very indignant at being mis-represented to the public.'[7]

Danby insisted that he had never allowed a copy to be made. Certainly Danby would have been unlikely to risk offending the owner, John Gibbons, who was a most indulgent patron. The *Art Journal* engraving appears to be of a little picture entitled *Fairies*, painted by Danby circa 1840, a rather insipid version of *An Enchanted Island*. Francis Greenacre, in the catalogue of the 1988 exhibition of Danby at the Tate Gallery, suggests that *Fairies* was probably a page from an unidentified album.[8] The question is further confused by *The Art Journal* calling the engraving *The Enchanted Island – Sunset*, a title similar to another painting by Danby, *An Enchanted Castle – Sunset*. Carter explained in the July number of *The Art Journal* that prior to the sale of the collection of the deceased James Wadmore he had obtained permission from the executors to copy some of the pictures. He presumed that this one was a slightly different design by Danby for *An Enchanted Island*. It had been knocked down for 46 guineas. Danby thought that the *Art Journal* engraving was of a little picture that a pupil of his had painted in his cottage in the spirit of *An Enchanted Island*, but that it was quite different from the original. If it had his name on it, he said, it was a forgery. Was this a copy made by a pupil under the supervision of Danby for the purpose of instruction? Or was it a fake of *Fairies* (a picture which would have been little known), and sold to James Wadmore by a dealer as a painting by Danby? Whatever its origin, Carter had offended Danby.

Nevertheless there were many artists who had reason to be grateful to Carter for his encouragement. Daniel Maclise always remembered Carter's kindness to him when he arrived in London in 1828. Carter called and immediately befriended him. The following year Maclise exhibited a picture of a scene from *Twelfth Night*, in Olivia's garden, and the Halls gave a party. 'I met a great many lions there,' he told a friend later.[9] He spoke of how important this friendship had been at the beginning of his career, and he remained on close terms with the Halls.

Carter said that more than once in the early 1840s not a single British painting was sold at a private view of the Royal Academy. The Redgrave brothers, quoting Richard Wornum's catalogue, stated that up to 1847 there were only forty-one pictures of the British School in the National Gallery. Carter's campaign against fraud, however, certainly contributed to the growing popularity of modern British art, though there were of course more powerful and lasting factors in the revival of the 1850s and 1860s. The Royal Academy provided schools and a forum for artists to exhibit their work (and also an institution against which to rebel). Some movements (like the Clique) were short-lived, but the Pre-Raphaelites, using different materials and methods, brought new life to the native school. Sir Robert Peel was the first Prime Minister to vote public money for the arts, and the foundation of the South Kensington institutions after the Great Exhibition was highly important. Prince Albert, too, was a valued patron of contemporary art, often visiting artists in their studios; and more and more the newly rich merchants and bankers preferred to invest their money buying brightly coloured modern British paintings rather than dark canvases of dubious 'old masters'.

Artists in London showed their appreciation of what Carter was doing for British art when, in July 1855, they circulated a letter asking for subscriptions to help Carter pay for the costs arising from the Hart libel case. The letter was signed, among others, by Stanfield, Ward, Frost, Foley, Goodall, Cooke and Harding.

6

Temperance and Intemperance

The revival of religious fervour in the early nineteenth century, combined with the desire to improve the lot of the poor, gave rise to the temperance movement. The Halls shared in this enthusiasm as well as in its accompanying censoriousness.

Drunkenness in Ireland was an even more serious problem than in England. Remembering his boyhood there, Carter says that drunkenness was universal. In his *Retrospect of a Long Life* he describes scenes at wakes, at farmers' club dinners and of faction fights, particularly at county fairs. The potato was not just the staple food, but was the basis for about a third of the whisky consumed in the country, brewed in illicit stills. A still, according to Carter, cost about £3 (most country people had a small potato patch), but once bought a man could always sell the 'potheen' that he brewed to his neighbours. Anthony Trollope worked in Ireland before the famine, and understood the country as well as any English writer. In *The Kellys and the O'Kellys* he writes of the Irish attitude to causes (in this case the movement for the repeal of the Union) when he says of John Kelly, 'It was the battle rather than the thing battled for, that was dear to him; the strife rather than the result.' He also understood the resort to alcohol, by various classes of society, as a palliative for poverty and despair. In his novel *The Macdermots of Ballycloran*, Larry Macdermot, a member of the minor gentry struggling hopelessly against the debts incurred by his father, sits by the fireside with his whiskey and water, sunk in despondency. He is unable to look after his daughter who is seduced by the dashing Miles Ussher, a sub-inspector in the revenue police whose duties were to search for the illicit stills and prevent the distillation of potheen. It was a service which gentlemen were glad to get their sons into, as to an officer with few scruples the job could be a very profitable one.

The first temperance societies were in America. In Ireland, the Revd George Whitmore Carr (son of George Carr's half-brother, the

Revd Edward Carr) is said to have established the first temperance society in Europe in 1829. In the same year the Ulster Temperance Society was founded. The movement spread to Yorkshire and Lancashire in 1830 when a newspaper called the *Temperance Societies Record* reported that there were about 127 societies. The founders of the movement in the south of Ireland, George Carr and Nicholas Dunscombe of the Established Church, and William Martin a Quaker, failed to influence the bulk of the Roman Catholic population with their rather prosaic appeals against drunkenness. The following poem was one of theirs:

'ONE PINT A-DAY'

One pint a-day! Well what of that?
Pray, stay awhile, and you shall hear:
For if you save the whole amount,
'Tis three pound sixteen shillings clear!
A good stuff hat this sum would buy,
A pair of shoes, and stockings too:
And two good shirts to wear besides,
Just fit for Christian or for Jew!

Such economical arguments were unlikely to convince a thirsty Irishman of whatever denomination. Very wisely, the founders invited Father Theobald Mathew to become the president of the movement.

Theobald Mathew was brought up at Thomastown Castle near Cashel in Tipperary, where his father was agent to his kinsman, the first Earl of Landaff. On leaving Maynooth College he joined the Franciscan order and was sent to Cork to look after a small chapel called 'The Little Friary'. He lived in miserable accommodation and worked indefatigably amongst the poor by whom he was beloved. He was a handsome, courteous man, with a rather sombre look, but with a sweet and gentle smile. People flocked to hear him and to take the pledge of abstinence. So strong was his influence that some of the more superstitious of his followers claimed that he had divine powers, and brought the sick and lame to take the pledge. Stories circulated about his curing a Wexford man in Waterford who was paralysed and dumb, and of another man in Donegal who was crippled.

The temperance movement always had a Protestant aura, though some Protestants considered there was too much superstition to give it their unreserved support. Families were divided. The Protestant press wanted a firm denial from Father Mathew that he could perform miracles. At a meeting in Beresford Place in Dublin, Father Mathew said that he had no powers of healing, but the Halls (who were among his staunch supporters) thought that he made very little effort to contradict the claim. In *Retrospect* Carter said that Father Mathew knew that such powers were attributed to him, but thought that had he denied them publicly it would have retarded the momentum of the movement.

The Roman Catholic Church was not altogether enthusiastic. The *Dublin University Magazine* was outspoken in its opinion as to the reason for this reserve:

> The social enjoyment of a convivial party within his reach is one of the few pleasures which the priest has in Ireland. The institution of celibacy deprives him of that most inestimable gift of Divine Providence, the exquisite and pure enjoyment of domestic happiness in a home made happy by a wife's love, consecrated by the reciprocal duties, and elevated by the ennobling sympathies of the parent and the child. His education has rendered the company of his brothers and sisters distasteful to him – there is scarcely any community of tie or frequency of intercourse between the companions of his childhood and himself. The antagonism by which our society is divided exclude him from familiar intercourse with the Protestant gentry, whom he has perhaps denounced at the hustings, and against whom he may have plotted at the elections. Is it to be wondered at that a priest so situated should keenly relish the social board – should regard it as his chief source of relaxation and that the moments passed in chattering about 'Old Ireland' and 'Young Ireland' should be some of the happiest of his existence? Such considerations ought to be recollected by those Roman Catholics and teetotallers who have so severely censured the parish priest for not adhering to Father Mathew's system of driving drunkenness from the land.[1]

Father Mathew always managed to remain aloof from politics.

Thackeray said of him, 'He is almost the only man, too, that I have met in Ireland who, in speaking of public matters, did not talk as a partisan ... and it was impossible in hearing him to know, but with previous acquaintance with his character, whether he was Whig, or Tory, Catholic or Protestant.'[2] This was not to say that he was unaware of political unrest in Ireland. In a speech at Tipperary he came out strongly against secret societies – 'They are filled with danger, with vice, with iniquity because they eat at the roots of social order.' The consumption of whiskey fell from twelve million gallons in 1838 to six and a half million gallons in 1841, according to the *Dublin University Magazine*, quoting Parliamentary returns. There was also a decrease in crime. In 1842 Judge Burton at the Down Assizes addressed the gentlemen of the grand jury saying, 'It is gratifying to me, as indeed it must be to you all, that we owe the peaceful state of the country to temperance!'

Whiskey shops in Dublin declined in 1841, and licences in public houses in 1842. This cannot, however, all be attributed to the temperance movement for it was a time of depression and there were minor potato famines leading up to the worst blight in 1845. Nevertheless, the success of Father Mathew's mission in Ireland was extraordinary amongst all classes. Thousands of people came to Cork to take the pledge, and in some towns the militia had to be called out to direct the crowds.

In 1843 Father Mathew came to England and preached in London in August. Mrs Carlyle went to the meeting held in the Commercial Road, and Anna Maria wrote a letter of introduction for her to Father Mathew. 'I saw thousands of people hushed into awful silence, with not a single exception that I saw,' she wrote to her husband, 'the only religious meeting I ever saw in cockney land which had not plenty of scoffers hanging on its outskirts.'[3]

Ireland was very much in the news at the time. Daniel O'Connell and the Repeal Movement was a burning issue in politics in the 1840s, and it is not surprising that the newly founded *Punch* quickly found in Ireland a source for its satire. There were cartoons about drunkenness, about bigotry and all the obvious characteristics of the stage Irishman. After Father Mathew's visit *Punch* published two cartoons entitled 'Father Mathew's Polly-Put-the Kettle-On Icon', with the words:

> It is not generally known that funds are at this moment being raised for the erection of a Temperance Hall, to be called the Pollyputthekettleonicon, to be devoted to Father Mathew on his return next year to London. The Father proposes to give a series of lectures, illustrative of the loveliness of temperance and the horrors of drunkenness; to do this he will take a drop of gin and water – understand us – not mixed, in which he will show the separate rewards of sobriety and intoxication.[4]

The first cartoon, 'The Water Drop', showed a happy family with volumes of *Punch* on their shelves and people waiting to drink pure water from a pump; the other, 'The Gin Drop', shows the degradation brought about by over-indulgence. Though Victorian England approved of Father Mathew's teaching of thrift and moral reform, his success was not as resounding as in Ireland.

Daniel O'Connell had tried unsuccessfully to interest Father Mathew in the Repeal Movement, and attempts were made to persuade the temperance societies to lend support to the movement with their banners and sober parades. In October 1843, though O'Connell postponed a 'monster meeting' which the Government had prohibited at Clontarf, he was arrested and brought to trial in the following January on a trumped-up charge of conspiracy. There was always the possibility of some of the temperance societies' enthusiasm being whipped up for 'the Liberator', given, as Trollope put it so well, the Irishman's love of the battle rather than the cause.

In November Carter addressed 'A Letter to Irish Temperance Societies concerning the present state of Ireland and its connection with England'.[5] 'It is not my intention to canvass and discuss the question of Repeal,' he states, and then proceeds to do so. Strongly in favour of the Union, Carter on his travels through Ireland was convinced of the improvement in the administration of the country since the measure had been passed.

> My design is simply to submit to you some reasoning and a few facts, in order to show that a connection with England is an advantage to Ireland and the Irish people. To show that the old, unwise, and wicked policy of governing Ireland has been entirely abrogated; that the vile motto 'divide and conquer' …

> was at length won over, and has been displaced by 'conciliate and unite' and that the atrocious principles which distinguish a dark age and bad governments – which treated Ireland as a conquered country – are now as intolerable to Englishmen as they can ever have been to Irishmen.

He ends the letter:

> You want a parliament of your own. Now the gain of this would be an immense gain, if it would give you ... extensive commerce, prosperous manufactures, high wages and plenty of good food ... [But]Repeal would never obtain them ... A repeal of the Union between England and Ireland – a division of Great Britain – there never can be.

In effect the letter gave offence to both the Liberal Catholic Party which Carter was trying to conciliate and the Conservative Party to which he belonged. An entry appeared in the *Dublin University Magazine*, edited by Charles Lever, charging Carter with having been bought and referring to Carter's letter 'as a wantonly wicked production'. It is unlikely that Lever wrote the entry, but as editor he was responsible for it. Carter, claiming that he had more experience as an editor than Lever, replied, 'I never knew so gross a departure from the just, the honourable and honest course; never saw more conclusive evidence of a spirit unbecoming to a gentleman and a man of letters than in your criticism on my "Letter to Irish Temperance Societies".' This aroused Lever to such a pitch of hostility that he came over to London and challenged Carter to a duel. In his memoirs, Carter ignored the circumstances of the challenge which took place at Chalk Farm, merely saying that the affair had been peaceably settled. However, he wrote to W. J. FitzPatrick, presumably when FitzPatrick was collecting material for his life of Lever, explaining what had happened.

> We never met; I never saw Lever, my friend on the occasion was Colonel (then Major) Clerke. I waited in a house near Chalk Farm for five hours alone. At the end of that time I found that the matter had been referred for 'arbitration' to Lord Ranelagh, and I was asked if I would withdraw my letter, on Lever's expressing his conviction that I had not been bought

> – or in any way paid – for the work I had done. That I readily did; stating that, but for the unfounded and unjust statement, I never would have written such a letter at all. That settled the matter. We were not such fools as to shoot at one another – content with paper pellets of the brain. When Lord Ranelagh was parting with my friend he said, 'I suppose this is the first time four Irishmen have met to shoot an Englishman and didn't do it!'[6]

Processions were a commonplace aspect of the London streets at the time. While strolling down Waterloo Road, John O'Neill, a poor Irish shoemaker and poet, was struck by the sight of a procession of orderly, respectable-looking teetotallers, some of whom he had known to be the most drunken and quarrelsome characters in his neighbourhood. O'Neill's memoirs give a vivid description of a life of respectable poverty in London in the mid-nineteenth century.[7] His is a heartrending story of a man struggling to make a living and to write his poetry, buoyed up by optimism one minute and plunged in despair the next. He joined the temperance movement, was introduced to the Halls, and was invited by Anna Maria to The Rosery, their cottage in Kensington, where she showed him much kindness. In 1840 O'Neill was encouraged by members of the movement to publish by subscription a poem entitled 'The Drunkard'. Though some people, like the Halls, he says in his memoirs, subscribed handsomely, for a man of no means and few literary acquaintances it was a daunting prospect. He had not even the means to supply the printer with paper, and a load of copies, which a temperance friend in Dublin had ordered, were returned to him (carriage unpaid) as the friend was away touring with Father Mathew. Then a City friend suggested that an illustrated edition of the poem might do well, and introduced O'Neill to George Cruikshank. Cruikshank seems to have treated O'Neill rather badly, but after much delay the second edition finally appeared in 1842. Even then O'Neill had trouble. He employed a cheap lithographer whose work proved quite unacceptable. It is to Carter's credit that he took the matter up, sent O'Neill to a reputable man and offered to pay for the stone.

Neither temperance nor intemperance much appealed either to writers or artists in the mid-nineteenth century. In the portrayal of dissolute upper-class society in literature, drunkenness and gambling are merely incidental. In *The Way We Live Now*, though Sir Felix Carbury's drunkenness is necessary for the development of the plot, Trollope is not making a moral issue of drunkenness as such. Dickens saw a comical side to it. Though many contemporary artists adopted a moral tone, drunkenness on the whole was a less popular theme than prostitution, fallen women and helpless orphans. George Cruikshank was an exception when he became a teetotaller: after illustrating O'Neill's poem he published a series of eight woodcuts called *The Bottle* in 1847, followed by *The Worship of Bacchus*, painted in oil for the Temperance League and now restored and on display at Tate Britain. *The Magazine of Art* reported in 1880: 'Sensationalism is the routine charge brought against this curious production, but its real absurdity lies in the poor feeble puerilities of the stories it tells.' The picture was exhibited at Exeter Hall and afterwards sent on tour. This proved disastrous for Cruikshank, as the expense was enormous and the public response very small. Publishers were not interested in commissioning works on temperance subjects and Cruikshank became eventually almost destitute.

Robert Patten in his book *George Cruikshank: Life, Times and Art* says Carter and other friends were shocked to find after Cruikshank died that he had been leading a double life. After the death of his first wife in 1849, Cruikshank married Eliza Widdison, who was a friend of the Halls, but within a few years set up a second household with Adelaide Altree who had ten children by him. However, William Bates who wrote a biography of Cruikshank called him 'honourable, truthful and generous ... he retained to the last days of his long and noble life the wit of a man with the simplicity of a child.' He also says that the artist's 'singularly pure and healthy nature refused the assimilation of evil'. This seems to have satisfied Carter and he wrote to Bates saying, 'You have taken a generous and, I believe, a just view of poor George. Who is he that will cast the first stone? Who are those that judgeth another? I am thankful there is no Asmodeus to take the roof off my house – and look in. How few are there who could bear that process?'[8]

Children were included in the movement after some juveniles took the pledge at Leeds, and the Band of Hope was formed in

1851. This extraordinary society carried on its crusade right up to the First World War. From time to time meetings took place in Ireland in Protestant church halls where little children, as young as six or seven, would climb on to a platform to make a promise that they scarcely understood and rarely kept.

The redesigned Crystal Palace was to be opened at Sydenham in June 1854, and it was rumoured that a licence for intoxicating liquors was likely to be granted. As the prospectus for the 'Palace of the People' grandiloquently claimed it would provide 'refined recreation' for the millions of people whose only pleasures at the time were 'the gin palace, the dancing saloon and ale house', it was not surprising that objection quickly came from the temperance societies. George Cruikshank and Sir Calverley Trevelyan headed a deputation to the directors of the company, but had no success. Sir Calverley was a firm teetotaller. He had thrown the contents of his father's wine cellar into the lake at Nettlecombe in Somerset, and at Wallington, as all the artists who stayed there had experienced, guests were only allowed two glasses of inferior wine. *The Art Journal* had an article on the opening of the Crystal Palace, probably written by Carter. It condemned the sale of beer and spirits as wholly at variance with the healthy progress of the age, an age 'which confutes the idea that enjoyment is enhanced by unwholesome stimulants'. It refers to the flow of petitions to the House of Commons to restrict the number of public houses and to prevent the sale of beer and spirits on Sundays. It ends with a rhetorical flourish, 'We have asked and been promised Art Manufactures in the Crystal Palace, and in lieu thereof, we are offered gin and porter.'[9]

Ginger beer was all that was now offered by the Halls to their guests, both Anna Maria and Carter having become total abstainers. A friend once slyly pointed out that this had not always been the case. Perhaps he was referring to Carter's participation in the convivial evenings of the Noviomagus Society, or to his bachelor days as a parliamentary reporter.[10] Wine had never exactly flowed at the Halls' dinner parties since, as William Bell Scott pointed out, Carter 'suffered from the prevailing disease of impecuniosity, which indeed affected almost every human creature I met in that long eight years' experience of the London world; every one I mean connected with the business of art!'[11]

Carter did all he could to help Father Mathew in his crusade. It was well known that Father Mathew dipped into his own meagre resources to continue his work, and Carter became secretary of a committee to raise funds to provide him with an annuity for life. A Major Russell, when he met Carter, showed him a letter which he had had from Father Mathew. 'I blush when I reflect upon Mr Hall's exertions on my behalf,' he said, 'he is more a brother to me than a friend.' The annuity was not raised, as Father Mathew protested against money being subscribed for him while people in Ireland were starving; for now the terrible potato blight was taking its toll. He was, however, granted a pension of £300 a year in the Civil List of 1847. Father Mathew told Richard Dowden, before he died in 1856, that they had achieved a considerable victory: 'We have turned the tide of public opinion; it was once a glory for men to boast of what they drank; we have turned that false glory into shame.'[12]

Grieved by Father Mathew's death, Anna Maria and Carter continued to work for the temperance movement. Anna Maria wrote *The Drunkard's Bible* in 1854, *Digging a Grave with a Wine Glass* in 1871 and finally published *Boons and Blessings, Stories and Sketches to Illustrate the Advantages of Temperance* in 1875. The latter was illustrated by E.M.Ward, Frederick Goodall, George Cruikshank and others of their friends, but the engravings proved too expensive and the publication lost money.

In 1875 Carter published *The Trial of Sir Jasper: A Temperance Tale in Verse*. Its interest today lies in its subject and in the accompanying illustrations, rather than in the verse – which, it must be said, is not very good. Birkett Foster, George Cruikshank, Thomas Faed, Sir Noel Paton and W. C. Dobson are some of the twenty-two artists who illustrated the poem. For instance, Alfred Elmore's picture (engraved by the Dalziel brothers) of a young girl who has suffered from her father's violence illustrates the lines, 'With memories black of many a bitter blow/ Dealt when the father's soul was dark with gin.'

Elmore was mainly a painter of historical scenes and rarely attempted such a moral subject. Here the bare-footed girl huddles against the wall in an attitude not unlike that of the woman in Rossetti's *Found* of 1851. In modern dictionaries of art Elmore's paintings are referred to as sentimental, in a derogative sense, as they would not have been in the nineteenth century. To Redgrave, writing about Elmore in 1866, there was nothing unusual in the Victorian acceptance of sentiment in the treatment of subjects of ethical behaviour. *The Magazine of Art* in 1880 has descriptions of paintings belonging to the 'genre of sentiment' and praises one of Arthur Stocks's pictures entitled *Her Sweetest Flower* for its gentle appeal to public sentiment. This appeal, in both literature and art, was all part of the Romantic Movement, but does not appear to have been so exaggerated in literature as in art. Jane Austen had warned against an indulgence in superficial emotion in her novel *Sense and Sensibility*, and certainly the novelists of the later nineteenth century treated sentiment with far more subtlety and restraint than their artistic contemporaries.

In *The Trial of Sir Jasper,* Sir Jasper, as a supplier of alcohol, stands on trial before witnesses whose lives have been spoilt, directly or indirectly, by drink. Other witnesses are called: a mother and child in the street – 'Hungry and foot-sore and without a bed' – are illustrated by Thomas Faed; *The Scholar in Bedlam*, 'Ten thousand devils haunt him, day and night', by Cruikshank. The Suicide, the Sailor, the Magdalen and even a drunken Maori in the stocks all confront Sir Jasper and condemn him.

The Trial of Sir Jasper was published at a loss, but was followed by *An Old Story*, which Carter wrote in 1875, also in verse. This fared rather better and went into a second edition in the following year. It was noticed in some of the national and in many of the provincial newspapers. There are letters from societies and individuals from all over the country ordering copies of the story. By now, however, the cause was in eclipse, although it lasted into the twentieth century. Writing in 1871 in *Memories of Great Men and Women of the Age*, Carter strongly denied that Father Mathew's work had had no permanent effect in Ireland though he accepted that much of his influence had gone. And in *Retrospect* he wrote: 'For drunkenness instead of being a glory has become a reproach … a ban has been put upon vice; authors do not describe it as venial, or jovial, or glorious; artists no longer class it with the picturesque.'

7
Is He Pecksniff?

When Charles Dickens published *Martin Chuzzlewit* in 1843–4, the idea that he used Carter as the model for that unctuous hypocrite Mr Pecksniff must have provided conversation at many dinner tables in literary London. Dickens wrote in the Preface of the 1849 edition of the novel, 'All the Pecksniff family upon earth are agreed, I believe, that Pecksniff is an exaggeration. I will not offer any plea on his behalf to so powerful and genteel a body.'

Dickens had a great faculty, as Walter Bagehot pointed out, of portraying characteristics rather than character. Dickens did not probe human depths. An impassioned writer with a vivid imagination, subject to his likes and dislikes, he used his characters to expose society and further the cause he was fighting for. The modern reader cannot conceive that Tom Pinch (Pecksniff's pupil), however simple and credulous, could not have seen Pecksniff for what he was, a rogue and a hypocrite. But most Victorian readers, with a strong social conscience, were prepared to overlook the limitations in his characterisation in the interest of a good cause, and accept an exaggeration which prevented too close an examination of their own foibles.

John Forster, Dickens's friend and biographer, goes further than the Preface, explaining that America (where part of the novel is set) had no Pecksniff and that he was purely English.

> The confession [he wrote] is not encouraging to national pride, but this character is so far English, that though our countrymen as a rule are by no means Pecksniffs the ruling weakness is to countenance and encourage the race. When people call the character exaggerated, and protest that the lines are too broad to deceive anyone, they only refuse, naturally enough, to sanction in a book what half their own lives is passed in tolerating if not in worshipping.[1]

He also implies that Pecksniff was not taken from a living person, but was constructed to show the evils ensuing from selfishness. 'Let me here at once remark that the notion of taking Pecksniff for a type of character was really the origin of the book.' On the other hand, Madeline House and Graham Storey, editors of Dickens's letters, suggest in their footnote to a letter from Dickens to Mrs Hall that Dickens virtually admitted the identification of Hall with Pecksniff, and refer the reader to later volumes.[2] I have not, however, found any conclusive evidence to support their suggestion.

Punch quickly used Pecksniff for its political jibes against Sir Robert Peel. There was supposed to be some physical likeness between Peel and Phiz's illustrations of Pecksniff, his hair rising straight up from his forehead. The accompanying article ending 'in short that he, Sir Robert Peel, is the original Pecksniff' caused little stir, and *Punch* turned its attention to Carter as the model for Dickens's odious character.

In 1845 an article appeared in *Punch* entitled 'The Art Union – Its Hand, Head and Heart'.

> In these days of selfishness ... it gives us some hope in our species to meet with a critic who really has a 'Hand, Head and Heart'! ... The Editor of the Art Union has them ... He is a man of intense sympathy – and of intense modesty to match 'Hand, Head and Heart'.

The piece lampoons the editor of *The Art Union*, relying on sarcasm and irony.

> He is a creature of feeling. When he cuts up a young painter – the poor creature not being one of his set – he does it with the delicate hand of a Liston, weeping anodyne tears into the wound, tears that, crystallized, might be worn as shirtstuds by the original Pecksniff himself!

The editor is made to talk pompously of the integrity and judgement exercised in the journal, and of the responsibilities of art criticism, with scarcely the screen of the anonymous for protection. *Punch* continued: 'The screen of the anonymous has certainly been very thin. Pecksniff behind a muslin curtain could not have been less hidden.' Other articles followed, and *Punch* on occasions referred to *The Art Union* as the 'Pecksniffery'.

Carter was naturally upset and had to be deterred by his friends (and probably by Anna Maria) from bringing an action against *Punch*. Certainly Carter was on the pompous side, and had very little sense of humour when it came to personal matters. Both the Halls took themselves very seriously. Charles Dickens was once asked if he thought either of the Halls was conscious of playing a part. His answer was that perhaps they exchanged a wink once a year, probably on Carter's birthday. The pair were very hospitable, sometimes giving quite grand dinner parties, and Anna Maria also had her regular 'evenings'. J. Comyns Carr, a frequent contributor to *The Art Journal*, found Carter a quaint and curious figure whose acquaintance afforded him a certain humorous enjoyment. Writing about the Halls, he quotes a story told to him by the author Thomas Purnell about a dinner party at their house. Purnell said that the gravity of their entertainment was broken up by the unexpected flash of humour from Anna Maria. Carter, in solemn tones, was expounding his belief in a future life, and the hope that he would join his wife in a happier world, whereupon Anna Maria interjected in a strong Irish accent, 'No, Carter, I shall go to Jesus.'[3]

Nathaniel Hawthorne's opinion of the Halls changed as he became more intimate with them. During his stay in England he wrote a detailed journal.

> April 4th Friday. On Tuesday I went to Number 14 Ludgate Hill to dine with Bennock at the Milton Club ... [He] introduced me to Mr S. C. Hall; whereupon that venerable personage in a tone audible to the whole reading room, began to express his admiration for me as the first – yes – it was really so – the very first writer of the age ... It was all said in the most fluent, irrepressible, and yet quiet way with a volubility of fine phrases and with as calm benignity of face. I have never met so smooth an Englishman as Mr S. C. Hall. He likewise presented me with a flower – a perfectly beautiful camellia which his wife had sent me ... I dreaded lest he (Bennock) would place Mr Hall in the next chair to mine, and besought him most

> earnestly to give me any other neighbour rather than he, for that I could not bear his incense. Bennock admitted that Mr S. C. Hall was a little too demonstrative – that it was his nature – but that perhaps my tendency was too much on the contrary direction.

Hawthorne's reaction to Carter's adulation is hardly surprising: such effusiveness would have been distasteful to him. Brought up by women in a reclusive atmosphere, Hawthorne had acquired a liking for solitude and avoided social life, when he could, during his stay in England. He also had a feeling of guilt about writing. This may have been an inheritance from his Puritan forebears, who might well have condemned writing as 'idle imagining'. And here was Carter advertising Hawthorne's talent, and involving him in an association with a fellow writer. Hawthorne went on:

> In respect of my severe criticism of Mr Hall's deportment, I ought to say that Bennock strenuously affirms that he is a good and honest man, though with some absurdities of manner. And he says that he has positively known both Hall and his wife to make greater personal sacrifices for the welfare of art and literature, than he has known any other person to make. Douglas Jerrold, on the other hand, and Dr Mackay, think him an arrant humbug.[4]

The Hawthornes and the Halls went to Oxfordshire together, and Hawthorne wrote in his journal:

> It was a very pleasant visit ... I saw a good deal of Mr Hall and feel bound to say that I repent of the harsh view which I took of his character, when we first became acquainted. I now acknowledge him to be a thoroughly genuine man, of kind heart and true affections, a gentleman of taste and refinement; not a very wise person, perhaps, too vain of his wife (though she is certainly a wife to be proud of) and of himself; saying many things that he had better hold his tongue about, talking too much about himself, his affairs and his achievements; telling his Irish stories over too often to the same auditors, though he tells them well; but still a most estimable man, and full of honour.

When Carter was a parliamentary reporter he had known Charles Dickens's father who was working for the *Morning Chronicle*, and he saw Charles Dickens growing up. Carter was editor of the *New Monthly Magazine* when Dickens submitted his first article to it entitled 'A Dinner at Poplar Walk'; and the Halls were at the christening of Charles Dickens's first child. There was every sign of an amicable acquaintance when Dickens wrote to Anna Maria in December 1838.

> My dear Mrs Hall,
> I am exceedingly obliged to you for your kind note, and the interesting anecdote which you tell so well. I have laid it by in the MS of the first number of Nickleby, and I shall keep it there in confirmation of the truth of my little picture

He goes on to talk about the rascalities of some of the Yorkshire schoolmasters and says that he thinks he met the subject of Anna Maria's story.[5]

Dickens used to visit the Halls at Firfield, their house in Surrey, and was one of their literary friends who carved his name on a tree in the grounds. Yet in 1853 he wrote a letter (to whom, it is unknown) saying:

> Concerning Mr. and Mrs. Hall – S.C. I presume to be the christian initial – I with confidence renounce that amiable couple as the most terrific humbugs known on earth at any period of its history and as to their being in my confidence or knowing my affairs I can only say that it must be in a magnetic table turning or spirit tapping way, wholly without participation of mine and altogether unaccountable and supernatural.[6]

So what went wrong? According to Charles Osborne, Carter often repeated a scandalous story regarding a certain incident which he thought had led to the separation of Dickens and his wife. Charles Churchill Osborne was a connection of Anna Maria by the marriage of her grandmother to George Carr of Graige.[7] Anna Maria had befriended Osborne when he was a young man, asking her friend Francis Bennock to help him find work in the City. Carter later wrote a testimonial for Osborne when he applied (unsuccessfully) for the Secretaryship of the Reform Club, and asked other influential people to do the same. So Osborne knew the Halls well. In 1906 Osborne wrote an article entitled 'Pecksniff and His Prototype' for *The Independent Review*. In the article Osborne says that he believes Hall's scandalous story (which he does not reveal) to be without foundation. Nevertheless, Carter's spreading such a story is most likely the reason for Dickens's 'humbug' letter of 1853 when his marriage was already foundering.

Osborne says in his article: 'I shall try to show that he [Pecksniff] is not a creature of flesh and blood, much less a truthful presentation of Samuel Carter Hall, from whom the character was undoubtedly drawn.'[8] Osborne condemns Dickens's lack of consideration for the feelings of others in that he did not hesitate to caricature his parents and friends, placing them under such a thin veil of disguise that their acquaintances could easily recognise them. If the representations were so grotesque, perhaps Dickens thought it unnecessary to disguise them; but probably it did not occur to him. John Forster, in his *Life of Dickens*, claims that the hurt he inflicted on Leigh Hunt, whom he caricatured as Harold Skimpole, was due to thoughtlessness.

Pecksniff was a schemer and full of moral platitudes. Dickens says of him: 'Perhaps there never was a more moral man than Mr Pecksniff, especially in his conversation and correspondence.' Osborne thinks that no man has such a large stock of tags of morality and well-known poetical quotations as Carter. It was Carter's style and manner of speaking that he thinks Dickens successfully caricatured, even giving Pecksniff phrases which might well have been Carter's own.

> I think Mr Pinch might have done better than choose for his companion one who, at the close of a long intercourse, had endeavoured, as he knew, *to wound my feelings. I am not sure that this was delicate in Mr Pinch. I am not sure that this was kind in Mr Pinch.* I will go further and say, I am not quite sure that this was even *ordinarily grateful* in Mr Pinch.

The phrases in italics are such as Osborne thought Carter constantly used.

Osborne had been shown Carter's bedroom at Avenue Villa,

Holland Street, Kensington, where sheets of paper, pencils and candles were laid out on a shelf.

> 'You see I am never idle,' Carter said. 'If I get an idea during the night I light my candle and jot it down, and then I work it out in the morning before I get up ... Be industrious my dear boy, and you will be happy.'

These little confidences to the young Osborne must have been embarrassing, but to Dickens they would have been a delight.

> 'This is my chamber [he makes Pecksniff tell Martin Chuzzlewit on showing him the house]. I read here when the family suppose I have retired to rest. Sometimes I injure my health rather more than I can quite justify to myself by doing so, but art is long and time is short. Every facility, you see, for jotting down crude notions, even here.'

And Pecksniff points to the table, paper etc. all put ready should an idea come into his head.

Poor Carter, his mannerisms were also copied – his snuff-taking and his habit of putting his right hand inside the velvet jacket which he usually wore, buttoned by one button at the waist. When he was involved in a lawsuit thirty years later, some of the papers referred to him as Pecksniff. This provoked Hall on one occasion to complain to Osborne: 'They say I am Pecksniff! What is there of Pecksniff about me? Do I resemble him in any way? Can any man say I ever wounded him? Thank God, thank God, I have a clear conscience!' According to Osborne he then continued, 'drawing out a huge coloured handkerchief and winking with both eyes at once, as it were against his will' ... 'I will not defend myself against such a charge. Ah well! It does not matter, it does not mat-ter.'

In looks, Pecksniff bore no resemblance to Carter, either as Phiz drew him or as Dickens described him – 'sleek, though free from corpulence'. Carter, on the contrary, was lithe, slim and well-proportioned. With aquiline features, a long jaw, thin mouth and deep-set eyes, he was a strikingly handsome man. He had nothing of the soft and oily manner of Pecksniff, being rather brisk and energetic in his movements.

In drawing Pecksniff for the novel, Osborne says that Dickens borrowed some of Carter's failings, but none of his virtues. Pecksniff has no virtues. Osborne thought Carter 'vain, officious, self-complacent' and sometimes 'offensively voluble', but he could never be described as a consummate humbug mouthing hypocritical phrases. Though Carter could drive a hard bargain as an editor, he was never mercenary. In private life, unlike Pecksniff, he was lavish rather than stingy, and was often generous to struggling artists and writers. Nor was he an intemperate man. Pecksniff was lazy and a cheat. As a so-called architect, he had never designed or built a public building, and the only prize he ever won was for a grammar school designed by Martin Chuzzlewit to which he had made a small addition. All his life Carter was a remarkably industrious man.

Periodicals flourished in the nineteenth century, providing opportunities for aspiring young writers, and for editors to publish in serial form the long novels that the Victorians enjoyed. Proprietors founding new magazines courted authors to join their editorial staff, and literary London had its circles where authors and journalists met in clubs and publishing houses. As editor of the only purely art periodical of the time Carter had no problems about competition, nor does he appear to have belonged to any particular circle, though artists and writers dined at his table. Perhaps he was arrogant; he sometimes gave offence, and was quick to take it. Either he offended the artist and journalist Henry Vizetelly or else Vizetelly was influenced by Henry Ingram, who was not well disposed to Carter. Vizetelly sold his shares in *The Pictorial Times*, which he had started with Andrew Spottiswoode, and joined Ingram's staff on the *Illustrated London News*, supplying a number of engravings, very few of which were derived from authentic sources. Vizetelly wrote vituperatively about Carter in 1893 claiming that 'Pushing young artists and ambitious art manufacturers competed for words of praise from his pen. Those who made offerings of little sketches in oil and watercolour, or choice examples of ceramic ware, were pretty certain to be lauded.'[9] Vizetelly was probably an embittered man when he wrote this, having lately served a term of imprisonment for publishing obscene translations of Zola. It was true that, like many vain people, Carter loved a present, but Osborne says that the monetary value of these gifts was small and that Carter valued them as a token that his efforts for the artists and for the profession of art or literature were appreciated.

Osborne protested against Dickens including Anna Maria in his 'humbug' letter. He regarded it as a privilege to have known her.

> A more sincere and kind-hearted woman I have never known … I have many pleasant recollections of her large-heartedness, her true interest in the welfare of all those she cared for, or whom she knew at all well: of her ready wit, of her bright spirits even when ill and suffering, and of many acts of personal kindness which I shall always hold in grateful remembrance. Intellectually, there was no comparison between Mr. Hall and his wife; and morally, as intellectually, she was, in my opinion, infinitely his superior.

In his memoirs Carter was noticeably reticent as to his personal knowledge of Dickens.

> I first knew Charles Dickens in the year 1826, when 'no shadow before' had heralded the 'coming' of fame … His satire – and he was often a keen satirist – was never personal, either as regards himself or the vices and follies he assailed; of him may be truly said, what the poet said of Sheridan in 'the Combat', his wit 'Ne'er carried a heart-stain away on its blade'.[10]

The rest is eulogy. Nevertheless, there is no doubt that Carter disliked Dickens, and probably this feeling was reciprocated.

Dickens's issue of a statement in the *Manchester Guardian* and in *Household Words* after the break-up of his marriage did little to allay the ugly rumours which were circulating about his relationship with the actress Ellen Ternan, and with Georgina, his sister-in-law. Much sympathy was felt for Catherine, his wife. The Halls were not alone in refusing invitations to Tavistock House if Mrs Dickens was not to be there.

Osborne thought that Carter's defects sprang from an inordinate egoism and self-complacency. He was an exemplary husband, perhaps parading his devotion in public with too much Pecksniffian exuberance. There were those who claimed him as a faithful, if not unselfish, friend. He was hospitable, a genial host and an excellent raconteur with a keen sense of humour where it did not concern himself.

Pecksniff is not Carter, but Pecksniff is not anyone of flesh and blood. Pecksniff's hypocrisy is so exaggerated, so monstrous, that he never comes to life. Walter Bagehot said that Dickens 'has a very peculiar power of taking hold of some particular traits and making a character of them'. That Dickens used certain mannerisms and sayings of Carter is probably true, but carried away by animosity he failed to produce the man and created a caricature rather than a character. Bagehot continues: 'Mr Dickens was too much inclined by natural disposition to lachrymose eloquence and exaggerated character. Such was the kind of writing that was read most readily; and of course he wrote that kind.'[11]

And of course people asked 'Is he Pecksniff?'

8

The Baronial Halls: *An Excursion in the Picturesque*

Very little of the art criticism or appreciation of painting in *The Art Journal* would have been written by Carter himself. He would probably not have thought himself sufficiently qualified, though knowledgeable enough to edit material meticulously. On the other hand, he had considerable knowledge and love of architecture, and enjoyed research into the historical detail and the genealogies of the families concerned. After the success of *Ireland: Its Scenery, Character, etc.* Carter began the research which led to the publication of *The Baronial Halls and Picturesque Edifices of England*.

The work was first published in parts in 1844, each part containing three plates and twelve pages of letterpress interspersed with woodcuts. The parts were subsequently produced in volume form, the first appearing in January 1845, with three volumes following in 1848. The illustrations were in lithotint, from drawings by such artists as J. D. Harding, Samuel Prout, George Cattermole, Thomas Allom and William Fairholt. The publication was based on *The Mansions of England in the Olden Times*, by Joseph Nash, to which Carter added some twenty or more buildings. Nash had published his *Mansions* in four series, in 1839, 1840, 1841 and (after Carter's volumes) 1849. Joseph Nash, a watercolourist and architectural draughtsman with all the nineteenth-century concern for historical authenticity, began drawing on stone and produced coloured lithographs of buildings, mostly of the sixteenth and seventeenth centuries. Into these drawings he introduced figures (always subsidiary to the architecture) – not, as he said, with an eye to picturesque effect, but 'with a desire to identify the edifices they are intended to illustrate with the characters and habits of a people who have now passed away, and to represent, in its various peculiarities "the very age and body of the time"'.[1]

Nash went to Paris with Pugin to make drawings for Pugin's *Paris and Environs*. He also lithographed plates for Pugin's views of *Examples of Gothic Architecture*. He illustrated novels and poetry and produced plates for *The Keepsake* and other annuals. His exhibits at the Old Watercolour Society were of architectural subjects mixed with designs inspired by Shakespeare, Scott and Cervantes. His figures always wore brightly coloured clothes and tended to be on the small side, dominated by the buildings that often filled virtually all the picture area. He was a friend of Anna Maria, and he is said to have done some of the drawings for *The Baronial Halls*, but his name does not appear in the table of contents.

Nash and his contemporaries in the 1830s and 1840s considered the taste in architecture after the reign of Queen Anne ugly and boring; beauty lay in the style of the Tudors. In the eighteenth century, figures in topographical drawings were generally depicted in eighteenth-century dress; but for people in the nineteenth century, to whom the past was romantic, costumes had to be historically correct. The landscape background to architecture in the eighteenth century was usually in the classical tradition of Claude and Poussin, but a picturesque style was more suited to the nostalgic view of history held in the nineteenth century. Picturesque was not just a term applied later, but was then in current use in both artistic and literary circles. In her novel *The Buccaneer* Anna Maria wrote of the 'Picturesque deformity' of the Eagle's Nest where the smugglers hid their goods. John Britton used it in the preface to his topographical work *Devonshire Illustrated* in 1837 when he said, 'There are few parts of England which afford such an extensive scope for picturesque and topographical illustrations as the county of Devon.' Nash, apart from being a talented architectural painter, was a master of the picturesque. Carter, who had a talent for gauging and developing popular taste, was confident there was room for yet another topographical work that, for him, could only be in the picturesque style.

But what did this word picturesque mean to Hall and his contemporaries? It was a philosophical concept which theorists had been analysing since the 1790s. Edmund Burke's theories in his

Enquiries into the Origin of Our Ideas of the Sublime and the Beautiful, published in 1775, had a profound influence on art and literature in the eighteenth and early nineteenth centuries, but Burke did not define picturesque. Sir Uvedale Price, a landowner in Herefordshire, who laid out his estate according to his principles, analysed the picturesque in two works, *An Essay on the Picturesque as compared with the Sublime and the Beautiful* (1796), and *A Dialogue on the Distinct Character of the Picturesque and the Beautiful* (1801). (The latter was in answer to Richard Payne Knight's claim that his distinction between the beautiful and the picturesque was an imaginary one.)

In his first essay Price says that intricacy and variety are the qualities which arouse the sensation of the picturesque. As to the meaning of the picturesque,

> In general I believe, it is applied to every object, and every kind of scenery, which has been or might be represented with good effect in painting, just as the word beautiful (when we speak of visible nature) is applied to every object, and every kind of scenery, that in any way gave pleasure to the eye; and these seem to be the significations of both words, taken in their most extended and popular sense.[2]

He quotes the Revd William Gilpin's definition of picturesque objects as being those 'which please from some quality capable of being illustrated in painting', but thinks this too vague. After reading Burke, Price came to the conclusion that 'the picturesque not only differs from the beautiful in those qualities which Mr. Burke has so justly ascribed to it, but arises from qualities the most diametrically opposite.' Smoothness of an object (a quality of beauty according to Burke), Price claimed, precluded variety or intricacy; whereas sudden broken or projecting lines can cause these and are the opposite of the qualities in beauty.

Picturesque colours were the colours of fresh beauty whether in human form or in the green of spring flowers and trees. David Cox (who was attracted to Herefordshire because it was the county of Price) used a 'broken tint' style during his picturesque period, short linear flicks of the pencil to show dappled foliage.

As to the picturesque in architecture, Price says that a perfect

Greek temple is beautiful and one in ruins is picturesque. The skyline of Greek buildings tends to be straight, and Price thinks 'Gothic architecture is generally considered as more picturesque though less beautiful than Greek'. Supreme emphasis was placed on the visible effects of time on rock and stonework.

The illustrations to *The Baronial Halls* were under the supervision of James Duffield Harding. Harding exhibited at the Society of Painters in Watercolours all his life. Using body colour freely, he was responsible for the abandonment of transparent colours by many younger watercolour painters. A popular and successful teacher, he was an advocate of lithography, a process much used by drawing masters. A good example of his teaching is his *Elementary Art; or the Use of the Lead Pencil Advocated and Explained*, published in 1834. In this Harding explains his methods as to how the different objects in nature can be drawn, and the fundamental importance of drawing. An illustration in this work, called *Ash Trees at Penshurst Park*, shows how he had developed the technique of lithography; neither the delineation of trees, giving each one a characteristic of its own, nor the treatment of sunlight and shadow is lost in the transfer to the stone. In 1841 Harding published *The Park and the Forest: A Collection of Sketches*, using a brush instead of a crayon on stone in a method which he called 'lithotint'. This highly skilled process gave a rich and surprisingly delicate effect and, as can be seen in many of the plates in *The Baronial Halls*, a much greater power of light and atmosphere. Ruskin regarded his work highly: 'There are few who equal him' he wrote 'in rapidity of seizure of material truth.'[3] The plates vary, as Harding, though he was the supervisor, did not engrave them all. Some have a very soft 'smudged' effect, as in Frederick Hulme's lithotint of Sizergh House, Westmorland, and the trees have an abstract quality. The soft edges were particularly suitable for creating an impression of crumbling stone and brick weathered by time. Some are more clear cut, like Frederick Fairholt's, drawn with very fine lines.

There is a certain gloom in the paintings of Constable and Turner before 1832, the year of the first Reform Bill. This is understandable in the climate of the time when bad trade, poverty and starvation brought society almost to the verge of collapse. The rural south of England nervously watched rickburning and disturbances, and the middle classes were demanding reform to appease the unrest in the classes below them. As John Barrell points out in his *Dark Side of Landscape*, Constable sought to preserve harmony by distancing his people in the landscape. Many of his workers are placed in the shade.[4] Though prices and rents were still fairly high after the Repeal of the Corn Laws in 1846, conditions of the working classes were improving, trade was developing and prosperity was spreading. Landowners were still enjoying country sports and entertaining lavishly, and there seems to have been little resentment against this by rural workers. The last three volumes of *The Baronial Halls* were published in 1848, 'the year of revolution' in Europe. When the barricades went up, first in France and then over much of the Continent, some people in England must have watched with apprehension, but on the whole the majority of the population felt that it would not be affected. In art, painters were taking an idealised view of the past, perhaps with a sense of unease at the present (the growing social conscience did not allow for satisfaction). There is none of the awesomeness of nature in the picturesque, but rather an emphasis on the unity of man and nature. In *The Baronial Halls* tidily dressed workers and retainers merge happily with the landscape. Established families inhabit the houses and well-behaved children play with Tudor and Jacobean toys.

Both Nash and Hall tended to choose buildings with picturesque attributes and romantic legend. Haddon Hall in Derbyshire, beloved by David Cox and followers of the picturesque for its dreamlike quality of medieval and Tudor times, was naturally included. Nash and Thomas Allom (Carter's illustrators) both drew the Long Gallery. The story that Dorothy Vernon had eloped from it on the night of a ball celebrating her sister's wedding added to its romantic aura. Rooms within the houses were carefully chosen. Of all the rooms at Knole in Kent, Samuel Rayner drew an upstairs room for *The Baronial Halls* and called it *The Retainer's Gallery*. A woman sits reading papers taken from an old chest, surrounded by broken chairs and unwanted furniture piled up on the worn wooden floor.

Nash devoted four plates to Hardwick Hall, Derbyshire, in his second series of mansions in 1840. His gallery at Hardwick shows the tapestries that Bess of Hardwick is said to have bought from the heir of Sir Christopher Hatton, and one of the fireplaces which resemble the designs by Serlio. There is a nice human touch of a child with a hobby horse, perhaps unable to play outside on a rainy day. His presence chamber is full of architectural detail. This is the High Picturesque, with the central figures of servants spreading layers of straw on the floor as a reminder of how people lived in the past. The staircase in another plate is architecturally correct, but has a picturesque touch of a stone askew. Members of the family walk down the stairs, preceded by a retainer who presents to the viewer the family coat of arms embroidered on the back of his clothing.

Carter only published one plate of Hardwick. His artist was William Lake Price, an architect who turned to painting after studying with de Wint. Like Nash, and many another painter of the picturesque, he illustrated for the popular annual *The Keepsake*. His interior of Hardwick is of a bedchamber with a lady seated in front of her dressing table while a page brings her a glass of wine.

Sir Christopher Hatton's name was more important to Carter in connection with Kirby Hall, the house begun by Sir Humphrey Stafford which Sir Christopher completed in 1570. This is probably the most interesting of all the houses in *The Baronial Halls*. It was planned about an axial line running roughly north-south which provided a view right across the forecourt and the inner court round which the house is built. It was deserted when Carter saw it – as it is today, though still owned by the Earl of Winchilsea. What makes Kirby (otherwise a fairly simple flat-façaded Elizabethan building) so exceptional is the use, on all four elevations, of giant pilasters running up through two storeys. Though the use of orders to embellish separate storeys was then usual, this is probably the first use of the giant pilaster in England. The north and south entrances have magnificent porches. The giant pilasters on the north porch are decorated with arabesque designs, candelabra and putto taken from the title page of John Shute's *The First and Chief Grounds of Architecture*, published in 1563 and then immensely influential. Carter thought that the windows on the first floor, inserted at a later date, marred the effect of the Elizabethan work. Harding's lithotint is of the porch on the south side. This has superimposed orders, very much in the French style, double Corinthian columns over double Ionic columns at the base. It seems that classical architecture in

England really developed as a way of decorating buildings rather than for structural use. At Kirby it probably appealed as much to Elizabethans as it did to the nostalgic Victorians, as a very attractive way of designing a porch.

The drawings for Naworth Castle, Cumberland, in *The Baronial Halls* are by George Cattermole. Cattermole was an architectural draughtsman and topographer of the Romantic Movement. While in Nash's compositions the emphasis is on architecture, Cattermole's buildings tend to be a background for his figures. Eventually he abandoned architecture for figure subjects and became a painter of historical genre of vitality and rich colouring. The colouring in Cattermole's watercolours was particularly admired by the French, who thought he continued the romantic revolution begun by Delacroix, Bonington and other natural colourists of that school. Ruskin wrote in *Modern Painters*: 'The antiquarian feeling of Cattermole is pure, earnest and natural.' He praised his early work, which

> though always conventionally brown in the shadows was generally well drawn and always powerfully conceived ... Since then he has been tending gradually through exaggeration to caricature, and vainly endeavouring to attain by an inordinate bulk of decorated parts, that dignity which is only to be reached by purity of proportion and majesty of line. It has pained me deeply, to see an artist of so great power indulging in childish fantasticism and exaggeration, and substituting for the serious and subdued work of legitimate imagination, monstre machicolations and colossal cusps and crockets.[5]

One of Cattermole's drawings of Naworth is of the grounds. The trees have gnarled trunks with what Uvedale Price would have called 'sudden protuberances'. A man who has just crossed the bridge drinks from a goblet, while a stag lies dead at his feet. Above the trees is a small view of the castle. In the other drawing, *A Gallery Armoury*, a man sits reading old documents taken from a box beside him, a suit of armour lies on the floor. An armoury was a favourite setting for Cattermole's paintings: he used it to great effect in *The Armourer's Tale* (now in the Victoria and Albert Museum) and several of his illustrations to literature have this seated figure who dominates the ones standing about him. Carter admired his early work, and had known him in his youth when Cattermole worked for John Britton, antiquary and topographer. Carter said that he made the dealers but not himself rich; his paintings would make nobody very rich today.

Audley End, Essex, was illustrated by Frederick Fairholt. He was a highly esteemed draughtsman who had been an assistant to the wood engraver Samuel Sly. He drew for the Society of Antiquaries and the British Archaeological Association and illustrated many topographical works. He was a regular contributor to *The Art Journal* from its beginnings, and Carter relied on his considerable antiquarian knowledge and fidelity as a draughtsman. He went to Ireland with Carter, and many of the illustrations in *Ireland: Its Scenery, Character, etc.* are by him. No doubt Fairholt's *Costumes in England*, published in 1846, served as a pattern for many of his contemporary artists. He was a close friend of the Halls, writing frequently to them when they were away, and always remembering 'dear little Fanny' whom he said he regarded as a sister.

Fairholt steadily maintained that he hated the country (he complained that the nightingales kept him awake when he stayed with the Halls at their house in Surrey). Nevertheless, his drawing of Audley End is set in an idealised landscape, with the house very much in the background. People stand on the bridge spanning the river (not Adam's Palladian one), trees bend in the wind and sheep graze.

Nash's Great Hall at Audley End is monumental. The carvings of the Jacobean screen and fireplaces are drawn in meticulous detail. The furnishings and pictures, additions by the 3rd Lord Braybrooke in the 1820s to create the look of a Jacobean hall (huge plates and flagons of wine), all add to the picturesque scene. As one would expect, neither Fairholt nor Nash chose Adam's charming drawing room (designed in the fashionable taste of 1764) for their illustrations. Based on the style of ancient Rome, it had nothing to do with the picturesque.

Fairholt's drawing of Westwood House in Worcestershire illustrates the advantages in the technique of lithotint. It is a highly atmospheric work, making full use of light and shade. Artists for these topographical works were naturally influenced by the fact that their original work was to be transferred to an engraving. While this encouraged care in the arrangement of chiaroscuro and delineation of forms, Ruskin thought it could be harmful 'so far as it involves a dependence rather on quantity of picturesque material than on substantial colour or simple treatment'.[6]

The Gate House at Westwood has two lodges with mullioned and transomed windows, ornamental gables and pinnacles, with the Pakington family arms above. Fairholt has placed this to the left of the picture in deep shade, and the darkness gradually lightens until the house itself is in full sunlight. With finely drawn lines, he shows the tripart porch with attached columns and arches arranged like the Arch of Constantine.

Carter found the Gate House at West Stow Hall, near Bury St Edmunds, infinitely romantic in its decaying state and its association with Mary Tudor, widow of Louis XII of France. A corridor linked it to the old house (then demolished) and then to the eighteenth-century house which Carter saw. He says that Mary Tudor and her husband Charles Brandon, Duke of Suffolk, lived in the house and that this claim is supported by her arms being carved over the Gate House. This is unlikely, though she certainly lived (and died) not far away at Westhorpe Manor. According to tradition, Sir John Croft (who improved West Stow) was either a member of the household of Mary Tudor or Master of the Horse, but there is no documentary evidence that this was so.[7] Perhaps he was hoping for such patronage from Mary Tudor, and put up her arms as a compliment. In one of the rooms of the Gate House there are wall paintings of four of the seven ages of man. One is of a youth hawking, with the inscription 'This do I all the day'. Another is of a youth making love to a young girl, inscribed, 'This do I while I may'. The third is of a man looking at a couple saying, 'This did I when I might'; while the fourth is of an old man sorrowfully exclaiming, 'Good Lord, will this world last ever?'

S. A. H. Hervey, writing about West Stow in 1905, evidently had little patience with the picturesque; he refers to Carter's 'fanciful and inaccurate view of he Gate House' drawn in lithotint by Harding from a sketch by W. Muller.[8] It is of interest that in a view published by John Britton in 1809 there is no clock face, while in engravings of 1818 and 1843 there is. As an inventory of the house in 12 October 1795 included 'Turret clock as fixed', Hervey thought that this was architectural licence on the part of John Britton. The clock is not there today.

As the title implies, *The Baronial Halls* is almost entirely an account of houses, but Carter included the fifteenth-century Beauchamp Chapel of St Mary's Church, Warwick, and the Church of St Nicholas at Arundel. As a lover of the picturesque, Carter could hardly have chosen a more suitable illustrator for the Lady Chapel at Arundel than Samuel Prout. Prout's career as a topographical watercolourist and painter of architectural subjects dates from when he went with John Britton to Cornwall in 1801 and made sketches for Britton's *Beauties of England and Wales*. His simple and direct style of these early years changed in the 1820s with his love of the picturesque and the curves and decayed ornamentation of buildings, and became somewhat mannered. It was an enthusiasm which sometimes even led him into including features of a building which, by the limitations of architectural perspective, he could not possibly have seen. Ruskin praised him for his perception of characteristics which had hitherto been lacking in art, 'of that noble feeling which results from the influence among the noble lines of architecture of the rent and the rust, the fissure, the lichen, and the weed'. Though Ruskin admits that Prout's popularity may have been due to mere love of the picturesque, he insists 'there is *no* stone drawing, *no* vitality of architecture like Prout's'.[9]

The church at Arundel was built all of a piece at the end of the fourteenth century. When Carter visited it the roof had gone, ivy covered pillars and mullioned windows, but restoration of the Lady Chapel had begun. He described the tomb of John Fitzalan, 7th Earl of Arundel, who died in 1434 at the Siege of Gerberoy during the Hundred Years War. The tomb is an open bier with the effigy of the Earl above a cadaver whose lank hair lies on a shroud falling in sinister folds. The tomb is just visible to the right of the engraving, occupying the opening in the wall between the chancel and the Lady Chapel. This is the picturesque at its height. Two men at the centre are digging up a grave, possibly part of the restoration (though they look more like grave robbers). A broken headstone lies beside a thigh bone. A workman's man's hat is slung over a sarcophagus and hatchments hang crookedly on a crumbling wall.

Though the publication of *The Baronial Halls and Picturesque Edifices of England* was well received, the year 1848 for the Halls, personally, cannot have been a happy one. Carter was still the proprietor of *The Art Journal* and was struggling to make it a success. For the first nine years the journal did not meet its expenses in any one year. The news from Ireland was very bad. The sufferings of the Irish people during the famine were terrible. Carter had been deeply affected by them when he visited Achill Island with Frederick Fairholt during one of the periodic famines. Anna Maria would have thought of the country people whom she had known so well living around her stepfather's estate in Wexford. The famine was not so virulent by 1848, but the economic aftermath was a disaster for both peasant and landowner alike. Benevolent and paternalistic landowners had born the crushing burden of paying huge sums in poor relief, while they saw their rents diminishing. Under the Incumbered Estates Act of the following year, many landowners disposed of their estates. Anna Maria must have been thankful that at least George Carr had been spared this.

9
A House in the Country

When George Virtue became proprietor of *The Art Journal* in 1849, Carter, as editor on a fixed salary from 1851, was relieved of anxiety and financial liability. He also had more time for other literary work. Anna Maria had established a reputation as a writer with her *Sketches of Irish Character* (which went into five editions), and several novels appeared after *The Buccaneer* which was published anonymously in 1832. Together, the Halls felt that their income would allow them a house in the country.

'Firfield' in the Surrey village of Addlestone was built by a Chertsey plumber and glazier, probably in about 1829. In 1851 the then owner, John Sparrow, sold it to the Halls. It must have been a fairly substantial house, standing in about an acre of land to which Carter added when he bought three adjoining plots in 1852. The house was demolished in the 1970s to make room for 'St Augustine's Home', but the layout of the grounds with a terrace, garden, coppice and tree-lined walk can still be seen.

> Their place [wrote Nathaniel Hawthorne] is an exceedingly pretty one, and arranged in very good taste. The house is not large, but is filled in every room, with fine engravings, statuettes, ingenious prettynesses, or beautifulnesses, in the way of flower stands, cabinets, and things that seem to have flowered naturally out of the characters of the occupants.[1]

It was tame enough country compared with what Anna Maria had known as a child, but still country where they heard nightingales and Anna Maria could garden, write in peace and entertain in pleasant surroundings. Friends came by train to Woking where the Halls' carriage would meet them. They walked in the grounds which Carter was laying out, and it became the custom for guests to be asked to plant a tree before dining early, sometimes at 5 pm. Maria Edgeworth planted one, also Jenny Lind, Hawthorne and

Dickens (presumably before the 'humbug' letter). Unfortunately, many of these trees suffered in the hurricane in 1986.

Mrs Oliphant said that at these parties Carter surrounded Anna Maria with an atmosphere of admiration, and was 'the sort of man whose specious friendliness, compliments and "blarney" were of the most specious kind, not calculated to deceive anybody, but always amusing'.[2] She said that a wonderful selection of people came to their house. People from Ireland were always welcome; even those of opposing political beliefs were invited if only, perhaps, for Carter to argue with them. Gavin Duffy dined at Firfield in the summer of 1853 when Mrs Oliphant was present. The 'Young Ireland' group was a splinter of the Repeal Movement, circling round the journalists who started the *Nation*, of whom Duffy was the driving force. In 1848, when the paper was prohibited, Duffy was arrested, but the following year was showing Carlyle around Ireland. He joined the Tenant League, but advocated a strong parliamentary representation at Westminster rather than the campaign to prevent payments of rents and poor rates. At the time of the Halls' party he was MP for New Ross, in Anna Maria's county of Wexford, which presumably made him respectable in their eyes. Mrs Oliphant remembered the discussion that Duffy and her husband had at dinner as to national characteristics. Duffy, with some heat, maintained that the frolic and wit usually attributed to his countrymen were a mere popular delusion.

The friend whom Anna Maria probably valued above all others was Francis Bennock. By all accounts he was a delightful, cultured man, well known for his acts of kindness both in the literary and commercial worlds. Born in Dumfriesshire, he came to London where he had wide business interests and was head of a wholesale trading company. He was admitted to the City Freedom by redemption, was a Common Councilman for the City ward of Cripplegate Within and became Deputy for the same ward in 1853. He was a friend of Wordsworth, Southey, De Quincey and Walter Savage Landor and was himself a poet. The Bennocks were constant visitors to Firfield as were the Halls to events in the City. Bennock travelled widely in Europe, sometimes with his wife who was known to be delicate, and also in America. The Victorians had a firm belief in the remedial effects of travel (for example, George

Eliot and George Lewis would undertake the most arduous journeys when they were far from well) and Bennock was travelling in Germany when he died.

Entertaining cost money, of which the Halls were always short. Sarah Fielding, Anna Maria's mother, lived with them and also Fanny, their adopted daughter, for the Halls had no children of their own alive.[3] A carriage was necessary which meant horses and a coachman. There had to be gardeners and some servants in the house, but Anna Maria was anxious that it should not be thought that they were keeping up a grand establishment. After a friend called Spiers (ex-Mayor of Oxford) had been staying with them, she wrote to Bennock:

> Hannah told me this morning that Mr. Spiers rode on the coach box most of the way to Staines and asked Edward what establishment we had – Edward in the pride of his heart said three gardeners – and a butler (Richard!) and four women servants – I told Edward it was doing harm both to himself and us to tell such an untruth – and he said 'The gentleman had no right to ask me' – this was true and I tell you simply, if you have an opportunity that you may contradict such a statement if you hear it made at Oxford – Edward is the only man servant we have ever in the house except when we have company – and Richard (who can do anything, then helps in the house) – Alice has been my mother's maid for thirty years – and we have a girl of fourteen to help Jane and Hannah. I should never have bought a brougham – but a dear girl made me a present of it when she married.[4]

The Halls, too, had others dependent upon them: Carter's two spinster sisters, one of them partially blind, were almost penniless, and he was educating his nephew, Sandford Rochat, whose mother had died and whose father was living abroad. Fanny, their adopted daughter, later married Sandford.

Carter considered that *The Art Journal* prospered after Robert Vernon granted permission for pictures from his collection of British artists to be engraved and published. Carter could not, however, have embarked on such a splendid series without the finances which George Virtue, as proprietor, now provided. *The Art Journal* of

1849 had 15 steel engravings, 12 of sculptures, and 800 engravings on wood. Dr Waagen, Director of the Berlin Art Gallery, wrote:

> Permit me to express my approbation of your Journal, as in every way realizing your object of the promotion in your country of an extended knowledge of Fine Art. I look to England as the only country in which the Arts can be permanently and securely fostered.

The price of the *Journal* rose from one shilling to two shillings and sixpence.[5]

Robert Vernon has been referred to as a self-made man, but, as Robin Hamlyn points out in an essay in the Tate Gallery Vernon Collection Catalogue of 1993, his father William Vernon was already an established hackney-man with a thriving business. His will mentions 'printed books, prints and pictures', so that Robert must have grown up in a household not devoid of cultural interests. His arrival among the collectors of the art world and London society seems to date from 1832 when he moved into No. 50, Pall Mall. He then bought Thomas Gainsborough's *Sunset: Cart Horses Drinking at a Stream* and pictures by Richard Wilson as representing the founders of the British School, and began buying pictures from living British artists.

An article in the first number of *The Art Union* in 1839 describes a visit to Robert Vernon's house which was almost certainly written by Carter himself.

> Mr. Vernon has not gathered his stores into 'A Gallery'. Every room in his mansion is filled with them – from parlour to attic ... His good taste is displayed also in the other arrangements of his apartments; there is no gaudy drapery or gilded furniture to attract the eye and distract the attention, the tables and sideboards are perfectly plain, the pillars simple and quiet ... – even the brass rails that hang the pictures are painted over.

Vernon had no children and never married; the description of his house does not suggest domesticity or one of great comfort, but of a house given over entirely to art. By this time his acquisitions were probably made with a view to presenting the collection to the nation. Carter gives the impression of Vernon at first making safe investments in pictures of established artists when he says that many of the pictures had been seen by the public at exhibitions. However, in the years leading up to the presentation Vernon seems to have gained confidence in his own discernment and bought some pictures straight from the easel. On the other hand, a study of the titles in the collection shows that he commissioned a number of small versions of pictures already owned by other collectors. J. C. Horsley said Vernon's 'apparent interest in art was really used simply as a means of lifting him out of obscurity into some sort of *locus standi* in the world'. But then Horsley disliked him after Vernon insisted on buying Horsley's painting *The Pride of the Village* without its frame and deducting £5 off the price. 'A jobber he certainly was,' Horsley said, 'by nature as well as by trade.'[6]

In 1843 Vernon opened his house to the public for two hours every Monday and Tuesday afternoon, and in 1846 gave Carter permission to publish engravings of the collection in *The Art Union*. The following year Vernon presented 157 paintings and 8 sculptures of British artists to the nation. All the works in the gift, save nine, were published as engravings in 57 parts with accompanying letterpress, between 1849 and 1854. These parts, on pale blue paper, cost five shillings. Anna Maria edited the first two parts and Carter edited the rest. They were subsequently published in three volumes as *The Vernon Gallery of British Art*. The engravings were published simultaneously in *The Art Journal* with a shorter text. Vernon wrote of the engravings in *The Art Journal*: 'They appear to me to be most beautifully executed ... [and will] by their diffusion at so moderate a cost, improve and increase the taste for the production of our native art.' This encouragement of British art was a manifestation of the growing nationalism and patriotic feeling of the time.

Vernon was typical of the new type of patron-collector, product of the growth of industry and wealth in the nineteenth century. Not only did such patrons tend to be more susceptible to changes in fashion in the art world – James Leathart, for example, sold several of his earlier acquisitions to make way for paintings of the Pre-Raphaelites – but they were more intrusive into the artist's work and would often stipulate the subject matter of the picture when commissioning a painting. In this connection it is interesting to note

J. R. Herbert's reply to his patron Francis McCracken, who had evidently explained what he wanted.

> I shall be happy to undertake for you some such subject as you describe, but I fear a subject of the Present Time, from the difficulty of treating the costume successfully ... the costume of this period is generally so bad that it would seriously interfere with any highly poetical work. There are a good many from our own history which I could enter upon with great interest and will shortly write to you and describe them.[7]

In this case the patron-collector did not get his choice, but a more powerful one often did.

So what was a patron-collector looking for at this date? The subject matter would have been all-important. Paintings with a lofty theme – historical or biblical – were regarded as 'High Art'. Vernon bought *Sir Thomas More and His Daughter*, painted by Herbert, at the Private View of the Royal Academy in 1844.[8] Herbert's choice of subject of a martyr for the old religion is understandable as he had become an ardent Roman Catholic. Ironically, at the same exhibition he showed his *Acquittal of the Seven Bishops*, one of the incidents leading to the invitation to William of Orange to come and safeguard the future of Protestantism. Carter wrote a descriptive piece of the painting.[9]

Next to history, in descending order, came literature and landscape, with pictures of everyday life coming bottom of the list. Paintings with a religious theme would be very acceptable in a collection about to be presented to the nation, and Vernon bought a copy of a picture that Sir Charles Eastlake had exhibited at the Royal Academy in 1841. The engraving in *The Art Journal* of 1854 (p. 107) is entitled *Christ Lamenting over Jerusalem.* The 1841 painting had no title, but with it were verses from St Mathew's Gospel in which Christ foretells the destruction of Jerusalem. The academic ideal of 'ut pictura poesis' – that poetry should have some of the aesthetic quality of painting – dominated writers in the eighteenth and early nineteenth centuries. When a poem was accompanied by an illustration, the picture became a mere adjunct of the verse: in using a text to add meaning to a picture, Eastlake was reversing this tendency and preparing the way for the Pre-Raphaelites who constantly used this device.

It seems that E. M. Ward painted a replica for Vernon of his picture *The Disgrace of Lord Clarendon after His Last Interview with the King – Scene at Whitehall Palace in 1667*, which he had exhibited at the Royal Academy (No. 545) in 1846 (whereabouts unknown). Ward was a very popular painter of historical genre at the time. His pictures were elaborate, told a story and were easy to understand. The title explained it all – even giving the date of the event. Henrietta, Ward's future wife, sat for the figure of Lady Castlemaine standing on the balcony with Lord Arlington and Baptist May, Keeper of the King's Purse. Anna Maria can be seen, as an onlooker, to the right of the picture with her back to the viewer, her hair bound with pearls. The text in *The Art Journal* suggested that 'the higher qualities of Art, however, are not so prominent as the ornamental in the work', and that Ward depended on the situation rather than on the character drawing.

There were some pictures in the collection which Carter decided not to engrave, and others to which he gave his own interpretation in the text. William Etty's *Candaulus, King of Lydia, Shows His Wife by Stealth to Gyres, One of His Ministers, as She Goes to Bed* does not appear in *The Art Journal*. It was a new subject for a British artist, and one which raised a storm of protest as an affront to decency and good taste. Instead, Carter published Etty's *Youth on the Prow and Pleasure at the Helm*, an untitled painting which was exhibited at the Academy with lines from Thomas Gray's 'The Bard' in 1832. The *Morning Chronicle* described it as an 'indulgence of ... a lascivious mind', but Etty himself maintained, 'The view I took of it as a general allegory of human life, morally, where what we see here portrayed in its fabulous sense, is often real.'

Public opinion at the time seems to have accepted nudity more readily in sculpture than in painting (a mythological attribute, of course, was a help). Carter was subscribing to this opinion when he said that French nudes looked as if they had taken off their clothes, while Greeks seemed not to have thought of them. Whatever their excellence, the distinction is one between painting and sculpture. Richard Redgrave wrote on the subject in 1866:

> There has always been a stronger objection to the nude figures of the painter than to the more tangible works of the sculptor; this had to be slowly overcome. It was difficult to tolerate such works from living artists, in pictures in their first glow of beauty and freshness ... unspoilt with age and fiddle-brown varnish; so that those who saw no objection to cover their walls with such subjects as *Lot and His Daughters*, *David and Bathsheba*, or *Joseph and the Wife of Potiphar* if reputed to be by the hand of a Guido or a Carracci, could not tolerate the nude from a native painter, even when the subject itself was unobjectionable.[10]

Carter, who knew Etty well, defended him from accusations that his paintings were indecent: 'He was a man thoroughly pure, of lofty mind, and with a tender, almost womanly heart, to whom a coarse expression or a libidinous sentiment would have been impossible.'[11] Nevertheless, Carter did not like *The Sepulchre* (*The Art Journal* 1853 p. 172) and thought the figure of Christ would excite the reverse of veneration, 'so coarse is it in composition, and so deformed in drawing'. His unease as to how the figures in religious paintings should be treated was shared by many of the Victorian public, who in the same way disapproved of Millais's painting *Christ in the House of His Parents*. Carter had no scruples about changing the titles of some of the paintings. He gave the title of *The Disciple* to the engraving in *The Art Journal* 1853 (p. 206) of Etty's painting called *The Saviour*, because he considered the head had none of the divine attributes associated with the appearance of Christ.

A scene from *The Devil on Two Sticks* in the Vernon Collection had been exhibited by Augustus Leopold Egg at the Academy in 1844. It was taken from René Le Sage's *Le Diable Boiteux*, first published in 1707. The central figure is Patricio, who has left his long-suffering wife to take two ladies of the town to a tavern, in the hopes of seducing one of then called Luisita. Patricio, encouraged by the women who are enjoying a good meal, calls for more food and wine than he can pay for. He is forced to pawn his rosary beads to pay the bill to the large landlord standing firmly behind him. Leaving the inn, the women gave Patricio the slip, and he has to return home without receiving the expected favours of Luisita. Egg was probably unconcerned as to the reaction of public opinion to such a subject. With his preference for illustrating famous literary works, he would have chosen it as one that afforded ample opportunity for his robust and colourful style of painting. The story is a satire on the follies and vices of men. In *The Art Journal* Carter concentrated on the moral issue that folly must be paid for, rather than on the sexual innuendoes, and gave the picture his own title of *The Victim*. In describing the picture he calls the women Patricio's 'acquaintances'. Such veiling of realities may now seem ridiculous, but Carter was well aware that *The Art Journal* would have its place in the drawing room of its readers and that, as he says, the style of *Le Diable Boiteux* was not 'calculated for general reading in an age of extreme sensitiveness to proprieties of thought and language'.[12]

David Wilkie was commissioned by Vernon to paint a picture of the size and character of his *Columbus in the Convent of Rabida*, and preferably with a female in it. On returning from a visit to Ireland, Wilkie suggested the subject of what he ultimately called *The Peep O'Day Boys' Cabin in the West of Ireland*. 'The Peep O'Day Boys' were a secret society in Ulster which the government, at a time of sectarian incidents and agrarian unrest in the 1780s, was unable to control. The members were Protestant peasants enraged that some of the Protestant gentry disapproved of, and sometimes circumvented, the harsh penal laws against Roman Catholics. Indeed, some liberally minded landlords preferred Catholic tenants, and this at a time when leases of land were scarce. Wilkie first called his painting *The Sleeping Whiteboy*. The Whiteboy Society, which developed in the South of Ireland in the 1760s, had a wide range of grievances, not necessarily sectarian, the chief being against the extension of pasture land and the payment of tithes. This resentment against tithes was at its height in the 1830s when Wilkie visited Ireland.

Wilkie would have seen plenty of cabins in the West of Ireland (though hardly as spacious as this one) and the scene of a simple dwelling was one that he loved to paint. To Robert Vernon and his circle the unlikelihood of finding a member of The Peep O'Day Boys' Society in the West of Ireland would have been immaterial, but the change of name gave Wilkie ample opportunity for rich drama. The very title invoked the dawn scene and the dangers which daylight might bring to the sleeping husband. The cock in the rafters announces the dawn, and a friend bursts open the door to warn the vigilant wife of approaching authority. But Wilkie painted an idealistic picture, almost classical in the posture of the wife and the recumbent man with the axe (attribute of a warrior) lying at his feet. So what would have been Vernon's opinion of it? Perhaps he thought of it as an allegory of Venus and Mars in a modern setting, unaware of the violence and bitterness underlying such a subject.[13]

It soon became apparent that relations between Carter and George Virtue, now the sole proprietor of *The Art Journal*, were not going to be easy. Virtue was by this time a very successful publisher, well known for the production of books illustrated with fine engravings and descriptive texts. He had started his career in the 'number trade' in which books were circulated entirely through the agency of his canvassers, without the intervention of other booksellers. He became part proprietor of the famous *Life in London or The Adventures of Tom and Jerry* series, written by Pierce Egan and illustrated by the Cruikshanks.

In 1851 Carter obtained permission from the Queen to copy some of the pictures in the Royal Collection with a view to publishing a series of engravings with descriptions in *The Art Journal* called *The Royal Gallery of Art*. These were later published in four volumes. The pictures were some from Buckingham Palace, Windsor Castle and Osborne House. The decision to publish this series shows Carter's awareness of the change taking place in the art world, and his ability to take advantage of successful innovations. It was most opportune for an art editor that the widening of patronage in the mid-nineteenth century brought about, or coincided with, the idea of bringing private collections of art before the public – collections hitherto often shut away in country houses. Even now, preparations were in hand for the first large exhibition of works of art in England from private collections, including that of Prince Albert and the inherited collection of the Queen. This was the Manchester Fine Arts Exhibition which opened in 1857. Its purpose, in the eyes of the Prince, was to instruct the uneducated in the history of art. Encouraged by the reaction of the public to this exhibition, Carter later, in 1862, was to publish *The Selected Pictures from the Galleries and Private Collections of England*.

This is, today, a valuable source for research of the collectors of the time and the exhibiting of their pictures.

The Royal Gallery of Art was to be published under the auspices, and with the advice, of George Virtue. There must have been some sort of financial agreement as to the expenses involved in commissioning artists to copy the pictures from which the engravings were to be made. Carter would have had difficulty in raising enough capital. It seems from correspondence that Francis Bennock played some part in an agreement being reached.

Before work on *The Royal Gallery* had gone very far, a separate issue arose which strained the Halls' relations with the Virtues (father and son). Anna Maria ran *Sharpe's London Magazine* in 1845, but for some reason she ceased to be associated with it after a while and complained that she had been slandered. She suspected that George Virtue, as publisher, had something to do with it. Bennock evidently smoothed matters over, for she wrote to thank him.

> You have had the power to make the right to be done, and to perhaps save your friends from a misunderstanding – After the manner the Virtues behaved about 'Sharpe' I cannot have very warm feelings towards them – I could not in my own heart trust them as of old – I could not have used them as they used me – I would have been well content with Mr. Virtue's *word* in a bargain – Now – I would prefer his bond. I shall be very glad to believe that as the publisher merely he could not have prevented the slander done unto my name in the periodical I had laboured so earnestly to perfect – but I can't *believe that yet*. I will however try, for it is very important to the interests of the 'Art Journal' that every thing is tuned to as good harmony as can be made.

She goes on rather scathingly about the difficulties of a man who had made money in the 'Number trade',

> putting farthings and pence together – to take as large a view of so large a subject as publishing the 'Royal Gallery' while it should be done with as liberal a feeling towards the public, as the Queen and Prince (God bless them) evinced towards the proprietors of the Art Journal.[14]

The Halls settled in to Firfield, Carter travelling up to London by train, and soon after their arrival bought two plots of land, about five and a half acres, on the south side. Addlestone had a butcher and a baker and, according to a letter of their neighbour the philologist and historian John Mitchell Kemble, the Chertsey tradesmen sent their carts to the village three or four times a day. St Paul's nearby, a very ugly church built between 1834 and 1836, was soon covered in ivy that the Halls were said to have brought from Ireland. A school had been opened in 1843 which by 1851 was in need of enlargement. To help raise funds for the building, Anna Maria wrote a handbook entitled *Chertsey and Its Neighbourhood*, published in 1853, much of which appears in her *Pilgrimages to English Shrines*, published in 1850. There are delightful little woodcuts – two by the Dalziel brothers, one of the gateway to Charles James Fox's house, and the other of the garden front of Cowley's house. Anna Maria describes the ruins of Chertsey Abbey, of which practically nothing remains today above ground. There is an illustration of Anningsley, the home of Thomas Day, author of *A History of Sandford and Merton* (and the intimate friend of Maria Edgeworth's father) of whom Anna Maria had heard so much. In the churchyard at Walton the Halls searched for and eventually found the grave of William Maginn. No stone marked the spot.

In 1853 Carter was in Paris and attended the Emperor's *déjeuner* at St Cloud. There was an enormous gathering and he and his English friends could not get near the tables laden with food. At last Carter (who was a tall impressive figure) called out, 'Make way for the Lord Mayor', and reaching the tables handed back food over the heads of the crowd to his hungry compatriots. It was here that Carter heard the story told about the late Lady Blessington. She had known Louis Napoleon in England and entertained him, a morose and silent guest, at Seamore House and Gore House in Kensington. When she went to live in Paris in 1849 she expected to be invited to his public as well as his private functions. Meeting her one day in the Bois, he was forced to stop and politely inquired, 'Do you make a long stay in Paris?' to which Lady Blessington quickly replied 'No – do you?'

Nathaniel Hawthorne's journal was written between 1853 and 1857. His wife, publishing it after his death, made her own revisions where she considered that descriptions of contemporaries were too outspoken, or subjects indelicate. She disapproved of the over-frequent allusions to food and drink and of the length of Hawthorne's appreciation of pretty women. Hawthorne went with Bennock and Dr Mackay (then editor of the *Illustrated London News*) to Sunday lunch at Firfield. He described the conservatory which Carter had built and the very fine casts of modern sculpture. *The Greek Slave* by Hiram Power was criticised by Bennock and Mackay as being too thin and meagre, but Hawthorne defended it as in the American taste in beauty. According to Hawthorne Anna Maria was 'tall and large and rotund ... [and was] a good figure of a woman'. He said she must once have been a beauty.

> I liked her simple, easy, quiet kind of manners – and I liked her husband too, a great deal better than on our first acquaintance. I believe that Dickens has greatly wronged him in that odious character of Pecksniff. He has his ridiculous side ... but still I do not think him insincere ... He has a wide and quick sympathy, and expresses it freely – too freely perhaps – but yet the world is the better for him.[15]

The Hawthornes went to Oxford with the Halls and found rooms together in St Giles Street. Fanny, the Halls' adopted daughter, whom Hawthorne described as auburn-haired and about seventeen, was with them, and also Joseph Durham the sculptor. The visit was not just a holiday for Anna Maria and Carter, but a preparation for their *Book of the Thames*. They went to Stanton Harcourt to see the church and house where, Hawthorne reported, Anna Maria was too large to climb the circular turret at the corner of the tower. By boat they travelled to Folly Bridge, and from there by barge to Nuneham. Carter thought the house only third-rate. This may have been because of alterations and anyway, built by the architect Stiff Leadbetter of Eton in 1756 as a Palladian villa, it would not have been to Carter's taste and was more suitable as a holiday retreat than as a family home. Lancelot Brown was brought in to improve the gardens and to make alterations to the house. Later, in 1832, Robert Smirke enlarged the house with a rusticated extension of the front, pierced by three segmental arches in the centre. Lord Waldegrave's widow, now married to George Granville Harcourt (son of the late

Archbishop of York), showed the party some of the treasures of the house. She told them that she had shown Dr Buckland, the famous geologist and Dean of Westminster, a silver box which she said contained the heart of Louis XIV (Hawthorne did not know how it could have got there). Taking the box from her, the Dean opened it – and swallowed the contents.[16]

The Book of the Thames was published in parts in *The Art Journal* and then in a volume in 1859. Frederick Fairholt provided much of the antiquarian information in the notes, as well as making sketches for some of the engravings. Most of the sketches were by William Stephen Coleman, a figure painter and illustrator who worked for Minton Art Pottery. *The Book of the Thames* is one of the earliest books to have been published with some photographic illustrations. Carter had been following the developments of this technique closely. Probably the first photographs to be published in a periodical had appeared in 1846 in *The Art Union* and the editorial in the June number was on Fox Talbot's technique.

Anna Maria was concerned when no notice of *The Art Journal*'s series of *The Book of the Thames* appeared in the *Illustrated London News*. As usual, she took her troubles to Francis Bennock.

> Private. Dear Mr Bennock,
>
> Dr Mackay told Carter some time ago that your friend Mr Herbert Ingram [the proprietor] would not permit any line of notice much less praise of anything we did, to go into the 'Illustrated News'. I do not know why the illustrious M.P. should so hate us – but it is evident he does. Though I earnestly and deeply respect a man who has been the architect of his own fortune ... yet were it not for the injury such a prejudice does us – in the way of our bread-earning – I cannot say I should give a second thought, as to whether the great man liked or disliked us – but the 'Illustrated' has a large circulation – and might do us some service – Could you get from Mr Ingram why he is so bitter and unjust – and could you convince him that it *is* unjust and ungenerous. I am anxious that 'The Book of the Thames' in the Art Journal should be noticed as it progresses through its pages.[17]

She went on to say that she thought it mere affectation for

literary people not to care about fame – for her it was a necessity. Poor Bennock, Anna Maria does seem to have been rather importunate in her demands upon him. Sometimes she did not tell Carter (who would probably have been embarrassed) that she was asking him for help. They were, of course, close friends, and she signed her letters 'Your sincere and affectionate friend' with reason. By all accounts Anna Maria was impulsive and warm-hearted, equally ready to be the giver or receiver of help. She also seems to have retained a certain youthful spontaneity into middle age. Nathaniel Hawthorne, after calling on her in London with his wife, spoke of her having 'a deal of sentiment, passing sometimes into sentimentality, and showing itself in little gifts and tributes of flowers, for instance, gathered from somebody's grave, or strewn upon it – and other such prettinesses, not to be looked for in a rotund English dame of ripe years'. (She had been visiting Bessy, the widow of Thomas Moore at Sloperton, and gave Sophia, Hawthorne's wife, a rose from his cottage.)[18]

Perhaps the visit to Oxford had been proposed by Carter in order to raise Anna Maria's spirits after the death of her mother in January of that year. Sarah Fielding had lived with them for thirty years, and was much loved by them both. Before she died, she had the pleasure of knowing that the estate in County Wexford, where Anna Maria had spent her childhood, was still being kept up. According to the diary of a descendant, George Carr had incurred debts through the extravagance of his wife (Anna Maria's grandmother), who spent large sums on forming 'costly flower beds, grottoes, ornamental temples and extensive puzzle-walks enclosed by high hedges of boxwood'.[19] George Carr's sisters, who inherited Graige on his death, sold it to a cousin, Samuel Boyse, who in 1835 (according to Thomas Moore's diary) was building a new house. The Halls were entertained by Richard Boyse (Samuel's second son) when they went to Ireland in 1854 or 1855. 'So dear Graige is kept up well. And you have seen it,' Mrs Fielding wrote happily in answer to Anna Maria's description of the place.

A stone plaque on the north wall of St Paul's Church, Addlestone bears the name of Sarah Elizabeth Fielding. The names of Anna Maria and Samuel Carter Hall were added later.

10

Tom Moore: In Memoriam

Carter first met the Irish poet Thomas Moore at a party at Lady Morgan's house in Dublin to which he was taken by the novelist and dramatist Charles Maturin. Moore sang his poems, and one of them, 'As a Beam o'er the Face of the Waters May Glow', affected Carter so much that (to the surprise of the poet) he fell on his knees and kissed Moore's hand.

Thomas Moore was born in Aungier Street in Dublin in 1779, the son of a grocer. After the Catholic Relief Act in 1793, Dublin University gave degrees to Roman Catholics and Moore (who had been baptised one) entered Trinity College in 1794. He read Classics and became proficient in music. In the College Historical Society he gained a reputation for his wit and vivacity, and was awarded a gold medal for composition. Carter afterwards gave this medal to the Royal Irish Academy (presumably it had been amongst the personal items given to him by the poet's widow). Though he became a friend of Robert Emmet, whose brilliant oratory made him one of the leaders of the College party of the 'United Irishmen', Moore's nationalism seems to have been mainly academic, and he took no part in the 1798 Rebellion.

When Moore went to England he brought with him a letter of introduction to Lord Moira (later Marquess of Hastings), who launched him on London society and even presented him to George, Prince of Wales. Moore's unremarkable translation of *The Odes of Anacreon* was dedicated to the Prince. When Moore published *The Poetical Works of the Late Thomas Little*, some youthful amorous poems, Lord Jeffrey, editor of the *Edinburgh Review*, attacked him in the August 1806 number calling him 'the most licentious of modern versifiers'. Moore (who in later years was ashamed of these poems) challenged Jeffrey to a duel, but when they met at Chalk Farm the police intervened. It all, however, added to the romantic aura surrounding the lively, witty little Irishman who became the darling of society. One of his friends, who mixed in every level of society, said, 'Tom Moore was the best table companion I ever met.' And Jeffrey, who became a close friend of Moore, said of him: 'He is the sweetest-blooded, warmest-hearted, happiest, hopefulest creature that ever set fortune at defiance.' His critics accused him of subservience to the aristocracy and, after his death, quoted as evidence an entry from his journal, 'Called at Lansdowne House, and *was let in*.' Carter, however, refuted this in his memoir of Moore, by pointing out that a few lines later in the journal Moore said, 'Lord Lansdowne called and *was let in*.'

In 1807 James Power, a music publisher, suggested that Moore should write verses for traditional Irish airs in cooperation with the composer Sir John Stevenson. These were published, at uncertain intervals, in numbers of twelve songs (fourteen in the last) and costing fifteen shillings, over the next twenty-seven years. These *Irish Melodies* established Moore's reputation as a poet, then and for posterity, and provided him with a steady, if small, income. In his Prefatory Letter to the *Irish Melodies*, Moore referred to the touches of political feeling in some of the songs: 'It has been accordingly said that the tendency of this publication is mischievous, and that I have chosen these airs but as a vehicle of dangerous politics.' (He had in mind letters under the signature of 'Timeous' attacking him in the *Morning Post*.) He begged people 'to believe that there is no one who deprecates more sincerely than I do any appeal to the passions of an ignorant and angry multitude; but that it is not through that gross and inflammable region of society a work of this nature could ever have been intended to circulate.'[1] Indeed, Moore loved nothing better than having a circle of beautiful women grouped round the piano in a London drawing room listening while he sang.

In Ireland, there was criticism that the youth who had been the friend of Robert Emmet came to Ireland so seldom, and kept aloof from politics. Carter says that Moore went there a few times for research. He attended a dinner in Dawson Street in Dublin in June 1818 when he said, 'My fame, whatever it is, has been acquired by touching the harp of my country, and is, in fact, no more than the echo of the harp.'[2] In London he was a constant visitor at Holland House, and his journal is full of names and gossip of the Whig politicians of the day. Married to a Protestant, he was equally at ease in a Roman Catholic or Protestant church, though he said, 'I was born and bred in the faith of my fathers, and in that faith I intend to die.'[3]

Moore wrote the *Irish Melodies* to be sung, not read. The poems were mostly set to traditional airs arranged by Sir John Stevenson, though some were by Moore. He was greatly influenced by a volume entitled *A General Collection of Ancient Irish Music ... Adapted for the Piano Forte* by Edward Bunting, published in 1796. These were airs only, but Bunting added words (probably impressed by Moore's success) in a new edition in 1809 which were not very satisfactory. Stevenson was accused of spoiling the simplicity of some of the traditional airs by introducing an elaborate variety of harmonies. Moore himself thought that the finest and most powerful melodies of Irish music were modern, when the harp was given extra strings. He only sang his own arrangements, and his voice was so sweet, though small, that he delighted his London hostesses. Sydney Smith wrote to him,'I swear that I would rather hear you singing than any other person I ever heard in my life, male or female.'[4]

For Moore the language of sorrow was best adapted to Irish music, and some of the melodies like 'The Meeting of the Waters' have a nostalgia tinged by the sweetness of melancholy. Though Moore had visited the beauty spot where the two rivers meet in County Wicklow, the words

> There is not in the wide world a valley so sweet,
> As that vale in whose bosom the bright waters meet;

were written, according to his wife, in a London attic. Though this was one of Moore's purely sentimental poems, many which might have been deemed political even then had such a romantic flavour that they were more suited to the drawing room than to the nationalistic podia, and it was for this that he was criticised by a section of society in Ireland. 'We know that even Moore himself thought that, perhaps, too much refinement pervaded the *Melodies* to make them entirely popular,' said the writer in the *Dublin Magazine* in his 'Recollections of Moore'.

William Hazlitt criticised Moore's poetry in an essay in *The Spirit of the Age*, but Hazlitt could be very severe (he gave little praise to

Byron or to William Gifford, editor of the *Quarterly Review*, in the same publication). 'His verse', he said, 'is like a shower of beauty, a dance of images, a stream of music or like the spray of a waterfall.' Further on he says that Moore's poetry

> seduces the taste and enervates the imagination ... His is the poetry of the bath, of the toilette, of the Saloon, of the fashionable world; not the poetry of nature, of the heart, or of human life ... There are here no tones to waken Liberty, to console Humanity. Mr Moore converts the wild harp of Erin into a musical snuff-box.

However, he liked Moore's musical squibs in the *Twopenny Postbag*. 'None can so well describe the set speech of a dull formalist or the flowing locks of a Dowager.' Certainly Moore was familiar with both. In a similar vein, *The Fudge Family in Paris*, which he published in 1818, was very popular. His best long work, for which Longman paid him 3,000 guineas, was *Lalla Rookh: An Oriental Romance* (1817). Other works followed in quick succession.[5]

Carter defended Moore against those who claimed that he had deserted the cause of liberty in Ireland which he had appeared to advocate in some of his early poems. He said that Moore only 'protested in emphatic verse against a continued agitation that retarded her progress when her claims were admitted, her rights acknowledged, and her wrongs redressed'.[6] This complacency on the part of Carter (and Moore) that all was well in Ireland seems extraordinary at a time when O'Connell was launching his National Appeal Association and was supported by the new 'Young Irelanders'. As the champion of Moore, Carter retaliated against Charles Phillips, barrister and miscellaneous writer well known for his florid oratory, who circulated an objectionable pamphlet a few months after the poet's death. Carter's attack on Phillips brought the threat of a libel action, but finally Phillips withdrew the pamphlet.

Moore was a close friend of Lord Byron. Byron used to say of him that he was the best-hearted man, with talents equal to his feelings. Byron gave Moore his memoirs as a gift when Moore stayed with him in Venice. After Byron's death Moore sold them to the publisher Murray for 2,000 guineas, but paid back the money when pressure was brought by members of Byron's family, and the papers were all burnt (not the only case of papers being destroyed by over-zealous relations in the nineteenth century). Carter is reticent about the whole affair, but Murray paid Moore £4,000 for a life of Byron in 1830.

Anna Maria wrote to Moore after reading his *History of Ireland*, published in 1842, and presented him with a copy of her *Sketches of Irish Character*. She said how pleased they were to see that Moore had included a poem entitled 'Jerpoint Abbey' in volume III of his *History* which Carter had written as a young man. During the 1840s the Halls became close friends with the Moores. Moore had married Bessy Dyke, a beautiful Irish actress, whom everyone praised for her gentleness and loyalty to him. There is no doubt about Moore's devotion to Bessy, but she seldom took part in his social life. It is debatable whether this was by her choice or his. Moore said that she preferred the company of her equals rather than of her superiors. On the other hand, in a letter to James Power he wrote:

> You will be glad to hear that Bessy has consented to my passing May in town alone; to take her would be too expensive; and indeed it was only representing to her that my songs would all remain a *dead letter* with you, if I did not go up in the gay time of the year and give them life by *singing them about* that she agreed to my leaving her.[7]

This advertising of the *Irish Melodies* was probably necessary as Moore was often in need of money and would not accept help from rich friends. He was extraordinarily good to his parents and sister, and he had a profligate son whose debts he paid on several occasions. He and Bessy settled in a small house at Sloperton near Bowood, home of Moore's friend the Marquess of Lansdowne. The Halls spent a week with the Moores at Sloperton in 1845, and Anna Maria became very fond of Bessy. After Moore's death Bessy gave the Halls the table on which Moore used to write when he sat out on the terrace.

Moore died in 1852. In his will he had stated that he wished Lord John Russell to edit his memoirs, journals and letters, and in 1853–6 they were published by Longman. The publication met with a storm of criticism both of the editor and of Moore. Carter thought Russell showed a singular lack of editorial knowledge and tact. He also made it known that Mrs Moore had wanted Carter to edit the papers if Lord John Russell had refused. For a man as busy as Russell to have produced eight volumes in three years, starting a year after the poet's death, suggests that he must have hurried it. Certainly much that is irrelevant and dull, apart from entries which might be called tactless, could have been omitted, and the publication suffers from a lack of an introductory narrative. As J. B. Priestley said in his work on Moore and the diary, it is a day-to-day account, never omitting a mention of a person of importance or of political gossip.

John Wilson Croker first criticised Lord John Russell in *The Times* in June 1853.[8] Then in the same year he launched an attack upon Moore and Russell in the *Quarterly Review*. 'The volumes [he wrote] are what is called *edited* in the most slovenly and perfunctory style. If Lord John had, as he intimates, a power of selection … [the entries are] in many instances very ill-chosen.' He also accused Lord John of suppressing a long account left by Moore of the destruction of Byron's manuscript and substituting some 'studiously obscure sentences of his own'. Next he turned to Moore. 'So voluminous a polyglot of gossip – such a gigantic distension of nothings and next to nothings … Its most substantial value is, undoubtedly, that it throws a great deal of light, and *corrective* light, both on Moore's genius and the character and tendency of his most popular works.'[9] He even accused Moore of lack of feeling for natural scenery, suggesting that he did not know which two different confluences he meant for 'The Meeting of the Waters' in Wicklow. Another charge was that he had never visited Killarney until he was forty-two, when the Marquess of Lansdowne took him there.

Carter was furious with Croker for this attack on his idol. 'There are many people who remember this busy body in the House of Commons [he wrote later in his memoir of Moore]. His party found him a zealous and unscrupulous partisan.'[10] Croker's venom, Carter thought, was due to Moore at one time having called him 'a scribbler of all works', an entry which Carter thought Lord John might well have omitted.

Moore's memory was attacked from another quarter in the same year. This was the preface written by Thomas Crofton Croker to a book of correspondence between Moore and his music publisher, James Power. The letters which appeared in volume VI of Lord John's publication were, according to Croker, presented in such a way (including a number of omissions) as to put Power in a very bad light. Croker's publication was suppressed in England, but was published in America. Croker maintained that Power had been a good friend to Moore, making him advances, while Moore would often be in arrears with the *Irish Melodies* and would instead press on Power other poems which he could only publish at a loss. He suggested that Moore had put off looking into his money difficulties with which Power had helped him over a number of years, and then begun to question the account with Power when he found that he was seriously overdrawn. Carter took a lofty view of this in his memoir of Moore, saying it was not worth while confuting the statements. Of Crofton Croker he wrote, 'He was a small man – small in mind as well as in body; doing many little things, but none of them well; his literary fame rests on his *Irish Fairy Legends*, a book of which he was only the editor.'[11] Carter himself had certainly written two of the legends. Such was Carter's veneration for Moore that he was prepared to belittle Croker despite the kindness that he had received from him in the past.

In 1853 Carter raised a subscription to put up a statue to Moore in Dublin, and in a notice in *The Art Journal* invited sculptors to apply for the commission. Christopher Moore, a Dublin-born sculptor living in London, won the competition for the monument, competing against leading Irish sculptors such as John Hogan. The statue, which was erected in 1857, depicts Moore in cast bronze wearing an ample cloak, standing on a large stone plinth. Christopher Moore's reputation rests on the sculpture of portrait busts, and it seems that he was not successful in larger, more important figure subjects. W. G. Strickland says of him, 'His grotesque effigy of Thomas Moore, in College Street in Dublin, is an unfortunate memorial to the poet.'[12]

When a centenary celebration of the poet's birth was held in the Exhibition Hall in Dublin on 28 May 1879, Carter said that one of the main objects was to replace what he called the 'odious' statue of Moore. (This was never done and the statue still stands today.) The

Lord Chancellor of Ireland, Baron O'Hagan, gave an oration, but Carter thought there was a poor attendance. The Lord Mayor was there, but no magnate of the City, no Fellow of Trinity and no representative of the Castle. Only Carter came from England. In 1869 Carter wrote *A Memory of T. Moore* and gave the proceeds from the publication towards putting a memorial window in the west end of Bromham Church where Moore is buried. Carter also placed an inscription on a marble slab over the door at No. 12, Aungier Street in Dublin, where Moore was born.[13]

The Halls continued to visit Moore up to the time of his death. According to all accounts, he was a delightful man – generous, affectionate and high-minded, and never spoilt by the flattery which surrounded him in London. The accusation that he courted the society of the aristocracy at Bessy's expense is probably unfair. Bessy would never have been accepted in the circles that Moore frequented, and he would not have been prepared to subject her to humiliations. After his death Anna Maria was very kind to Bessy, and was a solicitous friend.

As a poet Moore does not match up to his contemporaries, but then he never intended his *Irish Melodies* to be read. With his combination of poetry and music he should be remembered as the great Irish lyric composer. His poetry was not as popular in Ireland as in England, where its appeal was to the fashionable public imbued with the prevailing romanticism. Posterity has been inclined to view Moore's work as part of the Romantic Movement, the *Melodies* as dreams in a Celtic twilight. In fact, Moore kept his Celtic genius well within bounds. The poems are romantic in that they are an exposition of his sensibilities, but they are also full of good sense. His patriotism was not disturbing; as Hazlitt said, there are no tones in his poems 'to waken liberty'. Nevertheless, for an Irishman away from home, the *Irish Melodies* provide a journey in nostalgia on which he may choose his own way.

> Oh! 'tis only Music's strain
> Can sweetly smoothe, and not betray.[14]

11

Elegantia *and the Public*

The Halls lived at Firfield for about nine years. They were years during which Carter probably made his greatest contribution to art history in his role as an art editor, providing many valuable sources for future researchers. Nevertheless, overshadowing these days of satisfaction and excitement in his work was the constant worry about money. Carter does not seem to have had much financial sense and Anna Maria may have been (like her grandmother) extravagant; between them they seem to have taken on commitments which were beyond their means. Added to this, there was always an uneasiness in their relationship with George Virtue, who held the purse strings of *The Art Journal.*

For the first two years Carter spent little time at home. He and Anna Maria travelled extensively in France and Germany in their search for material for *The Art Journal.* In Dresden they visited Professor Vogel von Vogelstein, the painter of historical scenes and portraits, who had worked in Italy where he became a Roman Catholic and joined the Nazarene group of painters. His drawing of Carter, illustrated in this book, is signed with the date 18 September 1850 and shows what an exceedingly handsome man Carter was at the time. He also drew Anna Maria – both drawings are in the Art Gallery at Dresden.[1] Von Vogelstein took the Halls to see Moritz Retzsch, famous for his illustrations of the works of Goethe, Shakespeare and the German poets, and afterwards Anna Maria published an article in *The Art Journal* based on the visit. The main reason, however, for Carter travelling at that time was to prepare a catalogue of the Great Exhibition of 1851, to be published by *The Art Journal.* In Paris he knew many of the intending exhibitors, having reported the Paris exhibitions of 1844 and 1849. He employed an agent there and also in Brussels. He visited Munich, Berlin and Hanover in the autumn of 1850, obtaining drawings of works of industrial art which the manufacturers there expected to

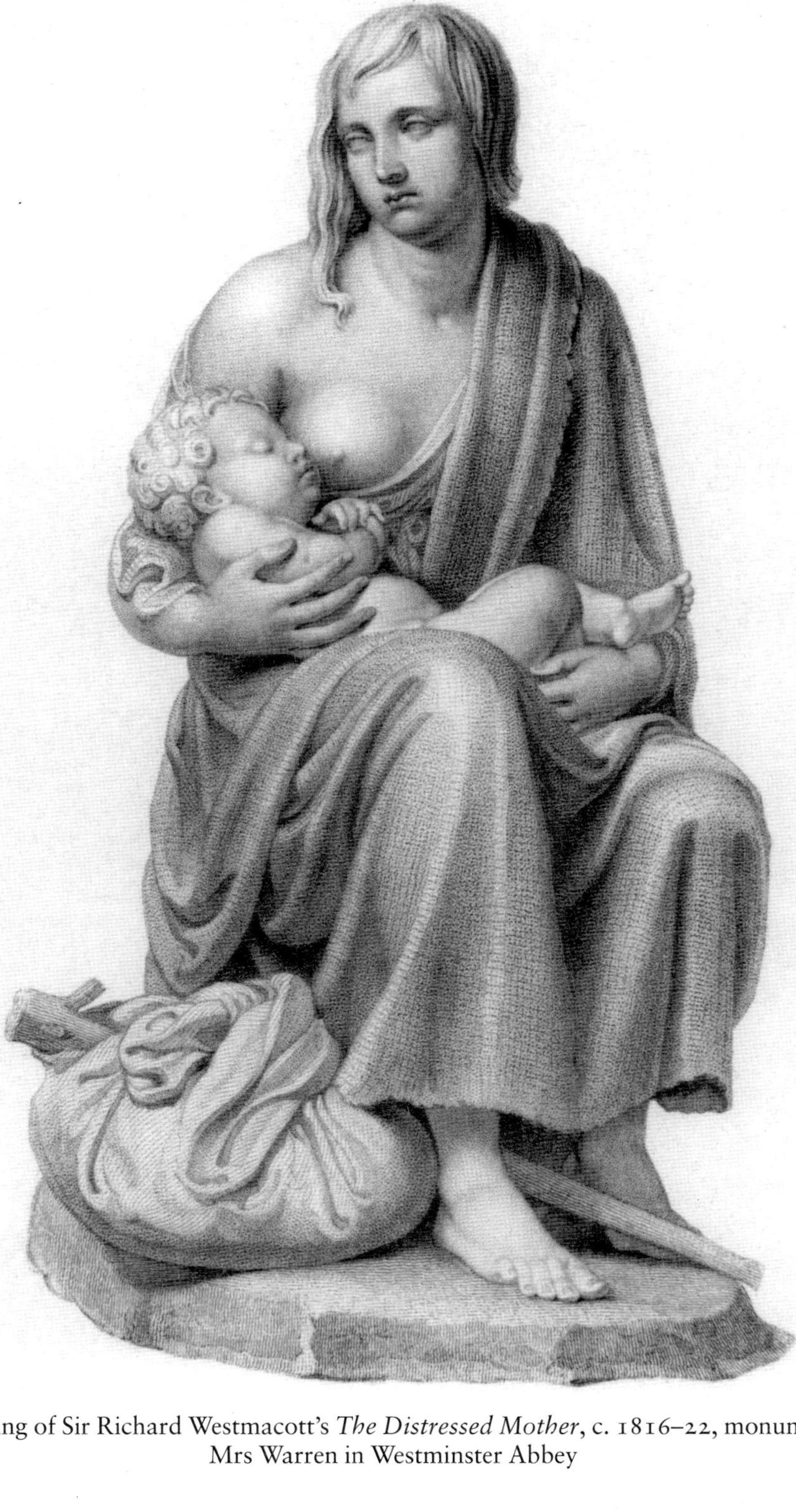

Engraving of Sir Richard Westmacott's *The Distressed Mother*, c. 1816–22, monument to Mrs Warren in Westminster Abbey

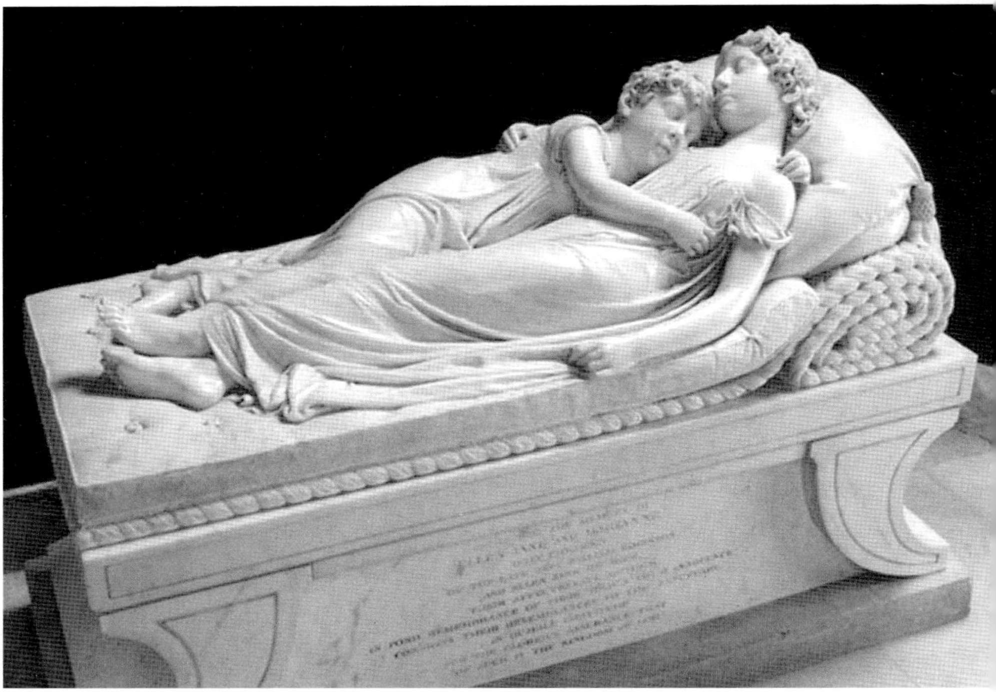

Sir Francis Chantry, *The Sleeping Children*, 1817, Lichfield Cathedral

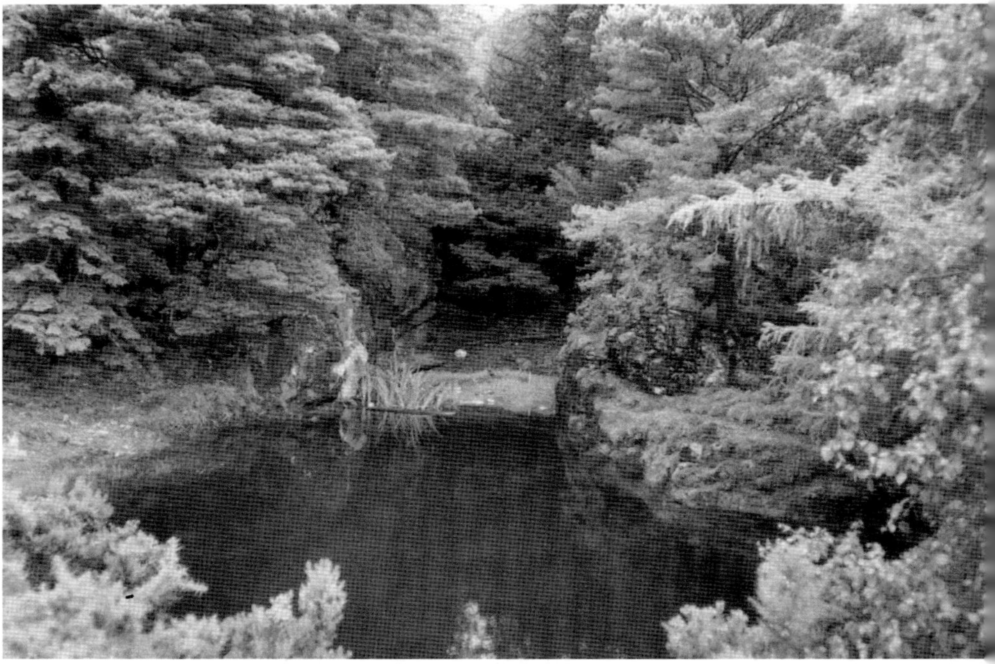

Site of Colonel Hall's copper mine at Ross Island, Killarney

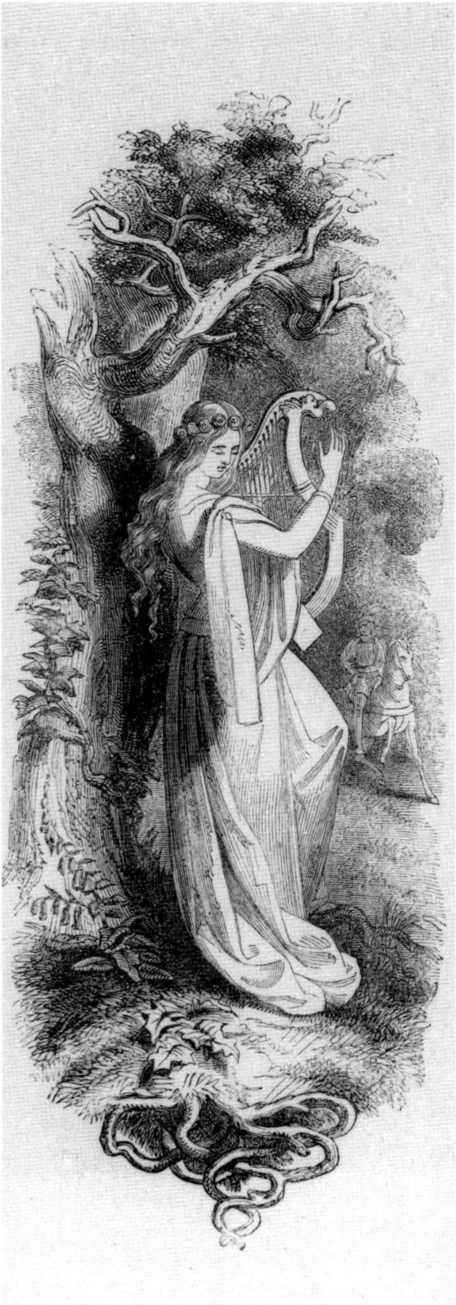

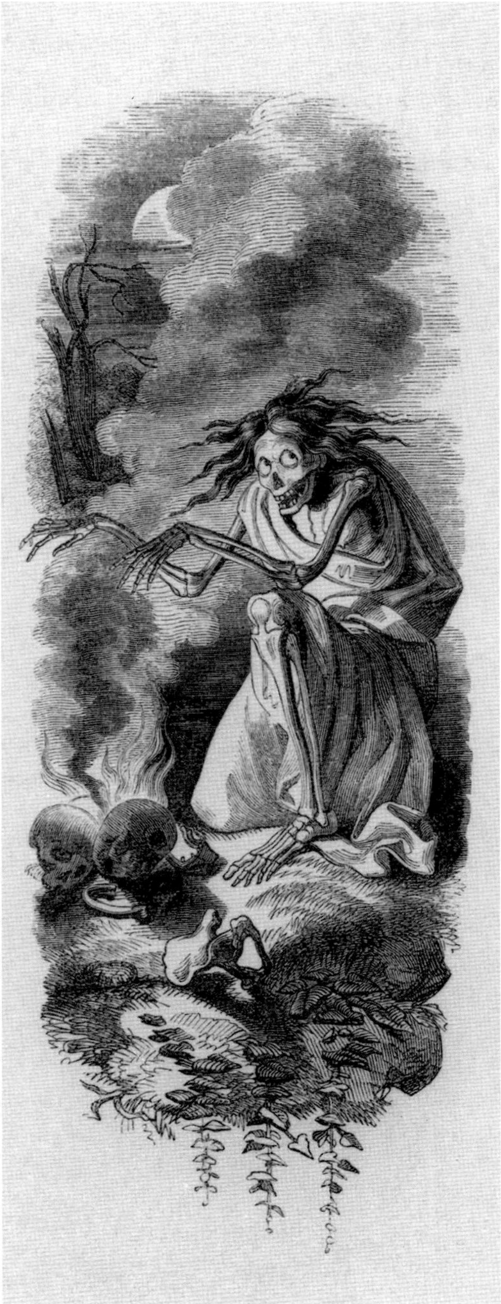

J. N. Paton, illustrations from 'Elfinland Wud', published in *The Book of British Ballads*, 1842

Robin Good-Fellow.

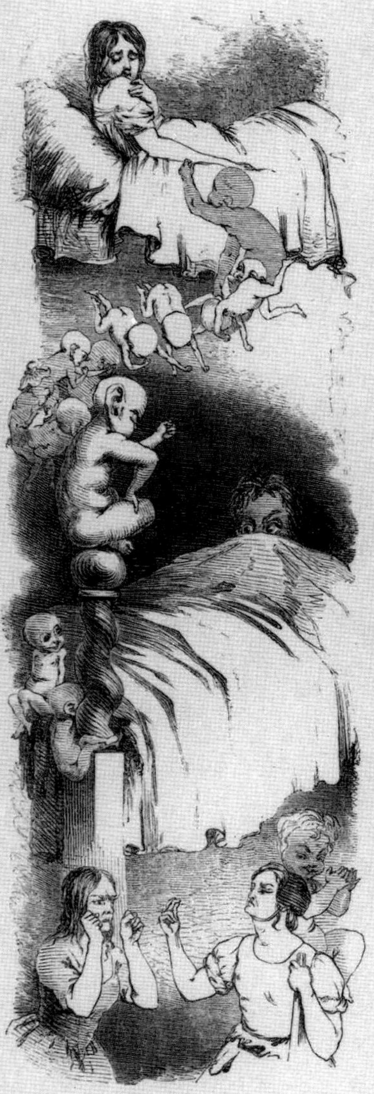

When house or harth doth sluttish lye,
I pinch the maidens black and blue;
The bed-clothes from the bedd pull I
And lay them naked all to view.
'Twixt sleepe and wake,
I do them take,
And on the key-cold floor them throw.
If out they cry, then forth I fly,
And loudly laugh out, ho, ho, ho!

When any need to borrowe aught,
We lend them what they do require;
And for the use demand we nought:
Our owne is all we do desire.
If to repay,
They do delay,
Abroad amongst them then I go,
And night by night, I them affright
With pinchings, dreames, and ho, ho, ho!

When lazie queans have nought to do,
But study how to cog and lye;
To make debate and mischief too,
'Twixt one another secretlye:
I marke their gloze,
And it disclose,
To them whom they have wronged so;
When I have done, I get me gone,
And leave them scolding, ho, ho, ho!

When men do traps and engins set
In loope holes were the vermine creepe,
Who from their foldes and houses, get
Their duckes and geese, and lambes and sheepe:
I spy the gin,
And enter in,
And seeme a vermine taken so;
But when they there approach me neare,
I leap out laughing, ho, ho, ho!

Dadd del. Green sc. B 89

Richard Dadd, illustration to 'Robin Good-Fellow', published in *The Book of British Ballads*, 1842

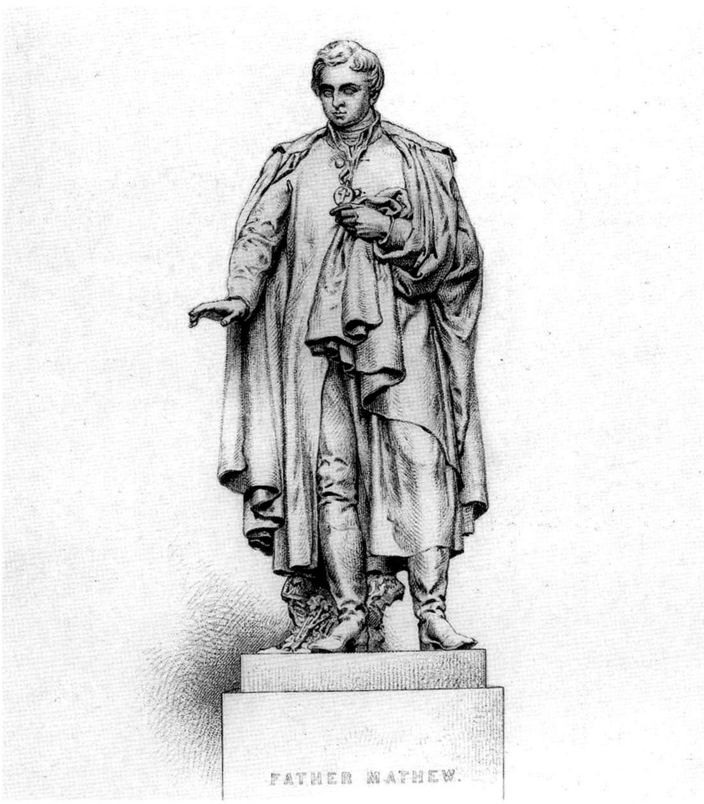

Engraving of *Father Mathew*, statue executed by John Henry Foley, RA, for the City of Cork. From the title page of J. F. Maguire's biography of Father Mathew, 1863.

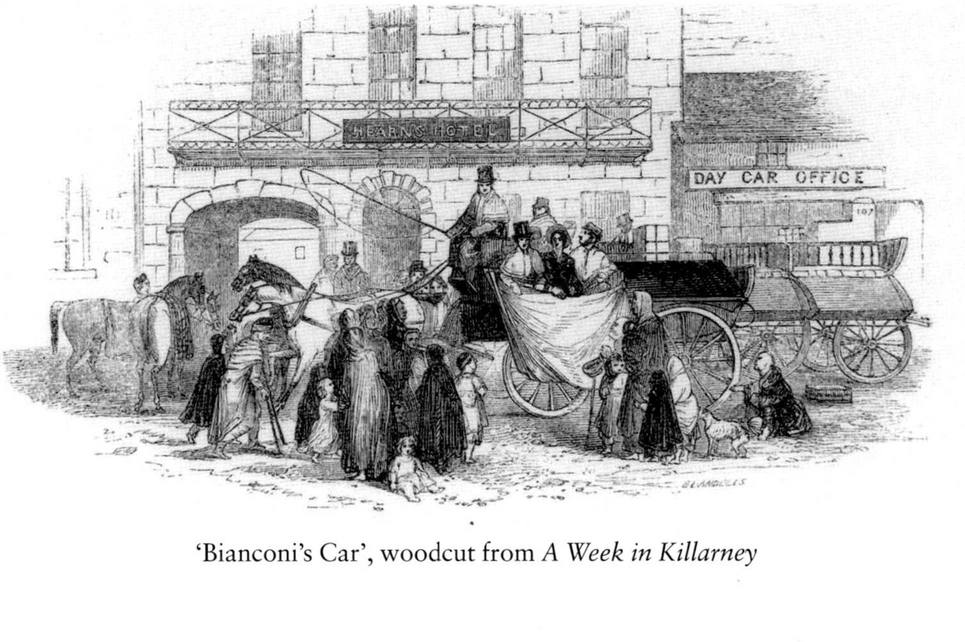

'Bianconi's Car', woodcut from *A Week in Killarney*

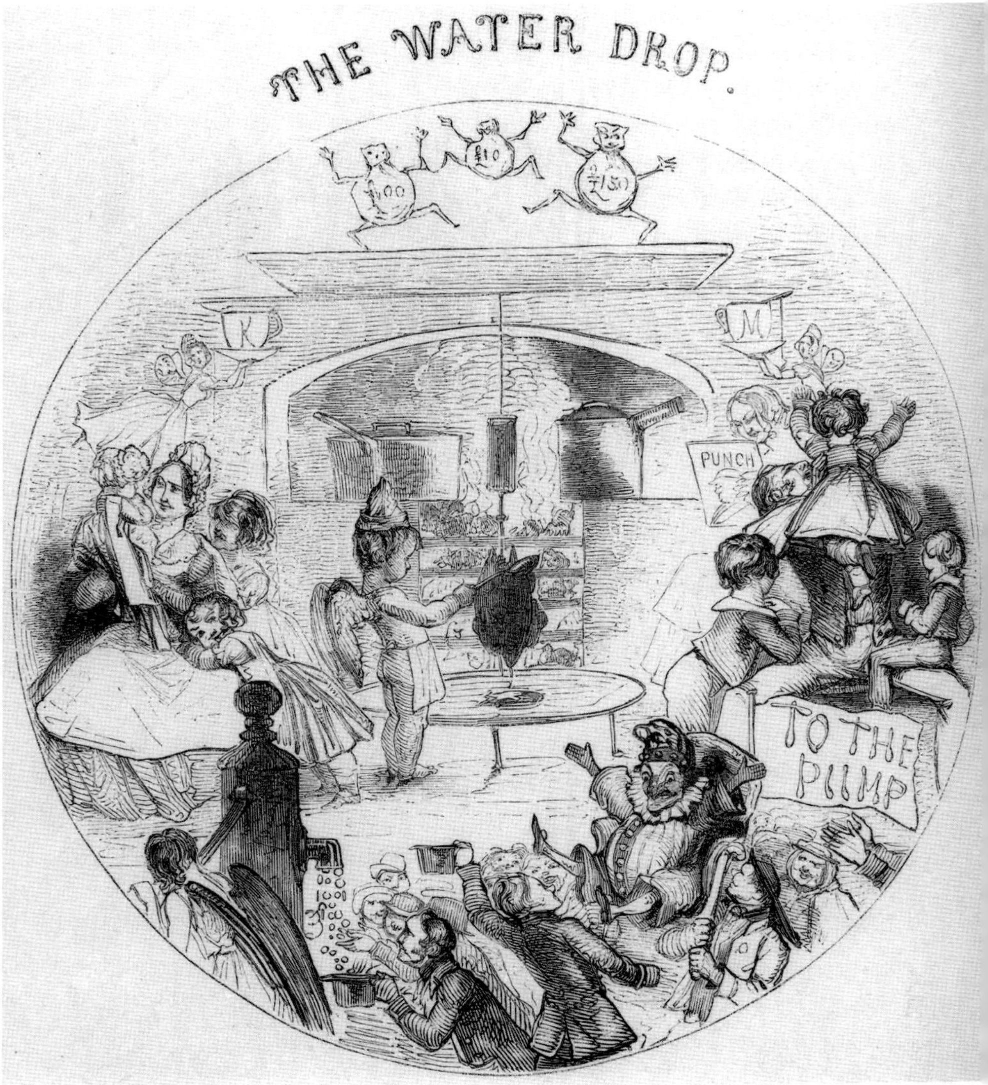

'The Water Drop', *Punch,* 1843

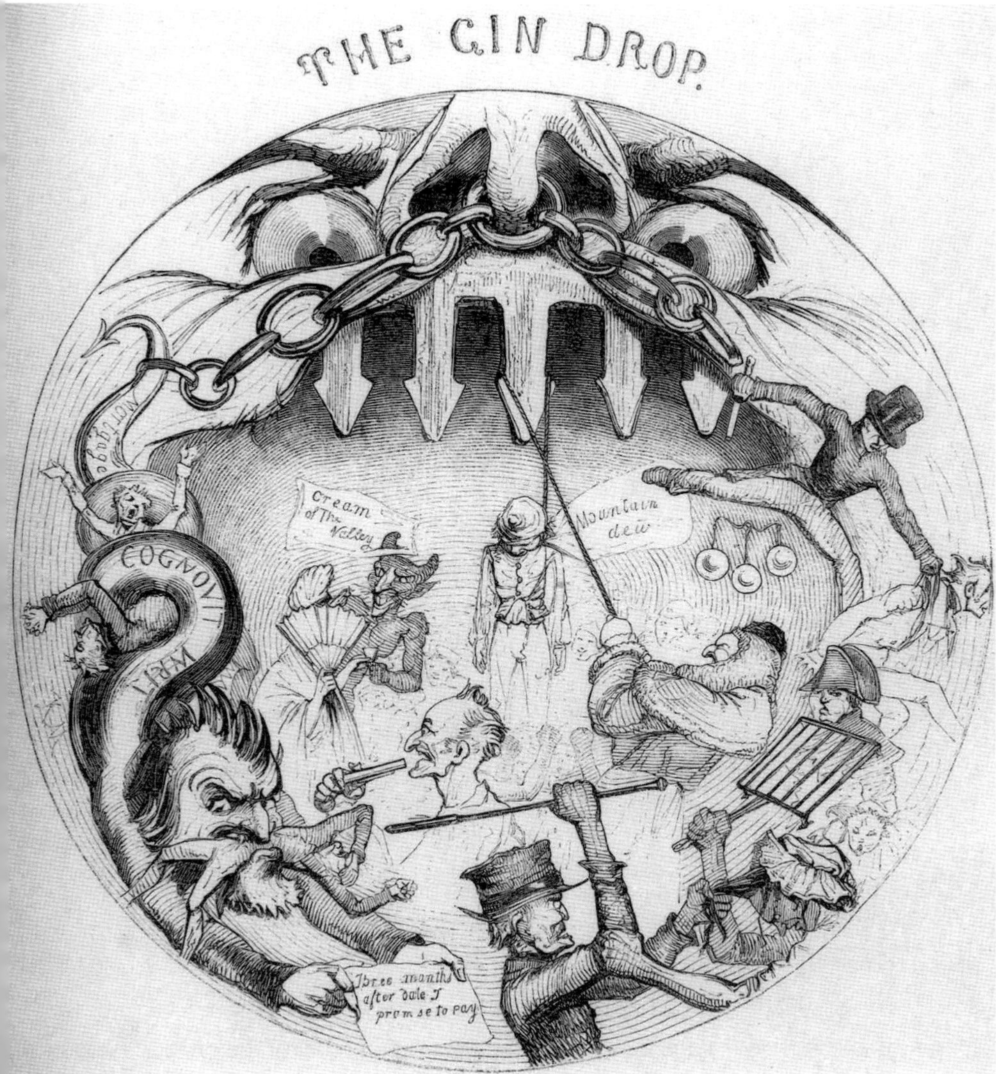

'The Gin Drop', *Punch*, 1843

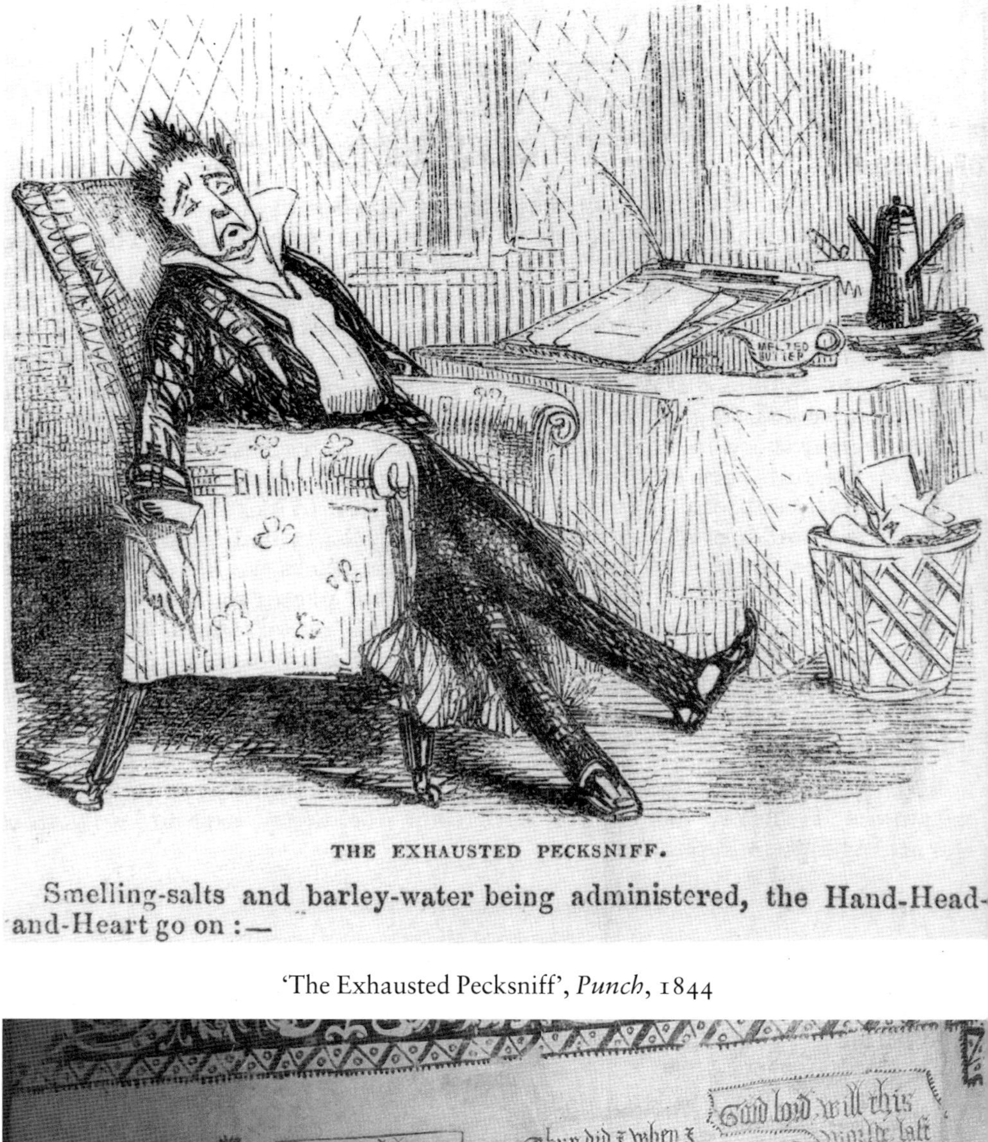

'The Exhausted Pecksniff', *Punch*, 1844

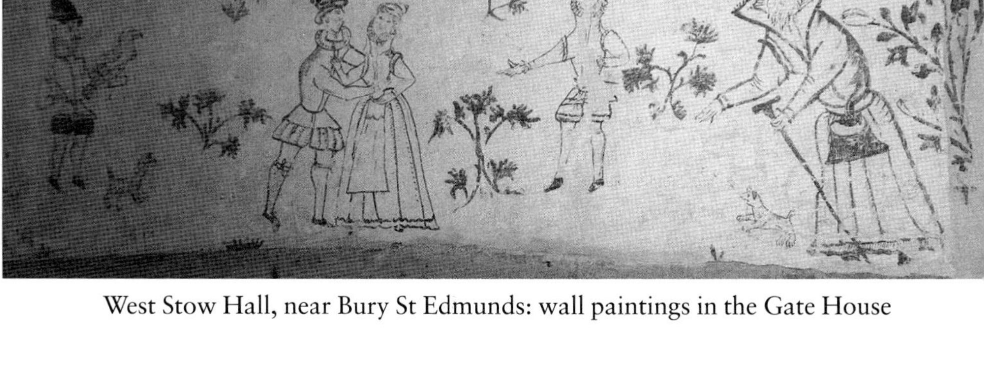

West Stow Hall, near Bury St Edmunds: wall paintings in the Gate House

contribute to the Great Exhibition. On his return he went to see all the London manufacturers, and had drawings of their exhibits made which were later engraved by the Dalziel brothers. He corresponded with all the main manufacturers of Great Britain.

That an exhibition was to take place on the scale of that of 1851 must have given Carter enormous satisfaction. In 1848 he had published an article in *The Art Union* by Dr Cooke-Taylor advocating the necessity for teaching the principles of the laws of beauty in design in the, then, highly criticised Schools of Design. 'It is idle to suppose the Industrial has no connection with the Fine Arts;' he said, 'they are twin sisters.' There followed an article by Carter on the advantages to be gained in England by an exposition of British manufacturers. He had been advocating the association of the industrial arts with the fine arts for some years, and his editorial of 1842 announced, 'We desire to promote the purposes of the useful Arts by showing how advantageously they may be influenced by the Fine Arts; and how largely our manufacturers may be benefited by the aid of taste and genius.' Articles on industrial art with engravings of manufactures continued in the *Journal* for many years. There can be no doubt that many manufacturers, both in England and abroad, were encouraged by Carter's personal interest to send their exhibits to the Crystal Palace in 1851.

Carter had not competed for the right to publish the official catalogue. It was published by Messrs Spicer and Clowes who, according to Carter, lost £2,000 over the publication. With his extraordinary satisfaction in his own achievements, Carter wrote later in *Retrospect*: 'Had the sole right of issuing an Illustrated Catalogue remained in my hands, it is my belief that the venture I embarked upon would have paid.' (In fact his own catalogue made a loss; and it was then that he sold his shares to his co-proprietors, whom he called 'men of business and calculating habits' and became the paid editor.)

The Art Journal devoted thirty-two pages with engravings to the exhibits in the exhibition, and continued this until it closed in December. These monthly reports were then published as a catalogue priced one guinea. The official Catalogue by M. Digby Wyatt was in three volumes and lavishly illustrated. In it can be seen the amazing inventiveness of the Victorians and their degree of technical efficiency. It also showed the quantity and quality of everyday articles which could be produced in England at reasonable prices, even if France still led the way in the production of luxury goods. *The Art Journal: The Illustrated Catalogue, The Industry of All Nations* is in only one volume and concentrates on British articles, though there are examples from other countries, particularly from France. There are five essays: 'Essay on the Science of the Exhibition', 'Essay on the Harmony of Colours as Exemplified in the Exhibition', 'Essay on the Vegetable Kingdom', 'Essay on the Machinery of the Exhibition', and a fifth essay by the winner of the Prize Essay (for which the proprietors of *The Art Journal* offered a hundred guineas) by Ralph Nicholas Wornum, afterwards Keeper of the National Gallery.

Wornum claimed that there was nothing new in the Exhibition in ornamental design, 'not a schedule, not a detail that has not been treated over and over again in ages that are gone'. This is usually the accusation made in later years, when everything Victorian was viewed with distaste – that so much that was produced in the mid-nineteenth century merely imitated other styles, and in reproducing them lost the spirit of the original. Wornum considered that the taste of the producers was generally uneducated and in cases where this was not so, the influence of France was paramount. He was surprised that there was so little in the Greek and Roman style which had been so popular fifty years earlier. On the whole the specimens which were most highly prized had 'Renaissance' decoration, while the bulk of the exhibits were in the style of Louis XIV.

As editor, Carter was responsible for the examples of exhibits in *The Art Journal Illustrated Catalogue*, and to a certain degree they probably reflected his taste. They range from coal scuttles in 'Greek' and 'Roman' style, to devotional figures such as one called *Morning Prayer* by P. MacDowell, RA of a kneeling woman with a sentimental expression. Pugin's Cross (which was originally hung high in the Central Hall of the exhibition and then removed to a more inconspicuous position) does not feature in the catalogue. There is a page of reproduction antique Celtic brooches made in Dublin, all part of the Gaelic Revival, a great deal of highly coloured silvered glass, then very popular, and an iron letter post from Brussels with the explanation beneath it that 'These posts serve the purpose in

Belgium that a receiving house does in England'. The emphasis throughout is on the aim of the manufacturers to combine beauty and elegance with utility. The text accompanying the engravings praises the exhibits and gives the name and location of the manufacturer.

The Great Exhibition underlined the necessity for education in art. It had shown that taste ranged from Gothic to Renaissance, together with a form of rococo which we now associate with early Victorians. One feels that the visitor to the Great Exhibition must have emerged with his mind reeling from such a plethora of 'good taste'. Nevertheless, amongst a section of the public there was a revulsion against the taste of some of the exhibits. William Morris, aged seventeen, visited the Exhibition and thought much that he saw was very ugly. John Eagles wrote in *Blackwood's Magazine* in 1853:

> I have looked into galleries old and galleries new – in some the Arts are not only 'Fine' but superfine – a great deal too fine – in others they are not fine at all, and lamentably dingy. And stranger still, I find the public running after both kinds with unbounded enthusiasm, and purses that take a pleasure in opening themselves. The extravagance on both sides throws me into bewilderment ... who then shall be the '*arbiter elegantiarum*', and what *elegantiae* will please the public? Yet pleased the public must be, and are, but how, or why, or who leads them? There is the mystery. This has been an incomprehensible thing since the world has been a world in England. Ever since I was young there has been a cry and a craving 'Tell us what we are to admire'.[2]

It was this that caused Owen Jones to feel that some attempt must be made to establish principles for future guidance. In his *Grammar of Ornament*, published in 1856, he wrote: 'No improvement can take place in the Art of the present generation until all classes, Artists, Manufacturers, and the public, are better educated in Arts, and the existence of general principles is fully recognized.'[3]

It is difficult to assess the role played by *The Art Journal* in this education of the public. It was a popular magazine, carrying many erudite articles. Carter, after all, in later years claimed to have created a public for art which seems to imply that he supplied criteria in taste. Yet in a reply to a presentation on his birthday from the grateful manufacturers of Birmingham on 9 May 1867 he said, with a burst of modesty, 'I have been an editor only. The knowledge I communicated was the knowledge that others had acquired; the taste I disseminated was the taste that others inculcated and taught.'[4] John Steegman in his book *Victorian Taste* says that though *The Art Journal* was not without influence, many serious-minded people mistrusted it and indeed felt that it was mostly of use to others who had axes to grind. Certainly the manufacturers of England had reason to be grateful to Carter, who announced at the end of his catalogue his intention to issue monthly 'Reports of the Art Manufactures of England' in *The Art Journal* together with engravings.

In the same year as the Great Exhibition Carter obtained permission from the Queen to copy and engrave for publication some of the pictures in the Royal Collection. It gave him the opportunity to publish a work with pictures rarely seen, at a time when the Prince was enormously popular after his triumph at Hyde Park, and the public was becoming increasingly interested in art. The engravings and letterpress were to be in four volumes, but these were also to be published monthly in *The Art Journal*, and they commenced in 1856, two years before the first volume appeared. It is clear from correspondence that Carter was paying a number of artists to copy the pictures, and that Virtue (as proprietor of the *Journal*) had undertaken to share in the expenses. No agreement has come to light, though Anna Maria refers to one in letters to Francis Bennock.

For the next six years Carter was engrossed in this work of reproducing the Royal Collection. He made constant visits to Windsor, Osborne and Buckingham Palace, making minute comparisons of the artists' copies with the originals before sending them to the engravers. We find him objecting to the work of one artist (unfortunately unnamed) when he wrote:

Art Journal, 4 Lancaster Place

My dear Sir,

I assure you I would much regret any misunderstanding that

> could exist between you and me – and do my utmost to prevent it … I do not object to the sum you receive; but I will presume to say that for your sake – as well as for mine – it must be more highly finished – before we can expect to make of it an engraving that will do us both honour and service. I assure you it is altogether too slight and unpainted: and I will very much thank you to go over it again.
>
> I am not in a hurry – for I have now about sixty copies made: and as I am going to Osborne in a week or so, I will take it with me to compare with the original.
>
> I beg to assure you that my anxiety on this point arises more for you than for myself. I am on all account bound to do the Royal Collection its fullest justice – and am exerting my utmost to secure the best copies and the best engravings in Europe.[5]

There was also the task of showing the copies and finding subscribers to the four volumes, and Carter himself made visits to many of the Midland towns, where he was well known. Anna Maria wrote to Francis Bennock:

> Here I am bothering you again! The matter now is this – the copies of the Queen's pictures are going the round of the provinces – commencing at Birmingham, they were shown at Everetts – the next move will be to Coventry where Carter will meet them (as he did at Birmingham) on Friday next – and he requests you to interest your friends there, as far as you can without much trouble – so as to get them to go and see them – perhaps you could forward Mr Hall a few notes of introduction to these chambers, which he could take with him on Friday.
>
> I am ashamed to trouble you – but kindness begets trouble – and I am sure had I known that Mr Hall would have had a tithe of the anxiety which has attended the production of the Royal Gal. – previous to the publication of the plates in The Art Journal – I would have done everything in my power to prevent his wearing out his soul and spirit as he does. I can manage his excitement on the subject – but when I see him morbid and despairing as to the result, and so fearfully

anxious that at times he forgets – or seems to forget – the noble arrangement you made for him, and which must come into action in January – I need what the world calls philosophy – to keep him calm, and at the same time not to abate exertions that are necessary – he undertook too much for the capital he had to work with – and he dreads not making it tell, as quickly as he desires – as in fact he needs – all, please God, will come right in the spring – but the difficulty now is to keep him calm and hopeful till then. Mr Dafforne, his Sub Editor, who really works almost as hard as my poor Carter, has got a terror of the Cholera, and so Mr Hall has given him permission to go to the country – and he goes to the Chambers to stay until Friday ... I shall go up with him and stay there too – as I do not like to leave him alone when he is very anxious and low.[6]

The expenses of Firfield were proving to be heavier than either Anna Maria or Carter had expected. These, together with the capital needed for the project of the Royal Gallery, were causing the anxiety that was affecting Carter's health. He was a man of many moods. It was almost as if in childhood he had developed the temperament of a Celt, ranging from exuberance to the deepest gloom. Anna Maria turned again to Francis Bennock for help and advice.

Firfield. September 8th Private.

I grieve to tell you that Carter is far from well – indeed so unwell that last week I wanted him to have advice – the simple fact is – that he is worried about the means to wind up the year until the next brings Mr Virtue's agreement into full work – I tell you this because you are not only our friend but our wise friend – you have not only a heart but a head – and your knowledge of the agreement *you* procured – and of the drawings, might make you to suggest some means by which he could borrow six or eight hundred pounds, – a thousand pounds would more than set him at ease until his return comes – and he would offer the drawings (for which he has paid over two – and which are worth more than he paid) as security – My poor husband is literally *breaking down* for want of the means which a few months would give! – this is painfully disquieting to me, his sanguine temperament puts him either up or down, and he is now so *down* that I don't know what to do – if he finds it impossible to borrow this money (which I hope it is not) he will be obliged to ask Virtue for help – or perhaps be forced to sell him the copies of the Royal Pictures for half, or little more than half their Value! Either of these alternatives is full of sorrow and anxiety to him – it will humble him in a way he does not deserve, ultimately he does intend to sell the drawings – but not yet – I am sure they would be a profitable speculation as a *whole* hereafter but that is a long look out.

Dear Mr Bennock – will you who think for so many think for us in this matter! We know no one like you! If there is no possibility of borrowing a sum of money until his return comes – I would hope that you would kindly give him the benefit of your advice and council as how best to obtain from Mr Virtue the necessary supply – and what terms – it is certainly not much to ask a publisher for, who has the *Means of Remuneration in his hands* and I do not see the objection to it that dear Carter does – it is a matter of feeling with him – and a fear of being imposed on – he does not know I am writing to you.[7]

Anna Maria told Bennock that she thought they should let Firfield for a few months, or a year. Carter was so little at home while working on the Royal Gallery, and it would cost much less living in town. She went on to say that she had not discussed this with Carter – it was such hard work keeping up his spirits – and she knew that she could rely on Bennock's sympathy and secrecy. Bennock must have helped, for there is a short letter from Carter to him in November.

My dear Bennock,

I am going home by no means well. And it just occurred to me that you have no sort of acknowledgement (except the cheques) for three hundred pounds I owe you – i.e. 200 I received from Mr. Reed and £100 the cheque you so kindly sent me.

Ever with love to you both, your friend, S.C.H.[8]

Things must have been very bad indeed. Three hundred pounds was a not unsubstantial sum, but if a single artist had to be paid 35 guineas, this was not going to go very far with all his other mounting expenses.

Eventually Anna Maria broached the subject with Carter of letting Firfield, and he agreed that it should be for six months, or even for a year or two. Bennock must have made her face up to realities, for she wrote to tell him of their decision adding,

> I know all you say about Firfield is quite true – I can bear it perfectly now – but my dread was that poor Carter would feel parting with it so bitterly – he has created it – but *he* proposed two years and said how the trees would be grown by that time ... the truth is – his whole heart is with the Queen's pictures – and his late difficulties – and the fag up and down – and his desires to do all right has overcome his love for his trees and flowers – and *that* has been a most grateful relief to my anxiety – until the blessed Sunday you came here – when in the garden I mentioned it to Mrs Bennock – I had no one to breathe it to – for even to my Mother I must put it that while this book is in process Carter must be on the spot, – I do so love the country – but I love a free mind more.[9]

By December 1854 relations between the Halls and George Virtue were again becoming strained. This was to do with Anna Maria's *Sketches of Irish Character*, a work which she first published in 1829, and on which much of her reputation as an Irish writer rested. There were further editions in 1831 and 1854–5. It is not clear what her grievance against Virtue was, but this time she was more cautious about quarrelling with him. As usual she wrote to Bennock (to whom the 1855 edition is dedicated).

> Dec. 1st 1854
>
> I enclose a statement of the misunderstanding about the Sketches of Irish Character, because I think that a little oil upon the waters might set it right – I do not think Mr Virtue intends to wrong us in *this matter* – but Salisbury would do or say – or write anything to please Virtue – and at that time Carter would have signed anything he put before him – please see if you can't make matters clear – I do not want any misunderstanding at any time – but particularly now – when the time

> like the weather consists of very little sunshine and a great many clouds.[10]

Whatever the trouble was Bennock as usual seems to have smoothed things over.

Carter thought he would try to increase the mortgage on Firfield. However, Anna Maria told Bennock that though the surveyor who valued the place called Firfield a *'Miniature Chatsworth*, nevertheless, he only valued it at £2,000 (not including the cottages and land that Carter had added) and therefore it would be unrealistic to increase the mortgage.

> £500 before Christmas and £500 after would put all right – but if it can't be done, it can't be – Virtue now sends back the people to Carter – saying he will pay no more – I suppose he thinks he has paid his half and will not wait the issue of the sale – I am concerned that he wants to force Carter to come to him for money, and so 'sell his birthright' – that I have been requesting Carter all the morning sooner than think of that mode of relief, to sell his pictures – I mean our collection – Ward and Frith and Goodall would I am sure rather he used their presents to free himself than have him die of a crushed heart – and leave them to be sold hereafter – however painful and humiliating such a sale would be, – I suggested he might say he sold them to make room for the copies of her Majesty's pictures, but with more bravery he said No – I would sell them and say so because without doing so the times are so much against me, that I had not the means to carry out and on the Queen's Collection. The moment we can get to Ashley Place we will do so, and then set about letting this for a year.

It seems, therefore, that Carter did receive presents from contemporary artists, probably sketches of their pictures which were engraved for *The Art Journal*. Henry Vizetelly maliciously suggested these were bribes; but Ward and Goodall were friends of the Halls, as were many other artists of the day, and their presents would have been given in a very different spirit.

Carter began publishing a series entitled *British Artists: Their Style and Character* in January 1855 (though articles on specific artists appeared before this, the first being on Edwin Landseer's *The Breakfast Party* in 1848). This series is a valuable source for research, as much of the information came directly from the artists themselves.

Anna Maria had another worry on her mind. The action for libel which the dealer Louis Hart was taking against Carter was to be heard at Warwick Assizes the following March. She wrote to Bennock:

> That picture dealing Jew is going on with his action and engaged Thessinger. I think evidence could well be got to beat him – if Carter's mind next month is free to think and act – it is the *artists' cause* – but if it goes against him – he will be the sufferer.[11]

As has been said, the case did go against him. The damages were put at forty shillings, the lowest which could carry costs, but these were considerable for Carter at a time he had so many demands upon him. The judge rebuked Carter for taking upon himself the self-constituted tribunal by writing a second article about Hart in *The Art Journal* while the trial was going on. Though artists came to Carter's rescue and helped to pay the costs, he still had to pay a considerable sum of money for the costs of the plaintiff and witnesses. He was, indeed, in serious financial difficulties. The month before the trial he was writing to Bennock:

> I ask pardon for my sins of omission – first – and next to say I enclose a cheque for the £25, which I believe is the sum referred to: I have made it payable on the 27th because then I know I shall have enough to meet it.
>
> But a matter of much greater moment presses on my mind and worries and distresses me sadly ... Here I am receiving an income of just about £2,000 a year. £1,500 from Virtue which I have no doubt will be paid regularly though grudgingly and certainly £500 from various other sources. My property at Firfield is certainly worth £6,000 and my property at Ashley Place is certainly worth £6,000 more.
>
> Now I owe about £4,000 or at the very extreme £4,500 and I have paid that sum for the Queen's drawings and the

advances on the Royal Gallery. So that the drawings cost me – and I believe are fully worth – the sums I owe to everybody. Just as fast as my surplus income comes in, it goes out to meet and discharge the necessary obligations which have of course been going up and up; and thank God I can see my way through all impediments – for time must do for me all I need. Up to this time, I have borrowed only from personal friends – I have had no bill 'go back' – and I have not even had what is called 'an attorney's letter'.

I need not say I have been reduced to no discreditable shifts to get money: but I am free to confess I have suffered much pain and anxiety – many a time and oft.

Now in this matter of Mr Freeman I feel that unless I can sell my drawings, it is utterly impossible for me to pay the debt I owe him – and the Bills become due on the 2nd. and 3rd. of March.

I have written to Agnew of Manchester, on the subject of these drawings; explained to him exactly how I stand; and asked his advice and attention – but he does not reply to my letter – and it is clear to me that he inclines to take the chance of their falling into his hands on his own terms. In short my dear Bennock, I know not what course to take – with ample means and a large income I ought not to be in any way embarrassed and should not be if I had a business mind. I must ask you to extend yet awhile and further the friendship and kindness and service I have had at your hands – and the same at those of Mr Freeman.

I believe as far as regards actual aid, I shall not require it for a very long time, but at present and for some months to come, I must do so unless I can sell my drawings – or borrow a sum of money on other securities.

Pray you consider this – as you have ever done with your sound understanding and large heart.

Ever truly and faithfully yours S. C. Hall[12]

What became of Carter's copies of the Queen's pictures is not known. Probably, over the years, he sold them as he was so often short of money. He still had them in 1862, however, as they were then exhibited at the French Gallery in Pall Mall. It seems that it became necessary for the Halls to let Firfield in 1856 and again in 1859, though it is not known for how long. Entries in the registers of Addlestone Parish Church show christenings of children of occupants of Firfield in these years.[13]

While Carter was preparing for *The Royal Gallery*, he was also editing the reports which *The Art Journal* was to make on the Art Treasures Exhibition to be held in Manchester in 1857. In 1856 several of the influential merchants and manufacturers of Manchester, impressed by the success of the exhibitions in Paris and Dublin, decided that their city would be a suitable venue for an exhibition of art treasures from private collections. A paper was written by Peter Cunningham and J. C. Deane, Commissioner of the Dublin Exhibition, and sent to connoisseurs suggesting such an exhibition.

> It may be taken as a fact (what indeed must be known to the readers of Dr Waagen's valuable but imperfect volumes) that there is, in the United Kingdom, in the possession of private individuals, objects of art which exceed in interest and value those of any other country in the world ... An opportunity would thus occur, of giving by examples a chronological history of British painting.[14]

Prince Albert was approached, and he welcomed the idea provided it had a higher purpose than that of merely gratifying public curiosity. A national purpose, he said 'might be found in the educational direction which may be given to the whole scheme'.[15] It was felt that the exhibition would be a logical sequence to the Prince's fundamental idea of education as the purpose of the Great Exhibition. He stressed the need for the classification of paintings and arrangement in chronological order. He and the Queen would lend paintings from their collections. This, then, was to be the first large exhibition in England open to the public of paintings from private collections and from the Royal Collection. It was also important as an attempt at classification and chronological arrangement such as the Prince had already advised the National Gallery Commission to carry out in 1853.

The Art Treasures of the United Kingdom Exhibition opened at Old Trafford in May 1857 and nearly one and a half million people are said to have visited it. The three-volume catalogue and a guide were compiled by Dr Waagen, Director of the Berlin Art Gallery. There was a series of articles on each section, originally printed in the *Manchester Guardian* and reprinted in handbooks. In an article in the *Quarterly Review*, Waagen said that there had been a great change in the arrangement of pictures in museums in Europe. The first object, he thought, should be to demonstrate the history and development of art in different localities and ages (in his opinion there was still very little system in the National Gallery in London). Some progress, he acknowledged, had been made at the Manchester exhibition, but the main weakness lay in the confusion of schools, pictures of the Spanish and French schools being jumbled up with Italian and Flemish.

An interesting aspect of the Manchester exhibition is the fact that the public now saw a change of taste in art, the new taste being for the masters of the Italian Quattrocento, particularly for the later Quattrocentists such as Mantegna, Cime and the Bellinis, whom they would not yet find in the National Gallery. (The fashion for Botticelli came a little later.) They also saw a large collection of the pictures of living British artists. Some of the Pre-Raphaelite painters were represented by pictures such as Charles Collins's *Convent Thoughts*, Arthur Hughes's *April Love*, Millais's *Autumn Leaves* and Holman Hunt's *The Awakening Conscience* and *The Hireling Shepherd*. Of particular interest was the British Portrait Gallery, giving the public a foretaste of what was to come in the National Portrait Gallery in London, founded the year before, but not open to the public until 1859 and then only on Wednesday and Saturday afternoons to ticket holders. But the opinion of the exhibition generally was that it was too rich, too overwhelming. As for Ruskin's two lectures on 'The Political Economy of Art', people found them very perplexing.[16] The lectures were mainly concerned with education, but were also an attack on the social and economic structure of modern life. The bewilderment of some of the audience was understandable as, in fact, Ruskin confused ethics with art.

The Art Journal gave extensive coverage to the exhibition. Its opening report, though probably written by Dafforne (Carter's sub-editor) are very much the liberal and moral views held by Carter.

> The Exhibition at Manchester ... while it contributes to social progress and promotes rational and intellectual pleasure, cannot fail to add much in removing those barriers which have hitherto separated 'the classes' by exhibiting the aristocracy – of rank and riches – not only willing, but desirous, that the people should, as widely as possible, participate in the enjoyments they themselves derive from their 'Treasures', and that, too, in a city which is understood to be the most democratic of the kingdom.[17]

The reports during the following months were enthusiastic, but cautious. The final article, however, was critical of the results of the exhibition. The purpose of the exhibition, it said, had been to teach the public to appreciate beautiful things, and in this the object was defeated because of several factors. The organisers, the writer claimed, did nothing to help the viewers to understand and appreciate art, and there was so much to see that there was no time to study (hardly the fault of the organisers). The arrangement of the pictures was bad, he said, rows and rows of paintings – and no grouping. Every picture should have been labelled with the artist's name, the name of the owner and the school of painting to which it belonged. This was an idea held by many reviewers of art at the time who, influenced perhaps by the Pre-Raphaelites who claimed a school of painting to themselves, tended to place works of art in schools and clear-cut categories for the benefit of people in need of artistic guidance.

The Manchester exhibition may have widened the public interest in the early Italian Masters (hitherto rarely seen in England) but serious study was still the concern of only a few scholars and connoisseurs such as the Prince, Sir Charles Eastlake and John Ruskin. In the series of pictures from *The Royal Gallery*, begun in *The Art Journal* in 1856, examples of the Italian Quattrocento would not be expected. Much of the great collection of Charles I was sold or burned during the Commonwealth, until Cromwell stepped in and saved a number of the finest works. George IV's taste was for the genre of everyday life and, when he could afford it, he bought Dutch and Flemish paintings of the seventeenth century. Queen Victoria, with the encouragement of the Prince, added many of the Modern

British School. Of the Royal Gallery pictures published in *The Art Journal*, the majority are of modern paintings, or reflect the taste of collectors just after Waterloo. For instance, in the 1856 *Journal* there are five paintings of the seventeenth century, one painting by Jean Baptiste Pater, one by Gainsborough and seventeen of the nineteenth century, mostly by British artists. There are paintings by Domenichino (so popular with collectors in the early part of the century) in the 1859 and 1860 numbers and two paintings by Raphael.

In 1859 Sydney Morgan died. She had lived in London since 1835, the year she was awarded a civil pension of £300. The Halls knew her well and had been at a musical evening on St Patrick's Night shortly before she died. Few writers at the time invited such criticism. John Wilson Croker was probably her most outspoken enemy. He accused her, indirectly, in the *Quarterly Review* of 'licentiousness, profligacy, irreverence, blasphemy, libertinism, disloyalty and atheism'.

Anna Maria (unlike her husband), always quick to grasp an opportunity of seeking patronage or help from her friends, took the occasion of Lady Morgan's death to write immediately to Bulwer Lytton. She suggested that she might be a worthy recipient of a civil pension, having always been a staunch supporter of the established religion and conservatism, and asked him to exert his influence on her behalf.

> Private 27, Ashley Place
> You have always been so kind that I presume to trouble you, as Mr Hall is not at home – and I cannot have the advantage of his advice [one wonders if Carter being away was the reason for the timing of her letter].
>
> Poor Lady Morgan is gone. She received for many years a pension of £300 a year. She was certainly clever and clear-headed but always at war with our Established religion and conservatism.
>
> I would ask any one to look into the pages of the 'Sketches of Irish Character', 'Tales of the Irish Peasantry', 'Lights and Shadows of Irish Life', 'Marian' – and judge if every power I

> possessed has not been devoted to the best purposes of religion – conservatism and at the same time – progress in Ireland. I do not intrude our last joint work on 'Ireland' on your notice, nor do I mention the various works written and edited by my husband and myself – though they number more than 230 volumes – I do not say how much we have enriched *publishers* and how poor we are left ourselves – but now that Lady Morgan is gone I do think that if the Minister did not believe it right to transfer so large a pension from one Irish lady to another – it might be possible to divide the pension in my favour. I presume to think it would not be an unpopular gift – it seems natural that a portion of Lady Morgan's pension should go to the only Irish writer unpensioned – we are apt to rate our values and our services too highly – I hope I have not done so – I write feebly – for I write not knowing how far I am taxing a kindness on which I depend so much – I hope and entreat you to pardon me. One hundred a year has been given to so many – more on the plea of poverty – than as a reward for services – that I should hope if my desire is at all taken into consideration – I might be deemed worthy of half of what Lady Morgan received – (a word from you would I imagine be sufficient) – but though I write in hope – I write in ignorance and feel confused and ashamed at what may be presumption.[18]

Perhaps there were more literary people deserving pensions then than there had been when Lady Morgan received hers, or perhaps the interest in tales of Ireland was waning. And yet a lecture given by Carter the year before, entitled 'The Fairy Legends of Ireland', had attracted a large audience at the Eaton Square Rooms in aid of the Tothill Ragged Schools. (One can imagine Carter's enjoyment at having an opportunity to tell his anecdotes of Irish beggars, waiters and car drivers, slipped in between the legends of fairies, so popular with the Victorians.) Whatever the reason, Anna Maria was only awarded a pension of £100 a year.

12

Collections

The Art Treasures Exhibition in Manchester in 1857 revealed the richness of private collections in England. Discussing the objects and results of the exhibition, the art critic in *The Art Journal* had been shocked by the organisers' disregard of their obligation to teach. The purpose of the exhibition, he said, was to refine the nation's taste by showing art through the ages. This was fairly good so far as the drawings and engravings went, but in oil painting some artists and schools were inadequately represented. The exhibition provided an opportunity to instruct manufacturers and elevate their ideas of design. Manchester had been chosen because of the special effect such an exhibition might have on it as a centre of manufacture, but, the writer asked, would art be better understood there?[1] Carter believed that only in London could such an exhibition be wholly successful, because only in London could it be understood. This was not mere arrogance on his part, but the view held generally that London was the centre of the art world in Great Britain (though Liverpool had a high reputation). The public knew little of the collections that were steadily growing in the Midlands and North of England.

At this first large exhibition of fine arts from private collections, patrons had shown a surprising willingness to exhibit their paintings. Carter, quick to grasp new opportunities in art, now approached museums and patrons to grant him permission to engrave and publish pictures from their collections. *Selected Pictures from Galleries and Private Collections of England* was published in four volumes in 1862 and also in a series in *The Art Journal* from 1862 to 1873 (with a short revival in 1886 after Carter's retirement). By 1873 *The Athenaeum* was also publishing a series on private collections. This was by F. G. Stephens, and Diana Sachko Macleod suggests that it is significant that there is a gap in the *Art Journal* series from 1873 to 1886.[2] It is certainly true that

The Athenaeum was a serious competitor after F. G. Stephens became its art editor in 1861 and (as will be discussed later) took on the role of art historian rather than that of a mere art critic.[3] On the other hand, the explanation given by *The Art Journal* that the series was suspended in order to leave space for reviews of international exhibitions was probably true. The series had appeared only intermittently, and Carter never revived it during his editorship.

The first article in the series of *Selected Pictures* in *The Art Journal* remarked on the new prosperity of leading artists, and the demand for British art in preference to earlier foreign schools. 'Patrons of art have been so continually deceived by fraudulent dealers that they prefer possessing native art.' The steel engravings were immensely popular, with more and more people becoming interested in art but unable to afford prices of original paintings. (They are still sought after today, with the result that one is fortunate to find a volume of *The Art Journal* of the 1850s or 1860s which has not had some of the engravings removed.) There is a text with each engraving giving the name of the artist of the picture, of the engraver and, in most cases, of the collector or of the gallery where the picture was situated.

Though much of the text was written by James Dafforne, the choice of pictures would have been Carter's. He and Dafforne had seen changes taking place in British art since the early part of the century when Carter first came to London; paintings illustrative of literature were popular then, creating a bond between artist and viewer. In the 1850s and 1860s the mood was for paintings of contemporary life. Though many artists still relied on literature for their subjects, they no longer chose works of the eighteenth century. Then came the Pre-Raphaelites and Ruskin's advice to young artists that they should go to Nature to seek her meaning, 'rejecting nothing, selecting nothing and scorning nothing'.[4] There was nothing new in looking to Nature, artists of the Romantic Movement were obsessed by Nature, but now the Pre-Raphaelites painted every detail faithfully in order to convey an imaginative or symbolic meaning. Because of their interest in the inter-relationship of art and literature, much of the Pre-Raphaelite painting is narrative. Many of their paintings are about love, and for inspiration they turned to passages in Keats and Shakespeare, to Dante and

Tennyson and to Arthurian themes. When the painters of the Pre-Raphaelite Movement exhibited at the Royal Academy in 1849, *The Art Journal*'s reaction was cautious. Of William Holman Hunt's *Rienzi*, however, the reviewer said: 'The work is assuredly that of a young man of genius, if he be young ... he is of a surety destined to occupy a foremost place in art.' And Millais's naturalistic but highly stylised *Isabella* he saw as 'a pure aspiration in the feeling of the early Florentine School ... an example of rare excellence and learning ... it cannot fail to establish the fame of the young artist.'[5] But Carter, like many traditionalists, could not accept some of the Pre-Raphaelite methods – the use of an overall light, the detail of subordinate parts of a picture, and the flouting of the rules of perspective respected since the Renaissance. In 1853 *The Art Journal* criticised *The Order of Release* by Millais because

> [being] against a flat background – we cannot see what is gained by this, but it may be seen what is lost – the figures lose roundness and substance. It is absurd to say it is done because certain prerogative celebrities of the Italian miscellany of schools did the same in imitation of Fra Tonelle dell Oscuita, the most eccentric of the post-Giotteschi. Among so much truth this is a too obvious fallacy.[6]

By 1854 *The Art Journal* was more definite in its criticism of the Pre-Raphaelites. When writing about Holman Hunt it said: 'The so-called Pre-Raphaelite school has made no converts ... not withstanding the eager advocacy of the Oxford graduate [Ruskin] no class of the public will give their admiration or sympathy to the works of this artist.' (It was yet unaware of the immense popularity that *The Light of the World* – exhibited the previous year – was to attain.) In the Notes on the 88th Exhibition of the Academy in 1856 the critic writing in *The Art Journal* was even more dismissive of the Pre-Raphaelites.

> The spirit of 'Pre-Raphaelitism' survives, but in a modified form; the manner of execution so called, is so easy of attainment, that many young artists, dazzled with the notoriety which has attended the efforts of the first professors of this taste, will be continually publishing themselves as followers of

the heresy, though gradually subsiding into something more reasonable, as with those who have gone before them.[7]

(Indeed the first phase of the movement had ended in 1853 when Millais became an ARA and Rossetti remarked 'So now the whole Round Table is dissolved.')

It would appear then that Carter was not a great admirer of Pre-Raphaelite art. Of Millais's *Peace Concluded* in the Academy Exhibition of 1856, *The Art Journal* critic complained: 'If this be another example of what is called Pre-Raphaelite Art, we should be glad of an explanation of the term. Every one of the works of this artist differs from the other, and yet are all called "Pre-Raphaelite".'[8] That the criticism in *The Art Journal* was not more severe may have been due to Carter's respect for the Royal Academy which, apparently, was never discouraged from hanging their paintings on its walls. Nevertheless, a study of the list of *Selected Pictures* shows that he published none of the paintings of the original Pre-Raphaelites and few of those of their successors.

So on what criteria did Carter choose the pictures? Availability would have been the first consideration. Some artists were unwilling to have their paintings engraved, and in other cases there may have been difficulties where the copyright was owned by a print publisher. Carter would have known a great many patrons of art, both from his work and from the social life he and Anna Maria led in London. Most of the patrons agreed to their name being given as the owner of the painting. In only a few cases is the name of the collection omitted.

Some paintings were more suitable for engraving than others. *The Art Journal* admitted that William Mulready's *Choosing the Wedding Gown*, an idea taken from Oliver Goldsmith's *The Vicar of Wakefield*, was not very successful in black and white, but nevertheless published it in 1869. The pure colours which Mulready used, luminous over a white ground, and the contrasts between the materials are lost in the engraving.

A few of the pictures are by painters of the old school such as Wilkie and Etty, but more are by what then would have been called modern British painters – paintings of historical subjects, of contemporary life, domestic scenes and paintings illustrative of literature.

Many of the pictures had been exhibited at the Academy in the 1840s and 1850s. The letterpress with each engraving was three-quarters a factual description with a short paragraph on the technique as to finish, light and colour. The aim was to show the way to appreciation, not to make judgements of art. No preference for a particular painter is shown and no theories of art are discussed. Stephens's articles, on the other hand, are an expression of his artistic beliefs by which he judged the merits of the picture he was reviewing. He condemns the paintings of the illustrator: 'Respectable in design, the best does not touch our heart.' He goes further and insists that 'if it would endure, painting must exist for itself only'[9] – a clear indication of his belief in 'Art for Art's Sake'.

Alfred Elmore was an Irish painter, little known today apart from his picture *On the Brink*, exhibited at the Academy in 1865 and now in the Fitzwilliam Museum in Cambridge. The picture caused a stir, and told exactly the kind of moral story which appealed to the Victorian public. The scene is the gambling rooms at Homburg, and shows Elmore's feeling for space and light. The contrast between the warm glow of the gambling room and the pale face of the woman lit by the moonlight as she escapes from her would-be seducer, placed in shadow, is highly dramatic. Elmore leaves it to the viewer's choice whether the young woman is on the brink of suicide or of adulterous love. This picture of modern life was one of Elmore's occasional departures from subjects from history and literature, as were his paintings of religious subjects. Though it was well thought of, his *Christ Crucified* of 1839 was his last attempt at sacred art. Elmore's father was the Halls' family doctor in London.

Carter published engravings of two of Elmore's paintings. *The Novice* was exhibited in 1852, and shows Elmore's ability for the handling of space. There is the street scene outside, where a carnival is being celebrated, in contrast to the quiet room and the novice sitting on her (not too uncomfortable-looking) bed, and a room behind with two elderly nuns approaching. *The Controversy* was exhibited at the Academy as *Religious Controversy in the Time of Louis XIV* in 1849 – a time of controversy in Oxford, and in England as a whole. John Henry Newman had resigned his living in 1843 and in 1846 was ordained in Rome. Hostility to the Roman Catholic Church was aggravated in October 1850 with the restoration of the Catholic hierarchy in England, and was popularly referred to as 'Papal aggression'. The text with the engraving of 1868 prefaced the inscription with the words, 'The whole atmosphere of the religious world is disturbed, and the elements of disputation are permeating every nook and corner of society, peace and amity.'[10] (Carter may also have been thinking of the threat of Disestablishment of the Church of Ireland, a threat which was to become a reality in the following year.)

In selecting paintings for engraving Carter undoubtedly never forgot his duty to publish pictures which would elevate public taste, and not offend its susceptibilities. So it is interesting to look at pictures which were not chosen (if available), while others by the same painter were deemed to be worthwhile. For instance, Carter did not approve of Abraham Solomon's *The Lion in Love*, a picture of an old soldier making love to what *The Art Journal* called an obvious 'jilt'. Nor did Carter publish his *First Class – the Meeting* or *Second Class – the Parting*. The first picture recognises the advantages of wealth in contrast to a second where a mother sadly parts with her son who is emigrating. *First Class* was received badly by the public and the critics. It was not thought permissible to paint a picture of a father asleep in the corner of a railway carriage, neglecting to chaperone his daughter who is being charmed by a handsome stranger. (Solomon later painted another version with the father in animated conversation with the young man, and the girl sitting at a safe distance in the corner.) *The Art Journal* thought it regrettable that 'so much facility should be lavished on so bold – or vulgar a subject'. This did not prevent Carter from publishing two of Solomon's other paintings, *Art Critics in Brittany* (exhibited at the British Institution in 1861) and also *Le Malade Imaginaire*, both subjects which were unlikely to offend any taste. No paintings by Abraham's brother Simeon Solomon were included in the *Selected Pictures*.

By the 1860s the Classical Revival affected not only English painting, architecture and education, but also entered into social life. Victorian novels are full of allusions to the advantages of being a good Grecian. Members of the public, as well as artists, visited the British Museum and felt that they could look blamelessly on nude and semi-nude sculptures in an age when the human body was assiduously being covered up (though Carter said that some ladies would hurry through a sculpture gallery not looking to left or right). The Greeks venerated the body and sought to elevate its form to the highest level. Faces were unimportant, but few Victorians understood this. To look at the calm and noble Venus in marble for inspiration was one thing; to transfer the spirit of antiquity to bright glossy paint on canvas was another. To the viewer the result often appeared merely as an expression in nudity.

Pheidias and his contemporary sculptors did not show the female form unclothed; they used drapery to reveal and enhance it. Praxitiles and Scopas in the Hellenistic age were the first to represent figures of the goddess of love in the guise of a nude woman and, even then, introduced the circumstances of her going to the bath. This became a favourite subject for the Victorians. The sources for most nineteenth-century studies of the female nude were either the Medici Venus or the Capitoline Venus whose hands modestly cover parts of the body. Victorians would have been familiar with casts of both these statues, and perhaps preferred them to Praxitiles' Knidos Venus (from which they are probably derived) which Pliny explicitly describes.[11] Victorians tried techniques which the Greeks would never have used such as wetting drapery so that it clung and delineated the body and, as with so many of their enthusiasms, they overdid it.

The females employed as models for the nude in the Classical Revival were generally women of the lower classes, women of no settled occupations, some of them prostitutes. The growing concern over stories of the conduct of students and models in life-classes in some government and private art schools came to a head in 1860, when Lord Haddo moved in the House of Commons that government grants be withdrawn from any state-funded school of art employing the female model. In an article in *The Art Journal* entitled 'The Study of the Figure', Carter criticised the motion, strongly advocating the need for the study of the nude in art, and denying that it had a corrupting influence. 'To every figure painter the study of the nude subject is a matter of such importance as to render, in these days of precision, utterly illusory any hope of even a modicum of success in his profession without such a course of practice.'[12] He then printed a long letter from one Edwin J. Jones, in which the writer objected to the employment of female models in life-classes as a degredation of women. Carter added a footnote pointing out that these were not the views of the *Journal*.

On the other hand, Carter believed that the artist had a moral duty to be mindful as to the sensations which his delineation of the nude might arouse in the viewer. He reminded Frederic Leighton of this when Leighton exhibited his *Venus Disrobing for the Bath* at the Academy in 1867, saying, 'The artist does good service to art who reconciles the untutored English eye to the beauties of the unclothed figure. Only let it be remembered that to such a painter is committed a grave responsibility. He is bound to paint on the side of virtue, and so to exalt beauty as to silence passion.'[13] But when Albert Moore, who probably had more of the spirit of the Greeks than any of his contemporaries, exhibited his *Venus* two years later, the critic of *The Art Journal* thought that there was no danger of its corrupting morality; 'The figure is in no way obnoxious to good morals; indeed it is too ugly and repulsive to be objectionable except to taste.'

Carter always defended William Etty as being a man of pure and lofty ideas, and published an autobiographical article by him in 1849. Nevertheless, Etty's paintings of the female form, sensuous and full-blooded with their rich colouring, were not always acceptable to the Victorian sense of propriety. Thackeray, reviewing Etty's *Aurora and Zephyr*, exhibited at the Academy in 1845, thought that some of his paintings would not be suitable in a young ladies' school! *The Art Journal* admitted in 1857 that 'Etty's choice of subject and even his manner and treatment was, and still is, the theme of much unfavourable comment. Barry Stothard and Howard, before him, painted the heroines of Greek and Roman mythology, but were more scrupulous in their ideas of propriety than Etty cared to show himself.'[14] Etty meanwhile cared nothing for a censorious public. He thought all human beauty was concentrated in woman, and so dedicated himself to painting her. Carter admired Etty's talent for the handling of paint and his rich glowing colours, and continued to include engravings of his pictures in *The Art Journal*. His *Cupid and Psyche* is in the *Selected Pictures* of 1863.

William Edward Frost was a follower of Etty. *A Cool Retreat*, which is a study of a female figure preparing for the bath, shows much of Etty's influence. Frost had been a portrait painter for a number of years, which probably accounts for the expressive faces of some of his females at a time when many artists were reducing the importance of the face in their studies of the female nude. His females, some of them heavily draped, move and gesticulate, but there is nothing erotic in their movements and little to give offence. Frost is in the 1857 *Art Journal* series *British Artists: Their Style and Character* with illustrations of his paintings *Sabrina*, *The Sirens*, *Chastity* and *The Sea-cave* which was painted for the Halls' friend Alderman Spiers in 1851. *The Art Journal* did not approve of *A Bacchante and Young Faun Dancing*, which was described as 'powerful ... but the subject not so agreeable to our minds as others'. *Chastity*, from Milton's *Comus*, was thought more suitable for the *Selected Pictures*. The central figure is clothed and the painting described as 'the interpretation of pure and exalted sentiment'.[15] Frost was less interested in colour than Etty and his canvases tended to be subdued in tone. Ruskin, in his Academy Notes of 1856, wrote of his paintings 'looking like Etty's with all the colour scraped off'.

The implicit sexuality in many paintings of the nude dismayed some art critics and members of the art world. It was felt that certain paintings should not be placed on the walls of public galleries, but would be better in the private collections of connoisseurs who would recognise their finer qualities. When the National Gallery refused Titian's *Rape of Lucretia*, which first came to England in 1845, Carter wrote in *The Art Union* in 1847: 'To place such a picture as the Tarquin and Lucretia in the Public Gallery of the British Empire would be nothing less than an act of gross delinquency.' But Carter had reservations, too, as to the suitability of hanging certain paintings of the nude in the home, particularly in a home with a young family. A little later, in an article on 'The Nude in Art' he wrote:

> I much esteem and honour my friend Alma-Tadema ... Yet I would not with all my love of art place prominently in my dining room that most skilfully and admirably painted work of his 'The Sculptor's Model', concerning which there has been so much angry discussion at Liverpool: ... Admirable and

> greatly coveted as it is for a gallery, it is not and ought not to be, considered by any home ruler as a household God.

The idea of a life-size figure entitled *The Sculptor's Model*, it is said, was suggested to Alma-Tadema by the discovery of the so-called Venus of Esquiline. To many people, however, the figure bore no resemblance to a Venus, but merely seemed an exhibition of a nude model. Carter was not alone in finding a picture of a naked model standing in front of a man, with no mythological connotation, quite unacceptable. He continued: 'Neither will I believe that a Pater Familias would fill the portfolios of his olive branches with studies made in the Life Academy of Mulready and Etty. Surely we are not justified in placing before the young that which may induce impure thoughts.'[16] These were the opinions of a man who was presenting art in all its aspects to the public, and must have been the attitude of the vast majority of the population which sought to protect its youth, and particularly women, from those dangers which might undermine society.

The Selected Pictures was a highly successful series introducing the public to the wealth of modern art in private collections, and to pictures often bought straight from the artist's easel. It also encouraged the public to buy good engravings at affordable prices. Today, the series is a valuable source for research, providing information about nineteenth-century private collections (collections which tended not to remain intact) and a clear indication of current taste. The series, however, marks the decline in the popularity of engravings of works of art. Writing in his *Memoirs of Great Men and Women of the Age*, Carter said in 1871:

> Engraving, unhappily, is now, in England, nearly a vanished art. Excepting the works executed for the Art Journal there are very few line engravings progressing in Great Britain. The mezzotint scrapers and professors of the mixed style, are, indeed, partially employed; but the new art of photography has been fatal to the higher, and indeed, to the humbler art of the engraver.[17]

By the end of the 1860s a pattern had been established for the contents and format of *The Art Journal* which continued into the

1870s and changed little until Carter's retirement as editor. A monthly number was about thirty folio pages long with three columns to a page, but shorter if a catalogue was included, as for the International Exhibitions of 1855, 1862 and 1867. In December there was usually an editorial note in which Carter announced some of the items to be published in the following year. The note in December 1868 gives an interesting list of some of the writers for the *Journal*. There was generally an article of about three pages on antiquarian or art-related subjects such as book-binding, armoury etc. The Selected Pictures ran through the 1860s and early 1870s. Exhibitions, both in and outside London, were reviewed; articles on picturesque cottages and gardens were very popular. Art treasures abroad might occupy two columns, such as the excavations in Syria and Palestine published in the March number of 1868. Exhibitions abroad were also reported. Nearly every month there were accounts of British picture sales, and these provide further evidence of the differences in taste of collectors in the north and south of the country. There were also obituaries. 'Minor Topics' of about two pages appeared every month covering events in London and a wide variety of subjects including innocuous art gossip. A column was generally devoted to the Royal Academy (tending to be critical of its policy in the 1860s) and several pages to reviews of the annual exhibition. Formerly the order of paintings under review roughly followed that of the Academy catalogue, but from 1863 paintings were grouped more systematically according to their pictorial genre. There were two or three pages of reviews of art and topographical books. These reviews were generally anonymous, as were some of the articles. The question of anonymity came very much under discussion at the time. In an early number of the *Fortnightly Review*, Anthony Trollope wrote a paper advocating the signature of authors. He had not changed his opinion when he wrote in his *Autobiography*, published in 1883:

> I think that the name of the author does tend to honesty, and that the knowledge that it will be inserted adds much to the author's industry and care ... A man should never be ashamed to acknowledge that which he is not ashamed to publish. In the *Fortnightly Review* everything has been signed, and in this way

good has, I think, been done. Signatures to articles in other periodicals have become much more common since the *Fortnightly Review* was commenced.[18]

The Art Journal was still the only journal purely devoted to art, but now several of the literary periodicals had articles on fine art and on art exhibitions, not to mention national newspapers which also reviewed some of the exhibitions. These years, from the end of the 1850s to the end of the 1870s, mark the zenith of a journal of which Carter could justly be proud. The high quality of the illustrations with steel engravings was to give way in the 1880s, after Carter's retirement, to the garish art of photochromy.

13
The Halls in London

It seems that Carter and Anna Maria had left Firfield in 1860 and were living at the Boltons, South Kensington when Carter sold plots 409–411 to a John Tulk of Firfield.[1] The assumption is that Tulk also bought the house that year. It must have been a wrench for the Halls leaving the place with the conservatory and garden which they had created. Carter said that the new owner appreciated the casts of modern sculpture, so these must have been included in the sale of the house.

The Halls were gregarious and hospitable. They knew, and entertained, many writers and artists in London. Llewellynn Jewitt, a constant contributor to *The Art Journal* and co-author with Carter of *The Stately Homes of England*, noted in his diary: 'Then to the Halls to dine, at a quarter past seven, dinner the most splendid and elegant I ever saw, and entirely arranged in my honour.'[2] Mrs Oliphant said that the Halls were fond of 'every kind of lion and wonder', great and small, and describes a party given for the painter Rosa Bonheur (then at the height of her reputation) with the most extraordinary entertainment provided.

> A round-faced good-humoured woman with hair cut short and divided at one side like a man's, and indeed not very distinct in the matter of sex so far as dress and appearance went. There was also a Chinese mandarin in full costume, smiling blandly upon the company, and accompanied by a missionary who had the charge of him. By some means or other the Chinaman was made to sing what we were informed was a sentimental ballad, exceedingly touching and romantic.[3]

Unfortunately, she said, it sounded like her Newfoundland dog howling. Mrs Oliphant liked going to the Halls' parties, she found their 'conventionality satisfying to the senses' because it was what she expected. She noticed that Carter was 'never tired, always insinuating, jovial and affectionate'. Nevertheless, she thought him an Irish humbug.

On further acquaintance Nathaniel Hawthorne decided that he had misjudged Carter. Though he seems to have found him rather overpowering, even, sometimes, as cutting rather a ridiculous figure, he believed him to be 'sincere in his demonstrations of regard'. He was at a party of the Halls given for the singer Jenny Lind, and described the crowded rooms and people of note who were there. He enjoyed meeting the Irish song writer and painter Samuel Lover. Lover was about to publish *Lyrics of Ireland*, in which he included a song written by Carter entitled 'The Blarney'. This had been sung in the play *The Groves of Blarney*, written for the actor Tyrone Power, which ran for a season at the Adelphi Theatre in 1838. Also in the *Lyrics* is a poem by Anna Maria from her first novel *The Buccaneer*. It is very much in the Tom Moore tradition, and one feels it could well be sung to the air of his 'Meeting of the Waters'. Lover found Anna Maria's tales of Irish peasantry exquisitely touching, 'sunny and shadowy like the people themselves'. He spoke of Anna Maria as one of the most gifted of Ireland's daughters, 'celebrated abroad and beloved at home'.[4] Henry Vizetelly had no doubts in his mind as to which of the Halls was the more gifted. He wrote scathingly of Carter, though he was never averse to accepting his hospitality.

> Hall talked even more priggishly than he wrote, and I have more than once felt surprised at hearing him launch out at his own dinner table without any attempt being made to check him by his sensible wife. True, he assumed an intellectual authority over her, and she blandly accepted the false position, but no one was taken in by it.[5]

It was not only the renowned and successful who were invited to the Halls' house. Anna Maria was always willing to help struggling writers of merit, particularly if their views accorded with her own. Mention has been made of the poet shoemaker, John O'Neill, in an earlier chapter. Anna Maria welcomed the poverty-stricken old man in her pretty drawing room and encouraged him to bring her his fairy tales and legends. She wrote to William Chambers, in the hope that he might include some in his journal. When O'Neill finished his *Handerahan the Fairy Man and Legends of Carrick*, Anna Maria offered to edit it and write an introduction. O'Neill was overjoyed to have her backing but because of some 'loose expressions' in the tales Anna Maria found herself unable to collaborate. Carter told him 'There was nothing in them that it was improper for a man to write, but there were some expressions that it would be indelicate in a lady to give her sanction to.'[6] However, after O'Neill had deleted several passages, Anna Maria wrote a charming introduction, regretting that the work was 'probably the last contribution of the kind that will be made to our literature, for the Irish fairies are, even now, beings of a past tradition'. But despite Anna Maria's efforts to find him subscribers, the book was not a financial success. However, it enabled O'Neill to apply again, this time successfully, for a relief from the Royal Literary Fund. Anna Maria was his sponsor, as she was to several applicants to the fund over the years.[7]

Like many of their prominent contemporaries in London, the Halls were enthusiastic philanthropic workers. Anna Maria had particular sympathy for impoverished governesses, many of whom ended their days in pitiful poverty. She ran a stall at a bazaar to raise money for a benevolent fund for which she wrote and sold copies of *The Old Governess*. Carter, for his part, had worked tirelessly to raise funds for the foundation of a consumption hospital in Brompton, and now more money was needed to enlarge it. Again, Anna Maria had a stall at a bazaar held in the grounds of Chelsea Hospital, for which she wrote and sold copies of *The Forlorn Hope, a Story of Old Chelsea*. These charity bazaars were frequently held for fund raising, they also satisfied social aspirations and provided a scene for fashion. A charity bazaar is the subject for James Collinson's *The Empty Purse*. Anthony Trollope, who disapproved of them, wrote a vivid description of one in his novel *Miss Mackenzie*. He describes the ladies of rank or importance who had the stalls, surrounded by their young helpers.

> The girls who went about among the crowd, begging men to put their hands into lucky bags, trading in rose-buds, and asking for half-crowns for cigar lighters, were fresh in their muslins, pretty with their braided locks, and perhaps not impudently over-pressing in their solicitations to male strangers. While they were not as yet either aweary or habituated to the

> necessity of importunity, they remembered their girlhood and their ladyhood, their youth and their modesty, and still carried with them something of the bashfulness of maidenhood; and the young men, the wether lambs, were as yet flush with their half-crowns, and the elder sheep had not quite dispensed the last of their sovereigns or buttoned up their trouser pockets. But as the work went on, and the dust arose, and the prettinesses were destroyed, and the money became scarce, and weariness was felt, and the heat showed itself, and the muslins sank into limpness, and the ribbons lost their freshness, and braids of hair grew rough and loose, and side-locks displaced themselves, – as girls became used to soliciting and forgetful of their usual reticences in their anxiety for money, the charm of the thing went, and all was ugliness and rapacity; young ladies no longer moved about doing works of charity; but harpies and unclean birds were greedy in quest of their prey.[8]

Carter was co-secretary with Sidney Herbert in raising money for the Florence Nightingale Fund to found an institution in her honour for the training of nurses. The Halls arranged for Jenny Lind to sing at a concert in Exeter Hall in March 1856, but did not find the enthusiasm for the cause as strong as they expected. Anna Maria wrote to Francis Bennock:

> I wish you would help to get rid of about 100 tickets ... Mr Hall and myself are grieved beyond all telling – Mr Hall thought the committee would have come forward and urged the concert on – instead of that there are only some 15 or 16 who have responded. Please dear friend – make those city people go – and the Lord Mayor gives a dinner the same night. Several I know are going – of course we sent a refusal.[9]

The concert, however, was a success and realised £2,000 for the fund.

William Goss, writing about Anna Maria, said she was a most influential woman, and the power of her pen was frequently sought to further various causes. An issue she would have nothing to do with however, which was the subject of much controversy in the 1850s and 1860s, was the rights of women. She believed in the

Christian duties of a wife and her obligation of obedience to her husband, which probably accounts for her apparent submissiveness to Carter even when he made himself slightly ridiculous in front of their friends. 'This new seeking of womanly independence among married women is an outrage against God and nature,' she wrote to a young wife. Nevertheless, with the furtherance of education for women their rights were inevitably becoming a burning issue. Fanny Trollope's story *One Fault*, published in 1840, is surprisingly advanced in ideas, even suggesting that women might become priests and Members of Parliament. Anthony Trollope, on the other hand, in a pamphlet *On the Higher Education of Women* (c. 1869), divided women's rights into two categories: the right to work, which he endorsed, and political rights, which he dismissed as unworthy of consideration.

Not that Anna Maria was living in sheltered ignorance as to the less fortunate of the world. She showed great pity and understanding for prostitutes and women fallen from the moral standards of Victorian society, and raised money for a 'House of Safety and Shelter' at Kerby Street, Poplar. She wrote an article in *Social Notes* (which Carter was editing) asking for contributions.

It may well have been due to the influence of William Howitt that Carter became interested in spiritualism. The Halls were close friends of William and Mary Howitt, and Carter had given Howitt both moral and financial support when he ran into trouble over the mismanagement of *The People's Journal*, of which he was editor and part-proprietor, with the loss of £3,000. The enthusiasm for spiritualism was a natural reaction against the industrialism and materialism of the second half of the nineteenth century, as the resurgence of religion, in the early part of the century, had been after the Age of Reason and the materialism of the eighteenth century. For some philosophers the term spiritualism was synonymous with idealism, to express the idea of the universe opposed to a material philosophy. Fashionable London responded to the movement as something that allowed for personal, spiritual experience in a material world.

One of the most influential and more respectable of the mediums was Daniel Dunglas Home. Said to be the natural son of Alexander 10th Earl of Home, he was adopted and taken to America by an aunt. On his return to England, prominent people, including judges and academics, attested to his good faith. He held seances at Cox's, his hotel in Jermyn Street, where, Sir David Brewster wrote in the *Morning Advertiser*, the table rose and rappings were heard. The word quickly spread and many great houses were open to him; but he took no money for seances. He was invited to Bulwer Lytton's house where the Brownings attended a seance. Elizabeth Browning had faith in him, but Robert Browning was sceptical and in 1864 expressed his disbelief in a publication called *Sludge the Medium*. Dr Wilkinson wrote articles signed 'Verax' in the *Morning Advertiser* recording levitations and messages received through Home, and Lord Lindsey, before the London Dialectical Society, attested that Home handled fire. Anna Maria, in a letter to Lord Dunraven (author of *Home, His Life and Mission*), also said that she had seen this. The Halls invited Home several times to hold seances in their house. After one of these, Anna Maria wrote to the sculptor Joseph Durham to give him the exact words of a message which they had received from the spiritual world. This was from her friend Letitia Elizabeth Landon, the poetess, who had died mysteriously in the Gold Coast after her arrival and marriage to George McLean, the Governor. When asked for her name in the spirit world, Anna Maria reported, the rappings spelt out the words, 'I was known in this world by the name L.E.L. I was murdered – but to me it was a boon for I may now work for those who did me a great wrong.'[10] Anna Maria accepted this; she always maintained that McLean had made L.E.L. very unhappy and was to some extent responsible for her death. Home founded the Spiritual Athenaeum in conjunction with Carter and a Dr Elliotson, a society for the propagation of spiritualism, at 22, Sloane Square. Carter remained a believer in spiritualism all his life, though he warned people against unscrupulous mediums.

Neither Carter nor Anna Maria wrote diaries, and it is only from references from their contemporaries and from Carter's *Retrospect* that any picture emerges of their married life. The extant letters are not very revealing. It seems to have been a happy marriage, despite the sadness that no children survived. Who their adopted daughter was remains a mystery, but she must have brought them consolation – and pleasure – when she married Carter's nephew Sandford

Rochat. As Carter said, he and Anna Maria had many shared interests, and he was able to understand the issues in Ireland with which Anna Maria was concerned, issues which to many Englishmen would have been incomprehensible. Unfortunately, Carter destroyed Anna Maria's letters to him, which he said were private. Anna Maria, on the other hand, kept all his, but these have been dispersed. William Goss, in a chapter on the Halls in his book about Llewellynn Jewitt, wrote, 'A host of valuable letters written by various distinguished people to Mrs S. C. Hall and preserved by her I have permission from her husband to preserve or destroy, according to my judgement.'[11] He makes no mention of Carter's letters to Anna Maria, though he quotes some in his book. Carter never mentions Goss, and there is no explanation as to why Goss had such discretionary powers. Anna Maria's letters to Francis Bennock, in the Library of the University of Iowa, give the best picture of the Halls' life together when living at Firfield. There is the pleasure that they both derived from living in civilised surroundings, in the house and grounds bought with the proceeds of their industry. It was only to Francis Bennock that Anna Maria revealed her anxieties for Carter when his mercurial spirits plunged from buoyancy to the deepest depression, and he drove himself beyond his formidable capacity for work. Money, which he does not seem to have handled well, was always a worry.

On 20 September 1874 Carter and Anna Maria celebrated their Golden Wedding. Their friends circulated a letter promoting the presentation of a testimonial to the Halls on the occasion of their Golden Wedding 'in recognition of the eminent services rendered by them to literature and Art, and of their varied, useful and energetic labours in so many good causes'. At a large gathering, presided over by Lord Shaftesbury, a testimonial was presented to the Halls, together with the sum of £1,600 – most of which went into an annuity. The testimonial carried the names of hundreds of prominent people in London, and showed the esteem and affection in which the Halls were held. With the Victorian enthusiasm for cards, the Halls sent their friends an anniversary card of the occasion. It is decorated on the left with a sprig of rosemary for remembrance, and on the right are photographs of Carter and Anna Maria.

For Anna Maria, Carter wrote a poem. The second verse pays tribute to her literary achievements, of which he was so proud.

> So it has been from manhood unto age,
> In every shifting scene of Life's sad stage,
> Since – fifty years ago – a humble name
> I gave to thee – which thou hast given to fame,
> Rejoicing in the wife and friend to find
> The woman's lesser duties – all combined
> With holiest efforts of creative mind.
> And if the world has found some good in me,
> The prompting and the teaching came from thee!

It cannot claim to be first-class verse, but speaks for Carter's romantic nature and was no doubt received by Anna Maria in the same spirit.

14
The Halls' Literary Work

Carter Hall always described himself as, first, 'by profession a man of letters' and, secondly, an editor. Nevertheless, though he shared with Anna Maria a love of literature and a zest for the researching of topographical works, it was as an editor that he made his principal contribution.

Anna Maria had a considerable reputation by the middle of the century as a writer of fiction. Her earliest stories were of Ireland, beginning with *Sketches of Irish Character*, first published in 1829, which went into five editions. These short stories were followed by *Lights and Shadows of Irish Life* in 1838, *Popular Tales* (which included many of the early stories) and *Stories of the Irish Peasantry* in 1848. Anna Maria's purpose was to awaken sympathy for the hardships of the Irish peasants and to portray their virtues to an English public. The stories, often comic though sometimes tragic, had conversations delivered in an Irish idiom. They delighted Anna Maria's English readers, who expected stories of Ireland to be either humorous or larded with Celtic romance, but infuriated the humbler classes in Ireland, the very people she had looked on as her friends. They mistrusted her impartiality over politics and religion, and regarded her writings as those of an Anglo-Irish woman with an English view of Ireland. But, as Mrs Oliphant believed, it was on the Irish tales that she built her reputation.

Maria Edgeworth was undoubtedly an influence. There is an early unpublished piece by Anna Maria entitled 'Sketches of Old Maids by One of the Sisterhood'. The introduction announces: 'It may be considered something very like double dealing for me to furnish the public with sketches of my own sisters – but if I don't do it somebody else will.' There follows a list of old maids that she intends to define: the disappointed old maid, the sentimental old maid (dangerous to young men until very old), the literary old maid, the juvenile old maid and several others ending with the good old maid.[1] Maria Edgeworth's amusing little piece entitled 'Thoughts on Bores' has a comparable list. (Given Carter's fondness for quotations, the following passage is a little near the knuckle.)

> The bore is usually considered a harmless creature, or that of a class of irrational bipeds who hurt only themselves. To such, however, I would not advise trusting too much. The bore is harmless, no doubt, as long as you listen to him; but disregard, or stop him mid-career, he will turn on you ... The everlasting quotation-loving bore – Greek, Latin and English – the everlasting quotation-lover dotes on the husks of learning.[2]

The Halls stayed at Edgeworthstown on several occasions. In 1842, when they were collecting material for *Ireland: Its Scenery, Character, etc.*, Maria Edgeworth wrote in Anna Maria's autograph album: 'I rejoice to see Mr and Mrs Hall at my home at Edgeworthstown, they are on a tour of Ireland which they will illustrate by their various talents, and truly represent, setting down naught in malice – and if nothing extenuating, nothing exaggerating.'[3] The two women kept up a regular correspondence in which Anna Maria often sought literary advice. Sometimes they were at odds. Generally, Anna Maria's stories of Irish character were taken from life, for the most part memories of girlhood, but she also used her highly developed imagination. Maria Edgeworth apparently

> did not see, so clearly as I saw, the value of the imagination in literature for the young, and was almost angry when she discovered that a sketch that I had written of a supposititious scene in Killarney was pure invention. She told me indeed, that she had been so deceived by my picture as actually to have enquired for, and tried to find out, the hero of it; and argued strongly for truth in fiction. I ventured, not withstanding my homage for that estimable woman, to ask if her portrait of Sir Condy in 'Castle Rackrent' was a veritable likeness, and endeavoured to convince her that to call imagination to the aid of reason – to mingle the ideal with the real – was not only permissible but laudable as a means of impressing truth.[4]

Both Anna and Maria Edgeworth wrote about characters 'almost peculiar to Ireland':

> the half-gentleman [Anna Maria wrote in 'Father Pike' in *Popular Tales*] is a noxious species ... ; these half-gentlemen are wholly idle, and on the strength of their relationship to some rich family ... they exist without any visible means of support ... they go from house to house, relying on the hospitality of the owners, and always manage to claim relationship with the opulent who for the sake of the family will not suffer them to wear a shabby appearance.

Maria Edgeworth's half-gentleman, easy Simon, in 'Rosanna' in her *Popular Tales,* is a shiftless character with a small patrimony which he neglects through sheer idleness. Her characters are not merely comic; she had a penetrating perception of people and situations, but a certain detachment. Anne Ritchie (Thackeray's daughter) wrote of her: 'Other people were *other people* to her; bright all the time she looked at them through her keen eyes and one is constantly reminded of this cheerful aloofness, this reserve and reticence.'[5] There is an authenticity about Maria Edgeworth's stories which Anna Maria's lack on account of a sensitivity bordering on sentimentality. Nevertheless, she does on occasion use a story to highlight an issue on which she feels strongly. Her contempt for the superficial education of young ladies, for instance, comes out clearly in her story 'The Hospitality of Barrytown' in *Popular Tales.*

> Mrs Croyden was the widow of a general officer. As her husband fell in love with her at a garrison ball, and as she calculated on a similar destiny for her daughters, she resolved on adding to their beauty every accomplishment under the sun, as they were portionless. What hosts of masters! Painting on velvet, japanning, oriental tinting, music, dancing, singing, fencing, riding, French and everything in the world except the solid usefulness of education.

Apart from her ten novels, Anna Maria wrote plays and children's stories as well as pamphlets for the Temperance and other philanthropic movements. Her first novel, *The Buccaneer*, was published in 1831. Her attempts, in the early draft, of portraying Oliver Cromwell (whom she much admired) seem to have been rather unsuccessful. She must have sent her manuscript to Lytton Bulwer for his criticism, as she wrote to thank him:

> The object however of your excellent criticism and delightful praise will I hope be in some degree answered … My great anxiety to make Cromwell (I speak with respect) *omnipresent* has I now clearly perceive drawn me into the error of making him common. I will try to do away with this.

Of the heroine Constantia, with whom Anna Maria clearly identifies herself, she wrote:

> I wish to represent Constantia's enthusiastic temperament cherished in solitude, and warmed by an acquaintance with *true poetry*, the poetry of nature as well as books. It seems to me a hard thing to check that species of enthusiasm which is engendered by the admiration of genius … I think Constantia's feeling would seem unnatural, from the observations you make – so certain am I that they would appear so that I will do my best to tame the chapter, and sober her enthusiasm.[6]

Dalton, the Buccaneer, is a romantic figure whose past is forgiven when he turns from his pirate ways. Lytton Bulwer praised the novel in the *New Monthly Magazine*, comparing it to Scott's historical novels. But after the second edition in 1855, Sarah Hales wrote in *Women's Record*: '*The Buccaneer* is well managed and some of the characters are skilfully delineated, but the work is too feminine and has too little energetic passion for the strong times in which it is cast.'

Carter was very proud of Anna Maria's literary reputation, and understandably appreciated her ability to combine the duties of a Victorian wife with her work (although Anna Maria regarded these duties as a privilege rather than a burden). She nevertheless felt passionately about the hardships that some women had to endure, and in some of her tales from *Tales of Women's Trials* the sufferings of the women, from different strata of society, are convincingly and touchingly told. The issue in 'The Trial of Grace Huntley' is the thinness of the line dividing moral laziness from degradation. This occurs in other stories and is only applied to men, never to women. Grace Huntley's husband, Joseph, slips easily from laziness into dishonesty, 'for the progress from idleness to comparative want, from want to vice, whether slow or not, is sure'. When Grace Huntley finds her husband has been teaching her son to steal she informs on her husband's poaching and stealing 'to save the children'. There is an attempt to have a happy ending, which Victorian readers expected, by Grace Huntley setting sail for Australia, fifteen years later, to join her husband at the end of his sentence.

By 1848 stories about Ireland were not so popular, and Anna Maria turned to writing stories for children and collaborating more with Carter on topographical works and guide books. The Halls were fortunate in knowing many of the eminent artists of the day whom they could approach as potential illustrators. Sir Noel Paton, Daniel Maclise and others did the drawing for *Midsummer Eve*, published in 1848 (1847 in *The Art Journal*). And *Pilgrimages to English Shrines*, published in 1850 and 1853 (also in *The Art Journal*), has delightful woodcuts from Fairholt's illustrations. Most of the notes and some of the text are by Fairholt.

Carter said that Anna Maria brought life and sparkle to his dry accounts of places and buildings in their topographical works. Certainly his style is somewhat ponderous and wordy, though fairly typical of early Victorian writers. His *Memories of Great Men and Women*, published in 1871, went into three editions. In his chapter on Sydney Morgan he tells a story of a party (to which he and Anna Maria were invited) at which she hoped to mix members of the aristocracy with people of artistic merit. It is an amusing little story which is interesting as the contemporary account of a social scene.

> Mr Mackinnon of Hyde Park Place had a large house, a suite of rooms capable of 'entertaining' many, and in partnership with that estimable gentleman her plan was to be carried out. He was to issue cards to ladies and gentlemen of his own order; she to those who were eminent in literature, science and art. The cards were printed accordingly. They expressed that Lady Morgan and Mr Mackinnon desired to be honoured with the company of so-and-so on the evening of Wednesday, July 16th. It was certainly somewhat startling to read the names thus joined. It was known that the one was a widow, and the other a widower, and there was consequently no just

> cause or impediment why they too should not be joined together. Still, it was curious and 'gossip' might have been excused, especially as the card was lithographed in their joint names, that of Lady Morgan standing first.
>
> We received our invitation from Lady Morgan's own hands, and accepted it. On the evening of the 16th we duly entered the drawing room at Hyde Park Place. We heard titles of all degrees announced, but hardly a name eminent in literature, art or science greeted our ears. There were present perhaps two hundred people of rank, but excepting ourselves and three or four others of our 'calling', Lady Morgan had no followers to fraternise with those of Mr Mackinnon ...
>
> A few days afterwards the mystery was explained. Mr Mackinnon had agreed to envelope and direct such cards as were to go to his 'order', Lady Morgan undertaking the transmission of such as were intended to lure the magnates of her own circle and craft. The cards, properly prepared and addressed, she handed to Mr Mackinnon's butler for the post; but either that important functionary forgot his duty, or grudged the postage, or thought it beneath him and his master to invite so many untitled guests – at all events they were subsequently found safe in his desk, where they had been in comfortable seclusion from the day when dear Lady Morgan placed them in his hands.[7]

In his chapter on Professor Wilson, Carter gives a long and rather tedious description of the Burns Festival held in August 1844.[8] This is probably the literary event at which, Dr Mackay told Nathaniel Hawthorne, Carter shed tears into a Scottish river, overcome by the emotional proceedings.[9] Mackay laughed gently at the memory, but it was the kind of incident which provoked taunts of humbug from some of Carter's detractors. Unless everything about the man is slightly bogus, one can only believe that Carter was genuinely affected by such effusions of cultural pride. There were all the dramatic elements in the scene of the seething multitude that had gathered to honour the memory of Burns which appealed to his nature.

Carter published *Retrospect of a Long Life* in two volumes in

1833 when he was eighty-three years of age. Like so many memoirs of that vintage, it is rather rambling and, in some places, dull. But it is worth reading for the interesting pieces of information about the art world and London life of the period. For instance, on the attitudes to women who stepped outside the moral code of the day. Of Lady Blessington he wrote: 'Her visitors were all men, or nearly all men, ladies were rarely seen at her receptions. Mrs Hall never accompanied me to her evening parties, although she was a frequent day-caller. We were not of rank high enough to be indifferent of public feeling.'[10] One tends to accept the Victorians' ideas of moral behaviour from their literature, where novelists did not allow their heroes and heroines to deviate far from strict rules. It seems, however, that there was some latitude within different ranks of society. Lady Blessington had intellectual pretensions even if her private life did not bear scrutiny; and evidently Anna Maria's place in society would not be prejudiced by visiting her in the daytime.

Unfortunately, Carter does not reveal where he went to school. He talks in *Retrospect* of Sunday school at Christ Church, Cork, as well as some happy holidays as a schoolboy in the house of a surgeon in Bristol. It would have been normal for him to come to England and perhaps stay for some of the holidays – the journey from Cork to Bristol, as he points out, was a serious undertaking.[11] But he was certainly in Ireland most of the time until he left in 1822. His opinions about the country as expressed in *Retrospect* changed little over the years. Though he thinks Ireland a better place in some respects in 1883, he cannot hide his pessimism that the agrarian crimes of his youth were still being perpetrated. He was writing only a year after the murders of the new Chief Secretary, Lord Frederick Cavendish, and his Under-Secretary T. H. Burke in Phoenix Park.

Although Carter had been writing and editing topographical works and books on art for many years, he published little other original work, and this only late in life and written in the style of his youth or middle age. While this would no doubt have been thought old-fashioned by younger writers and critics of the 1870s and 1880s, it may well have been accepted (and even welcomed in some quarters) in an age that was becoming uneasy about the cheap literature which was flooding the market. *The Art Journal* published an article in 1876 on 'Bad Literature', attacking 'penny dreadfuls' and poor illustrations.

There is an interesting contemporary comparison to be made between Carter and Thackeray, writing, as it happened, on the same subject, Ireland and its people and scenery. Thackeray's *The Irish Sketch Book* was published in 1842, just at the time when the Halls were publishing *Ireland: Its Scenery, Character, etc.* They could well have met on their tours. However much Thackeray concedes to the beauties of Ireland (which he sees with an artist's eye) he is always ready to make fun of the inhabitants, or slip in some words of denigration. Nor can he abide the dirt, the beggars and the dilapidations. Of Innisfallen in Killarney he writes:

> Here we landed for a while, and the weather clearing up allowed us to see this charming spot; rocks, shrubs and little abrupt rises and falls of ground, covered with the brightest emerald grass; a beautiful little ruin of a Saxon chapel, lying gentle, delicate and plaintive on the shore; some noble trees round about it, and beyond, presently, the tower of Ross Castle ...
>
> The boats' crews were grouped about the place and one large barge especially had landed some sixty people, being the temperance band, with its drums, trumpets and wives. They were marshalled by a grave old gentleman with a white waistcoat and queue, a silver medal decorating one side of his coat, and a brass heart reposing on the other flap. The horns performed some Irish airs prettily; and at length, at the instigation of a fellow who went swaggering about with a pair of swirling drum sticks, all formed together and played Garryowen – the active drum of course most dreadfully out of time.

Though rather long-winded, there is a lightness of touch, and the scene comes alive. The Halls' description of Innisfallen in *A Week in Killarney*, on the other hand, is idealistic and ponderous.

> After our visit to Innisfallen in 1840, it became associated with our dreams of happiness – it was to us a vision of beauty – of peace – of loveliness ... Yes, there is Innisfallen, but oh, how changed! The storms, they tell us, uprooted some, and rendered

> topless others, of those noble trees, now but the relics of their former greatness; shorn of every bough and leaf, headless trunks – truly the glory has departed, for a time, from Innisfallen. Did we say 'for a time'? Alas! Much has departed that can never return. The beautiful little oratory changed, in latter days, into a banquetting house, that graceful ruin. – a gem of beauty – has been almost pulled down.[12]

The reader, while sympathising with the disappointment of seeing a lovely place changed, finds his patience tried by the extravagance of language, and comes to the conclusion that this is no first-class writer.

Carter's influence in the world of literature and art in the nineteenth century was undoubtedly as an editor, in an era which produced editors of real literary merit. He had, of course, considerable experience before becoming the editor of *The Art Journal.* In 1826 he founded and edited *The Amulet* and in the same year became editor of *The Spirit and Manners of the Age.* From 1829 to 1830 he edited *The Morning Journal,* and was editor of *The New Monthly* from 1832 to 1836. The following year he was sub-editor of *John Bull*, and in 1839 had become manager of *The Britannia* when Richard Hodgson (of Hodgson and Graves) offered to put up the capital if Carter would edit a journal wholly devoted to art. The first number of *The Art Union* was published in that year.

All this prepared him for the work which was to occupy him for the next forty years of his life. He had learnt the hard way that an editor must make his periodical pay and not merely indulge his artistic preferences. *The Amulet*, which was a very expensive production, had failed. One engraving alone, a Crucifixion after John Martin by Henry Le Keux, had cost 210 guineas. Joseph Comyns Carr, author and critic and one of the directors of the Grosvenor Gallery, became a regular contributor to *The Art Journal* until he objected to Carter's interference in his column.

> For a time, our relations on The Art Journal were friendly and undisturbed, and Mr Hall was good enough to express in unstinted terms his appreciation of my work. But it was impossible, even at that time, in personal converse with the man, not to be haunted by the suspicion that his constant

> assertion of the most ideal aims in life were consistent with an occasional reference to the more mundane considerations ... It was only upon longer acquaintance I discovered that ... the air of venerable piety, which never deserted him in social intercourse, was consistent with a very shrewd appreciation of commercial success. Little by little I found the sanctity of his manner sometimes giving way to the very pointed suggestions that the mercantile interests of the Journal must not be wholly sacrificed to my independent views on art ... At first these views were only tentatively put forward, and always with an elaborate deference to my better judgement as a critic, but day by day they became more encroaching, until at last the conviction was forced upon me that the columns under my charge were intended to serve as a useful support to the advertisement department of the Journal. After a while these constant interferences became so galling and exasperating to me that I determined to break our connections, and in a letter which I strove to make polite but which I intended to be deeply sarcastic, I ventured to hint that as the criticism I was called upon to write was now required to take so entirely the colour of an advertisement, I thought it would be better that it should pass directly into the hands of the manager of the advertisement department.

Whatever protest Carr expected from Carter, he must have been disappointed by the non-committal note sent in reply: 'I hasten to acknowledge with many thanks your courteous letter. So much I feel compelled to say, more than this I will not say.'[13]

At a time when literary figures were courted by proprietors of periodicals to join their editorial boards, Anthony Trollope had this to say about the role of an editor. 'When once the feeling has come upon an editor or critic that he may allow himself to be influenced by other considerations than the duty he owes to the public, all sense of critical or of editorial honesty falls from him at once.'[14] This duty, he thought, lay in giving the public advice as to whether a work was worthwhile; it might not be the best advice, but it was better than none at all. Carter would have agreed with this, but would have gone further in that there should be a didactic element in the advice. His statement 'I had to create a public for art', at the foundation of *The Art Journal,* implies the necessity to teach. He firmly believed that the public, lacking confidence in its own judgement, was influenced by the opinions expressed in *The Art Journal* and looked to it for advice in buying works of art. He said as much in one of his editorials (probably with his campaign against fraud in mind). His claim may have been true in the days before dealers had the influence on patrons which they acquired later, but such complacency naturally annoyed some of his contemporaries.

On the editor's role Carter wrote:

> The less he writes the better ... In a word, he must study solely the interests of the work under his charge, and give no thought to the satisfaction or the reputation a task may confer upon himself. He must however be a despot; to approve or reject without being called upon to assign a reason for his decision. Moreover, the privilege to erase he must always use though never a power to add.[15]

However, though the functions of an editor may be different from those of a critic, there are some areas where they must merge. Carter says that the editor should be qualified to write, when necessary, on all subjects which the journal covers, and in such cases he may take on the role of the critic. Most editors maintained their independence and integrity, and Anthony Trollope (who was an editor for three and a half years) made it plain that an editor should not be influenced by social pressures. He says that an editor should never accept a present. We are told that Carter did. As to Carter's claim that the editor must give no thought to the satisfaction a task may confer on him, he presumably meant that he should not use his magazine simply as a vehicle for showing off his own literary expertise.

Trollope thought that the best editors were publishers, or publisher-proprietors, who would not be too soft to say 'This is trash.' Carter would have been unlikely to use such a succinct dismissal, though he had no qualms about refusing contributions. No Mrs Brumby would have bamboozled him into publishing unsuitable material. Mrs Brumby, in Trollope's short story about an editor, 'made life a burden to us, and more than once induced us to calculate whether it would not be well that we should abandon our public duties and return to some private corner into which it would be impossible that Mrs Brumby should follow us'. The editor in the story was quite sure that he never said that he would use her work, but somehow she managed to leave her manuscript in his hands. And somehow he never got round to reading it, and in the end he found himself paying £10 to her lawyer for delay in the perusal of her story simply to get rid of her.[16]

So who were this new public for art? As an editor how would Carter have reacted to the late Fabian ideal of art for the masses. An obituary of him says that he was trying to bring art to the lower-middle classes.[17] Certainly he was in sympathy with Ruskin as regards art in the Working Men's College. (Ruskin, too, is said to have liked Carter and contributed nine chapters of his *The Cestus of Aglaia* to *The Art Journal* in 1865 and 1866.) In the appreciation of paintings, particularly those of the modern British school, *The Art Journal* was catering for the middle and lower classes who formed the market for prints of contemporary art. As for the articles on architecture and archaeology, they could only have been enjoyed by people with some knowledge of the subject.

Carter's industry was exceptional. With all his work as the editor of *The Art Journal* (which involved a lot of travelling) it is hard to imagine how he could find time to research and edit so many works of art and architecture. Probably the most useful of these for study and reference today are *The Gallery of Modern Sculpture*, *The Baronial Halls and Picturesque Edifices of England*, *The Vernon Gallery of British Art* and *The Royal Gallery of Art, Ancient and Modern*. As the series 'The Vernon Gallery of British Art', published in *The Art Journal*, provided much material for the exhibition 'Robert Vernon's Gift' held at the Tate Gallery in 1993, so there are references to the *Journal* today in nearly every exhibition catalogue of Victorian art.

15
The Critic and His Function

Carter's promotion of British art in *The Art Journal* was both informative and didactic, but as the reputation of the modern school of British painting grew, the *Journal* became more of a critical force while still retaining the role of the teacher.

In May 1855 the Paris *Journal L'Union*, in a review of the Exhibition of Fine Art at the Palais des Beaux Arts, gave considerable space to the English Gallery. French criticism was to have a strong influence in the art world throughout the century. On the whole this critique was not complimentary. As well as commenting on individual artists the critic said: 'England is eminently national, and she is too proud to imitate others; make her the subject of stricture or of praise but of this be assured, that if you find her ugly, her ugliness is all her own.' *The Art Journal* quoted the review and challenged it.[1] 'Some criticism of individual artists', the writer suggested, might have been set aside 'on the score of good taste and considerate feeling.' This consideration for the artist was a constant precept all through Carter's editorship of the *Journal*. Even in the Whistler/Ruskin case the *Journal*, while agreeing with Ruskin's assessment of Whistler's painting exhibited at the Grosvenor Gallery in 1877, condemned his vehement language.

Art criticism in England was a nineteenth-century development, in the early part of the century closely related to, and influenced by, literary criticism. It centred on description, on the narrative in paintings and the moral implications. It was limited to short reviews of the principal exhibitions – in particular the Academy – and to occasional articles on art in literary journals. By 1860 it was becoming more specialised, with some critics concerned with art history. Giorgio Vasari had assumed the dual role of art critic and art historian as early as the sixteenth century in his *Delle Vite de' più eccellenti Pittori, Scultori, e Architettori* (1550) and it is significant that his work was not translated into English until 1850 when Mrs J. Forster's version of it appeared as *Lives of the Eminent Painters, Sculptors and Architects*. Vasari's historical text contained inaccuracies, but it was probably because his theme contradicted Ruskin's views on the matter that English readers did not at first accord him the credit he deserved. Vasari's volumes reflected his humanist line of thought. He praised artists who had abandoned what he called the barbaric Byzantine and Gothic art and revived classical culture and learning. Ruskin, on the other hand, condemned the Renaissance for the breaking off of the ideals of the medieval artists and builders and their direct approach to nature. 'As Christianity had brought this love of nature into paganism, the return of paganism in the shape of classical learning at once destroyed this love of nature.'[2]

The role of the critic was increasingly becoming a subject for discussion. At a Royal Academy dinner in 1836, the President (then Sir Charles Eastlake) said, 'The office of the professed critic is, almost of necessity, to detect imperfections.' *The Art Journal* strongly rejected his opinion:

> That criticism is not only unwholesome, but thoroughly evil, which labours to discover blemishes, and takes little or no note of beauties or perfections ... On the contrary, the duty of the critic, and surely his pleasure, is to do good; to create happiness where it can be done faithfully; and to avoid giving pain where it can be done honestly.[3]

These sound like Carter's own words. *The Art Journal* always attacked harsh critics, insisting that the duty of the critic was to teach the people and not to flagellate the painter.[4]

John Ruskin's view of art as an expression of morality lay at the heart of art criticism in the middle of the century. Critics valued the ability of a picture to convey a moral or narrative message above technical skill. In *The Contemporary Review* the Revd R. St John Tyrhwitt, writing about Thomas Faed's picture *Worn Out*, stressed the salutary moral effect that art could have on people when he said, 'But only form a notion of the average moral effect of that work on hard-working men and weary mothers of families.'[5] The critic Leslie Steven, in an article entitled 'Art and Morality', wrote:

> Art exerts a most powerful influence upon the deepest part of our nation ... Art provides the most powerful, though the least obtrusive means by which the standard of morality is effected. The songs of a nation, I quote once more the old truism, effect men's manners more than their laws. [Nevertheless] the normal sphere of art is in great part distinct from that of morality. The artist has to reflect what he sees around him – he paints vice and virtue as they exist. His responsibility ends with the duty of fidelity to facts.[6]

Frederic Leighton's picture *Dante in Exile* (1864) was praised by the critics because of the moral lesson it taught. The picture is taken from Dante's *Paradiso*. Dante, exiled from Florence, stands on the steps of the Can Grande in Verona. His austere figure is in sharp contrast to those of the revellers in their rich clothes on the way to a fiesta. Leighton, however, had come under attack from critics when he exhibited his *Odalisk* in 1862. Some critics thought his style foreign – un-English – which was considered a serious crime. The tone with its rich clothing was luxurious and the painting, with its lack of a moral focus, showed Leighton as a sensualist. Tom Taylor used the word 'voluptuous' several times in his critique in *The Times*.[7] Millais's pictures, on the other hand, were essentially British, and words like 'vigorous' and 'powerful' were used in praising them. *The Art Journal* endorsed the view of certain critics that Leighton's pictures were not drawn from nature, but presented a second-hand view of the sensuality of the sixteenth century.

Overall, there is a shift at this period in critical criteria from the old school, with its emphasis on morality, to a new approach which valued paintings primarily for their aesthetic qualities. The new critics, some of them now employed on the staff of newspapers and periodicals such as *The Athenaeum*, expanded the critical vocabulary to include form and technique. But the old beliefs about art's moral purpose persisted.

The theory that the natural world was not divine handiwork had caused unease in the Victorian world. Some Victorians felt that art might fill a need which religion had hitherto satisfied, while many clung to the past and to the old Christian tenets. The old-school critic of *The Spectator* thought Leighton's *Helios and Rhodos*

(1869) an offence against decency, claiming that 'under a pseudo-classic mask it has a lascivious leer which belongs not only to the art which the painter affects to imitate; and that its partial cleverness of realization only makes plainer its intrinsic impurity ... I have no desire to moralize, but immoral art is bad art.'[8] *The Art Journal*, however, found no offence against morality in *Helios and Rhodos*. It called the picture 'a flight of fancy which to the matter of fact common sense of the nineteenth century may appear rather preposterous. Nevertheless, we are truly thankful to any painter who will bring us deliverance from the plain plodding of the modern realistic school.' It may seem surprising that Carter would not have had stronger views about morality in art, but then his business was the promotion of modern British art in *The Art Journal*, with due regard to the increase in its circulation amongst people with different views.

The question of nudity and semi-nudity posed a difficult question for both sides in the debate. Many critics defended Leighton's *Venus Disrobing* (c. 1866–7), indeed F. G. Stephens in *The Athenaeum* said, 'Nakedness is not the leading characteristic of this figure.'[9] *The Art Journal* thought that such a picture, which might offend prevailing prejudices and principles, could only be justified if it were successful: 'That Mr Leighton's *Venus* holds its grounds, that the bold attempt has been treated with respect, amounts to a tacit admission that the artist has at any rate not failed ... His picture is eminently chaste.'[10] Similarly, another *Venus* – this time Albert Moore's of 1869 – struck no chord of disapproval in the *Journal*. Possibly some critics approved of more doubtful examples of nudity for fear of being thought prudish.

The change in critical vocabulary is particularly noticeable from the late 1860s. In the 1850s, in the old style, *The Art Journal* was praising paintings which it described as 'virile' and 'powerful' and the critic praised the 'tender supplication' in C. R. Leslie's *Hermione*. *Love's Labour Lost* by F. R. Pickersgill he called the 'least ethical composition that we ever remember', but approved of the 'earnest sobriety' in *Hide and Seek* by T. Webster. The choice of subject in the 1850s was considered very important. The critic thought W. L. Windus's *Burd Helen* (a painting which disconcerted the critics) 'an example of the worst taste in the selection of a subject'.[11] By contrast, Ruskin put execution in a painting above subject. He never deviated from his critical examination of the didactic value in a painting.

The abandonment of narrative by many artists in preference for aesthetic qualities, and the painting of subjects who appeared idle or bent on trivial occupations, evoked words like 'sensuous', 'luxurious' or 'voluptuous' from the critics. In 1864, when Leighton painted the male figure in *Golden Hours*, a bearded youth with thick curling hair and with strong affinity to sixteenth-century Venetian art, the critics censured it with the word 'effeminate'. Elizabeth Prettejohn, in an article entitled 'Morality versus Aesthetics in Critical Interpretations of Frederic Leighton, 1855–1875', says:

> The word 'effeminate', and the closely related vocabulary of sensuality, began to be used more broadly after 1864, to designate not merely individual figures but the artist's whole style and technique. The early appearance of this kind of terminology in the criticism of Leighton is particularly interesting given the prominence of the vocabulary of 'effeminacy' in later attacks on the painting and poetry associated with aestheticism.[12]

The Art Journal, however, thought the head of the musician in *Golden Hours* was its redeeming point: 'This is a face in every feature responsive of Art's ennobling impulses; sensuous indeed it is, and dreamy to the last degree – as men muse-inspired are wont to be.'[13] Meanwhile the critic of *The Spectator* found Leighton's 'super-soft' productions far from pleasing, and in his Notes on the Academy of 1866 found it a relief to pass to 'the manlier works of Mr Pettie and Mr E. Nicol'. He had been looking at Leighton's *The Painter's Honeymoon.*[14]

The art market flourished in the second half of the nineteenth century as more and more pictures were painted and sold. In the 1870s *Punch* nearly always had jokes about artists. As critics proliferated, so their functions came under discussion. The critics of *The Art Journal* played a slightly different role from their contemporaries in that the *Journal* gave assistance to artists and was also concerned (as Carter said) with creating a public for art. Thus *The*

Art Journal combined the role of critic and promoter of art, unlike other periodicals.

P. G. Hamerton (critic of *The Saturday Review* and founder of *Portfolio* in 1869) listed some eleven duties and functions of the critic. The most important, he considered, was to utter unpopular truths. Carter might have been chary of this, but would have agreed with the second duty, which was to instruct the public in the theoretical knowledge of art. (The value of education, of course, was predominant in the way of Victorian thinking.)

The fourth duty was in effect aimed at the protection of the critic:

> To prevent false living artists from acquiring an influence injurious to the general interests of art. For some good-natured people think it is very wrong and unkind in a critic to point out the defects of living men, and so reduce their incomes; but as soon as any painter acquires any influence, his shortcomings ought to be clearly, though not discourteously, stated.

Of the seventh duty, 'to speak with absolute sincerity', he said that some critics will seek any pretext to say things which are merely smart, and he had a dig at French critics who he said produced masterpieces of this kind of writing.[15]

Sidney Colvin thought that the critic must have the faculty of sight and judgement.[16] He must be on his guard against literary ambition and acquire the habit of literary self-denial. This view was expressed several times in *The Art Journal*, and by Carter himself. The critic, Colvin went on to say, should not address the artist. It was not the role of the critic to tell the artist what his aims and ideals should be: the critic was only the interpreter. However, criticism of painting in *The Art Journal* was sometimes addressed to the artist, although there is little evidence that Carter, or the critics whom he employed, consciously aimed at teaching the painter his craft.

Colvin was both art historian and art critic, fulfilling the double role which many critics aspired to. F. G. Stephens, who was art critic of *The Athenaeum*, certainly regarded himself as an art historian writing in a new area of expertise. His critiques were knowledgeable and much more to the point than those of his other contemporaries. His articles in *The Athenaeum* on the paintings of the collectors of the North-East of England are still a useful source for research. Colvin believed that a critic should be as impartial as possible. Stephens tried to be, though he did little to conceal his preference first for Pre-Raphaelitism and then for the Aesthetic Movement. *The Art Journal*, by its very nature, had to be impartial, though a glance at the list of artists of the *Selected Pictures* shows a preference for certain artists and lack of enthusiasm for the Pre-Raphaelites.

By the late 1860s there was beginning to be a demand for critics with some technical knowledge. The Revd R. St John Tyrwhitt wrote in the *Contemporary Review*: 'Until lately we have had but few critics possessed of real technical skill, or of that knowledge of nature and form which is, in fact, only to be obtained by drawing. But now we are beginning to have painters who can write, and write well.'[17] As early as 1790 Sir Joshua Reynolds was saying much the same thing. He said at the distribution of prizes at the Academy:

> I am convinced that one short essay written by a painter will contribute more to advance the theory of art than a thousand volumes such as we sometime see; the purpose of which appears to be, rather to display the refinement of the author's own conceptions of impossible practice, than to convey useful knowledge or instruction of any kind whatever.[18]

One wonders what part he would have taken in the great debate on this very subject in the trial which was about to rock London's artistic world.

When Sir Coutts Lindsay opened his Renaissance-style Grosvenor Gallery in Bond Street on May Day 1877, James McNeill Whistler exhibited his painting *Nocturne in Black and Gold*, later entitled *Nocturne in Black and Gold: the Falling Rocket*. *The Art Journal* made no attempt at criticism, merely saying 'As to Mr James Whistler's Nocturnes, they are simply too subtle for us ... The art instincts of Mr Whistler are unquestionable, but his performances to most people are simply conundrums.'[19] Other critics hesitated, waiting for Ruskin's opinion. It came in his *Fors Clavigera* (a publication which often included passages of controversy and abuse) – Letter 79: 'Life Guards of New Life' (July 1877) – and was quickly spread by the leading newspapers and journals. 'I have seen, and heard, much of Cockney impudence before now, but never expected to hear a coxcomb ask 200 guineas for flinging a pot of paint in the public's face.'

Linda Merrill says the criticism was unusual for Ruskin in that it contradicted his words in the preface to his Academy Notes of 1855.[20] In this he said, 'No criticism is any value which does not enable the spectator, in his own person, to understand, or to detect, the alleged merit or unworthiness of the picture.' The criticism certainly did nothing to guide the spectator towards an understanding of the painting, and it is primarily concerned with price. Nevertheless, it is not at variance with some of Ruskin's theories on art economics which included the duty of the workman to give the full capacity of his labour in return for payment; and this duty, Ruskin considered, Whistler had not fulfilled.

Whistler's main reason for bringing an action for libel against Ruskin was, almost certainly, in the hope of gaining large damages should he win the case. He was in dire financial straits at the time. There was also his dislike of critics. When Frederick Leyland suggested the general title of *Nocturnes* for Whistler's night paintings, Whistler wrote to him in delight: 'You have no idea what an irritation it proves to the critics, and consequent pleasure to me.' This was not the first time that Ruskin had made unfavourable comments about Whistler's work. He had done so in an Oxford lecture in 1873 in a similar vein, though in more temperate language. Whistler had had enough.

The court records of the trial Whistler versus Ruskin have been destroyed, but reports can be read in most of the newspapers and journals of the time. The jury, after rather muddled instructions from the judge, brought in a verdict in favour of the plaintiff, but with damages of one farthing. It was a Pyrrhic victory for Whistler. The trial, though fascinating in many ways, is only relevant here in the discussion on the function of the critic which took place during and after the event. Sir John Holker (the Attorney General and Ruskin's counsel) asked Whistler; 'You don't approve of criticism?' To which Whistler replied:

> It is not for me to criticise the critics. I should not disapprove in any way of technical criticism by a man whose life is passed in

> the practice of the science that he criticises, but for the opinion of a man whose life is not so passed I would have as little respect as you would have if he expressed an opinion on the law. I hold that none but an artist can be a competent critic. It is not only when a criticism is unjust that I object to it, but when it is incompetent.

Holker pointed out that artists needed critics, but went on to say: 'The critic used to be feared and respected, but now it is not so, as he cannot express an opinion lest he have brought against him an action for damages.'

The judge (Sir John Walter Huddleston) in his directions to the jury had this to say about criticism:

> If a critic honestly expresses an opinion, though he does so in strong language, he ought to be protected; but if his object is to use his powers of denunciation without regard to facts and feeling, and to reflect unjustly upon the individual whose picture he is criticising, then his conduct is unjustified and he cannot claim the critic's privilege.

The jury thought that Ruskin's critique expressed his general beliefs, though it exceeded the bounds of the critic's privilege.

D. C. Thompson, writing in *The Art Journal*, thought that there might have been more sympathy for Whistler over the critique if he had not published a pamphlet on 24 December entitled *Whistler v Ruskin, Art and Art Critics*. In this he declared: 'Now the war, of which the opening skirmish was fought the other day at Westminster, is really on between the Brush and the Pen, and involving literally, as the Attorney General himself hinted, the absolute *raison d'être* of the critic.' Only painters, he insisted, are qualified to criticise a painting. Of Ruskin he said, 'To him and his example do we owe the outrage of proffered assistance from the unscientific ... Master of English literature, he has a right to his laurels, while as the Popularizer of Pictures he remains the Peter Parley of painting. Let there be no more critics.'[21]

Whistler sent copies of his pamphlet to the art critic William Michael Rossetti and to Comyns Carr, from whom he received very different answers. Rossetti wrote:

> Though I have been figuring for so many years as a non-professional art critic, I nevertheless agree to a very considerable extent in your thesis that the publishing of art critiques by non-professionals, whom the easy-going public allow thus to assume and dominate authority over their own minds, is noxious and deserving of protest; indeed I have myself said the same in an article (say towards 1864) in the *Fine Art Quarterly Review.*[22]

The answer from the eminent art historian Comyns Carr cannot have given Whistler much satisfaction.

> An expiring critic hails you as his deliverer. You have come to set us free from our bondage and drudgery: 'tis a noble mission. I only hope I may live to witness the new regime and to note how painters like Christians love one another. I pray God at least that painters may still have time to paint and that they may find leisure from praise of each other to do their own work.[23]

The Art Journal came out strongly in defence of Ruskin, and in the belief of the benefit to art from art criticism. D. C. Thompson, the author of the article, admitted that Ruskin could be dogmatic, and said:

> It is probably due to this serene dogmatic self-sufficiency – if it may be termed so – that Mr Ruskin fell into the unfortunate mistake of so very vehemently expressing his disapprobation of Mr Whistler's contribution to the Grosvenor Gallery in London in 1877. Mr Ruskin, with his command of language, could easily have said what he wished to say as strongly, and with the same certainty of showing he considered the Art bad, in his beautiful and flowing language, as he did in condemning the work in words one would hesitate to attach to any presumably honest man.[24]

Thompson was dismissive of Whistler's pamphlet, which he called an 'extraordinary and extravagant production'. Whistler, he said, called his case 'the beginning of the war between the Pen and the Brush' and wrote as if he were leading the vanguard against the pen. He quotes Whistler as saying 'No, let there be no critics; they are not a necessary evil, but an evil quite unnecessary, … harm they do and not good.' Thompson said that few had been able to explain what artists feel, but that it was the special function of the art critic to do so. He believed that Ruskin, because of his lifetime labour and his genius, fulfilled this function. He went on to say that there was no golden rule in art criticism beyond the necessity of judging every picture from the artist's standpoint.

This article went a long way towards expressing the functions of the critic which Carter, as editor, expected the art critics of *The Art Journal* to fulfil. After this year the *Journal* would be in other hands. He believed that the critic should have knowledge, good sense, sympathy and delicacy of taste, and that it was with these qualities that he could appreciate the merit of a work of art, and interpret it for the benefit of the public and for the artist himself.

16
Libel

'In 1878, in an unfortunate hour,' Carter wrote in 1883, 'I yielded to the request of the Marquis of Townshend that I would edit a work on which he had set his heart.'[1] This was a weekly publication entitled *Social Notes*. It seems extraordinary that Carter, with such an exacting job as the editorship of *The Art Journal*, should, at the age of seventy-eight, have taken on another publication and a weekly at that, though he was a man of enormous vitality. One can only think that he was preparing for retirement (he finally retired from *The Art Journal* three years later). *Social Notes* would provide him and Anna Maria with a suitable periodical in which to publish their own articles, and a place to advocate the cause of temperance about which they both felt very strongly. Money may also have been a reason for acceptance. The salary was probably not very substantial, but Carter was always short of money.

An advance notice appeared in *The Art Journal* recommending the forthcoming *Social Notes*: 'Neither religious nor political, according to the ordinary sense of the term ... it is of no party ... In short, we repeat, the little weekly work (which by the way is well aided by Art) is sufficiently described by its title, "Social Reforms, Social Requirements, Social Progress".'[2]

The first number appeared on 7 March 1878, priced one penny. There were articles on such subjects as the future of the Albert Hall, factories and workshops, accidents in coal mines, vivisection, working men's clubs, free libraries and education. Carter and Anna Maria both wrote articles for it, and the opening article was on 'Total Abstinence' by the Revd Canon Farrar DD. It was ironical that Carter, editing a periodical which was to further the cause of temperance, should find that the man whom he had employed as his manager/sub-editor, Pepperell, was a drunkard.

On 27 March Carter dismissed Pepperell. The reports in newspapers of the two actions which followed are not very clear, and that in *The Times* is probably the best. One is left to make up one's own mind as to what really happened. Pepperell brought an action against the Marquess Townshend (in fact Carter) for wrongful dismissal. The reasons that were given for the dismissal were that Pepperell had neglected to see to the registration of the paper though directed to do so, that he could not account for all the money that he had been given for advertising purposes, that he had improperly interfered with the contents of the paper and that he had come to the office intoxicated. It turned out that Pepperell had been a Methodist minister and had been allowed to resign from the ministry, but no pension was granted. In some of the public houses in Hammersmith and Notting Hill he was known as the 'drunken methody parson' (perhaps the money intended for advertising kept Pepperell in funds). It was hard on Carter that, according to his own account, he had told Pepperell that one of the purposes of the paper (the main one being to help the working man) was to advocate total abstinence, and that he had asked him if he was a teetotaller. Pepperell had answered that he was. It seems that Carter had not made any inquiries about Pepperell before employing him.

The case was not due to be heard until 17 January 1879. In the meantime the circulation of *Social Notes* was increasing; and Anna Maria was hopeful about its future when she wrote to Francis Bennock on Christmas Day 1878 asking him to find a new publisher for them as their present one was ill. Perhaps, she suggested, the publisher with whom Bennock was associated might be interested.

> It seems to me, dear friend, that the older I get, the more bothering I become to my friends. ... It is a pretty good proof of how 'Social Notes' is regarded – when I tell you that Mr. Theodore Martin has written a touchingly beautiful article on our dear Princess Alice for the next number of 'Social Notes' *with his name to it* which will be published on Saturday – do dear friend take this into consideration and forgive the bungling way in which I have put this matter.[3]

From this Anna Maria does not seem to have had any worries as to the outcome of the impending case. Otherwise she would have almost certainly have mentioned them in her letter, as she so often took her troubles to Bennock.

There can be no doubt that Pepperell's habits would have been most distasteful to Carter. It is doubtful, however, that this was the main reason for the dismissal. It is much more likely that Carter was infuriated by Pepperell's alterations to an article which he had edited, for he never allowed any interference with his editorial decisions. The article was on the subject of breach of promise of marriage, and suggested that a woman would be better off married to a man who had tried to jilt her, rather than remain as a spinster:

> In theory, no doubt, love should be the great incentive to matrimony, but Cupid is mostly too capricious and unpractical to conform to the exigencies of every-day life. There are many who make happy homes without ever having fallen victim to the 'tender passion' and others whose future has not been less blissful because they have not wedded the object of their affections. In fact, couples who enter on matrimony with a consciousness that each has failings and with a firm determination to make mutual concessions are certain to travel through life more pleasantly than those who at starting regard each other as perfect, only subsequently to make the painful discovery that they are mutually mistaken. Every-day experience teaches us that the most satisfactory unions are those where convenience was the main inducement.

It is surprising that Carter, with his romantic view of life, should have accepted these sentiments, and one wonders whether they would have been palatable to the majority of the readers of *Social Notes*. Pepperell, who said that he found the views detestable, had radically altered the manuscript.

As to the accusation that the plaintiff came to work intoxicated, Carter's ideas of sobriety might well have been different from those of many employers. Two witnesses at the trial, however, said that they had seen Pepperell in the office drunk and incapable of speech. In a third trial which occurred later in 1881 (after Carter's retirement) when Pepperell brought an action against the printers, Simpkin Marshall & Co, there was more evidence of Pepperell's intemperance at the time of the dismissal. One witness described an occasion in a local public house when some convivial spirits decided to test how much Pepperell could drink at other people's expense, but gave up when they became tired and badly out of pocket.

Summing up the evidence at the end of the trial, 'Pepperell versus The Marquis of Townshend', the Chief Justice asked the jury to consider whether a degree of intemperance had been proved to justify dismissal, and whether the jury thought that Mr Hall's authority had been set in defiance. The jury returned a verdict for the plaintiff and the payment of £100 less the money he owed the defendant. The Chief Justice was dissatisfied with the verdict, and suspended execution for fourteen days. On Carter's counsel applying for a retrial, the application was considered in the High Court on 13 June 1879. Of the jury's verdict the Chief Justice said, 'In this case I cannot express too strongly my dissatisfaction ... I think there ought to be a new trial on all the grounds urged, and I think there was strong evidence of insubordination.'[4] He granted a rule nisi for a new trial to take place.

All might have been well, with a new trial impending and the future of *Social Notes* fairly secure, if Carter had resisted the temptation to try and vindicate himself after the trial by publishing an article in *Social* Notes (which he signed) fulminating against 'the miscarriage of justice'. The article was aimed at those people in the literary world who had enjoyed Carter's discomfiture in the trial and the verdict. Here was a chance to prove himself right, for the retrial would probably go unnoticed whatever the outcome. Smarting from his defeat, Carter was carried away in moralising over a 'monstrous principle' which he considered that the verdict had established, and in his condemnation of Pepperell's behaviour. For a man involved for over forty years in publishing, knowing all the pitfalls, the article seems to have been the height of folly. It is hardly surprising that Pepperell immediately took an action for libel against Carter.

The case of Pepperell versus Hall was settled out of court, and Pepperell accepted £200. He had done very well out of the dismissal. In *Social Notes*, on 8 February 1880, Carter announced his resignation as editor. He had contracted to edit the paper for a year, and the year was now up. 'I will not trouble my readers with reasons for this step,' he wrote, 'if I did state them they would, I think, see that I could adopt no other course.' He added a footnote saying that none of his reasons had reference to the Pepperell/Townshend case. He paid tribute to the newspaper press. He had, he said, printed extracts from many newspapers representing all shades of public opinion,

> all that is to say, except those I was bound to oppose and expose in efforts to suppress infidelity, socialism, disloyalty – especially such as strive to corrupt the young. ... If I have my own opinion on the two great subjects, Religious and Political – I humbly think they have not been made apparent in *Social Notes*.[5]

The whole tone of the 'Farewell' suggests that there had been some criticism as to the conducting of the paper. Many of the contributors, certainly, were Carter's friends, and Carter himself wrote for many of the numbers, but most of the articles were about philanthropical causes and social problems, leaving little opportunity to impose religious or political views. Despite what Carter said, the two civil actions must have embittered him against the paper, and he would have had little heart to continue with it. Some newspapers enjoyed the rumpus which the case had caused, while others even remembered the humorous references to Carter as the original of Dickens's Mr Pecksniff some thirty years ago. *Social Notes* had been an unfortunate enterprise.

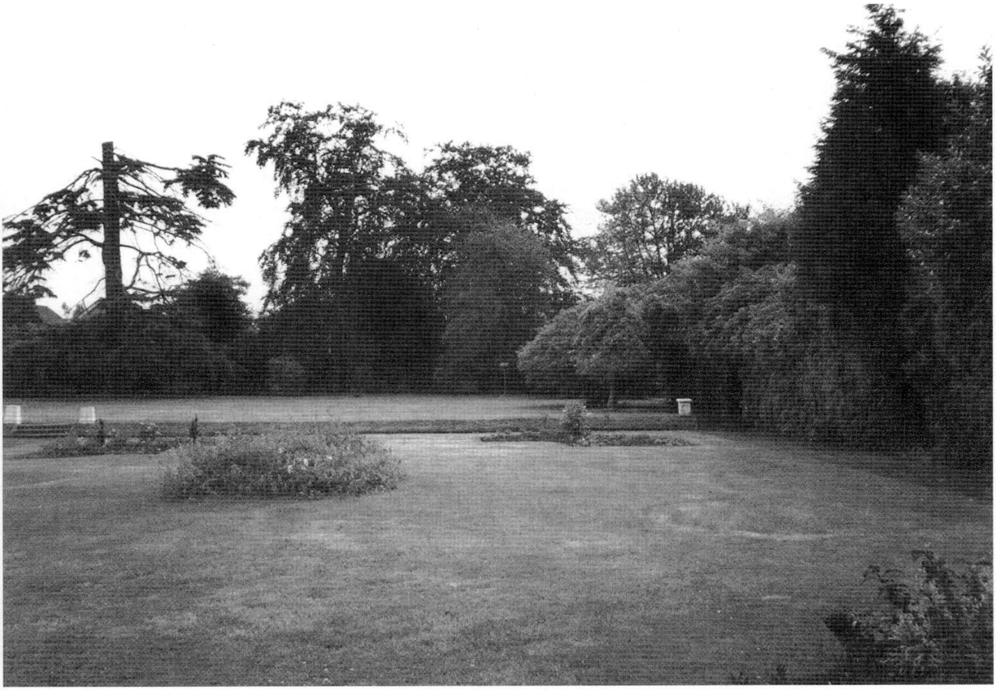

The grounds of Firfield, Addlestone, Surrey

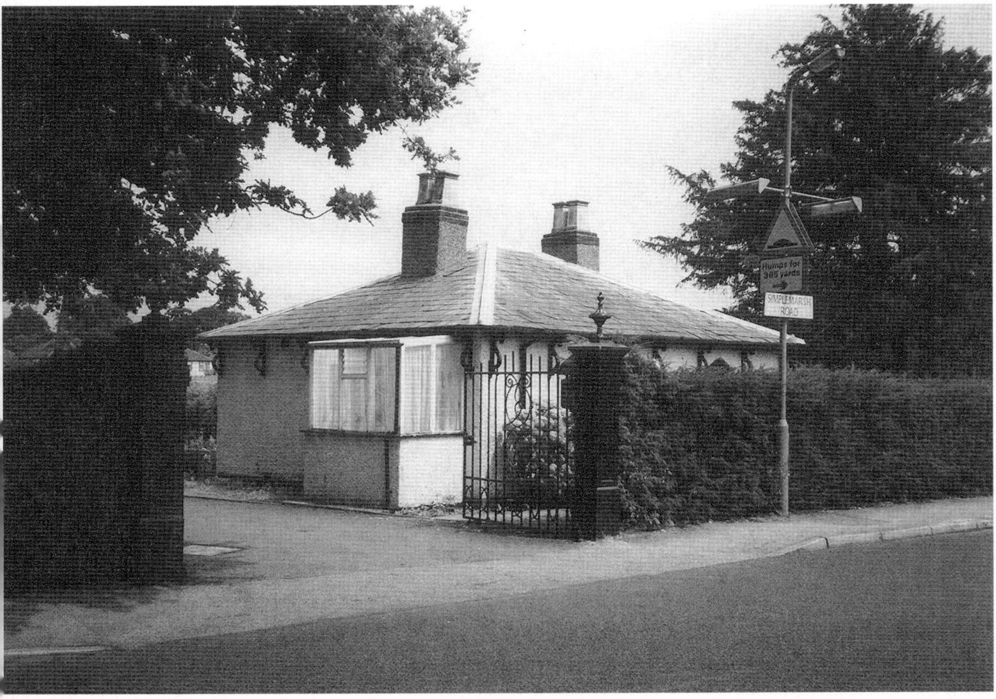

The Lodge at Firfield today

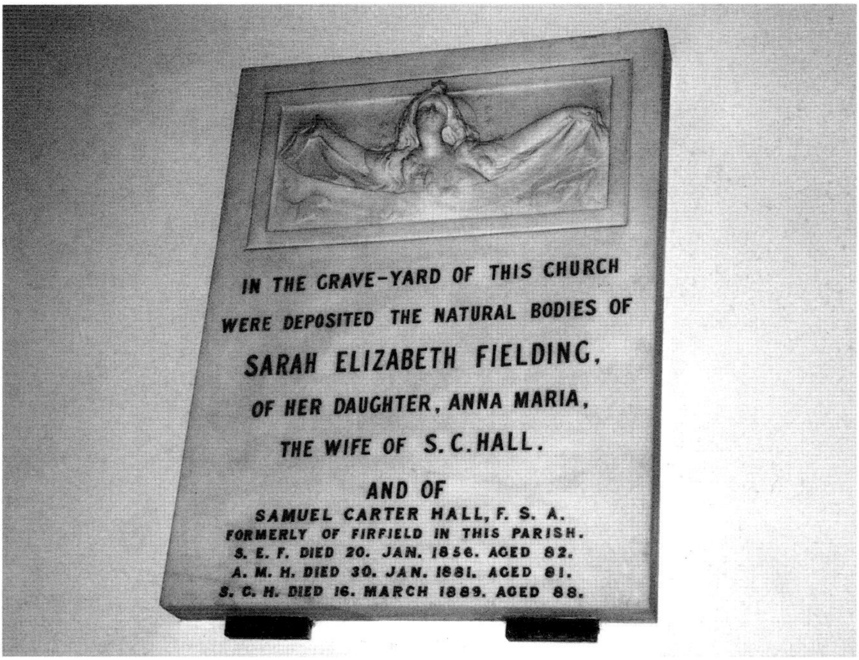

Memorial to Sarah Elizabeth Fielding and the Halls
in St Paul's Church, Addlestone

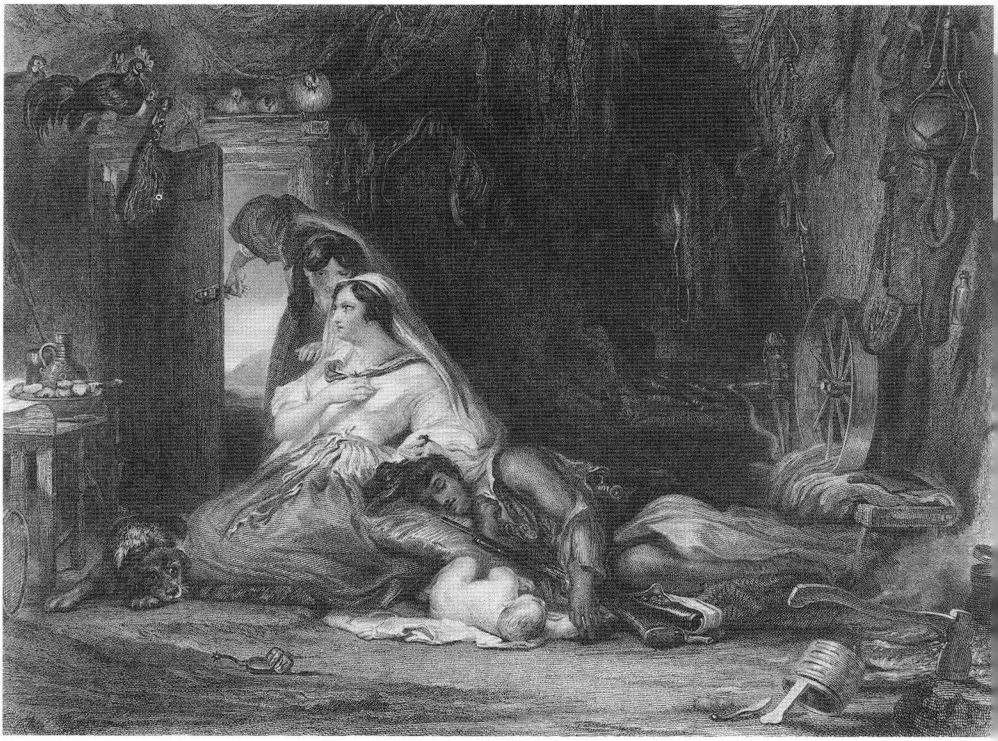

Sir David Wilkie, *The Peep O'Day Boys' Cabin in the West of Ireland*;
engraving in *The Art Journal*, 1850

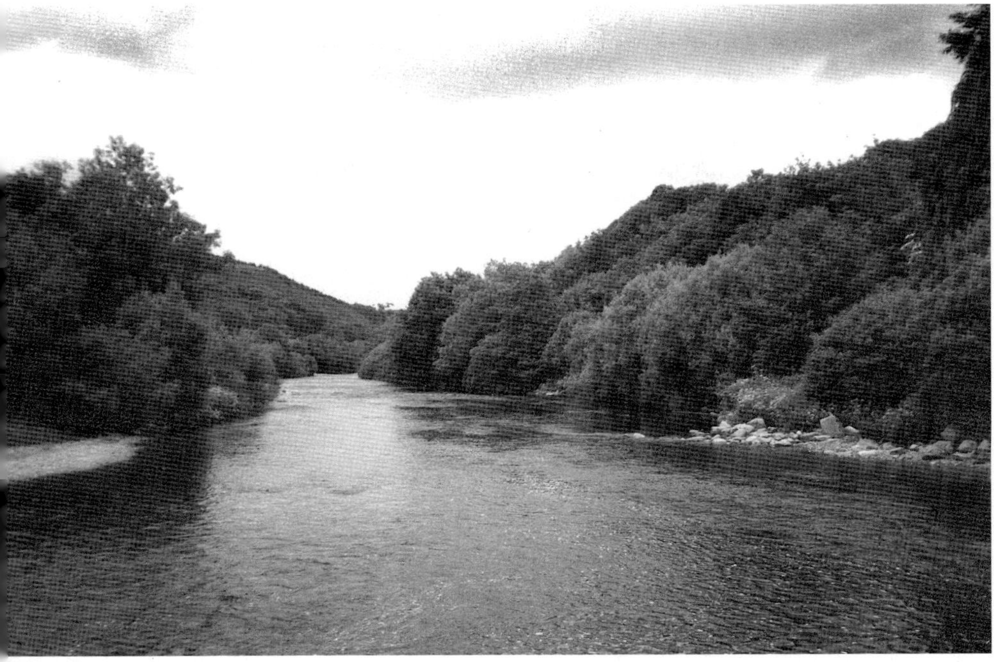

The Meeting of the Waters, Vale of Avoca, Co. Wicklow

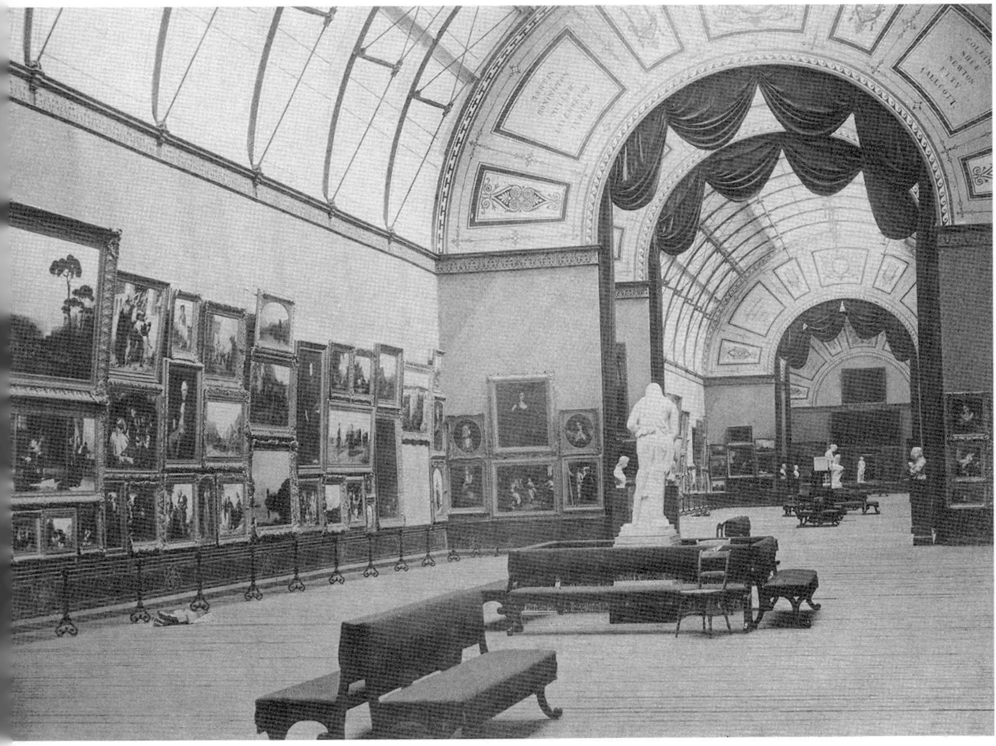

Art Treasures Exhibition interior, Manchester 1857

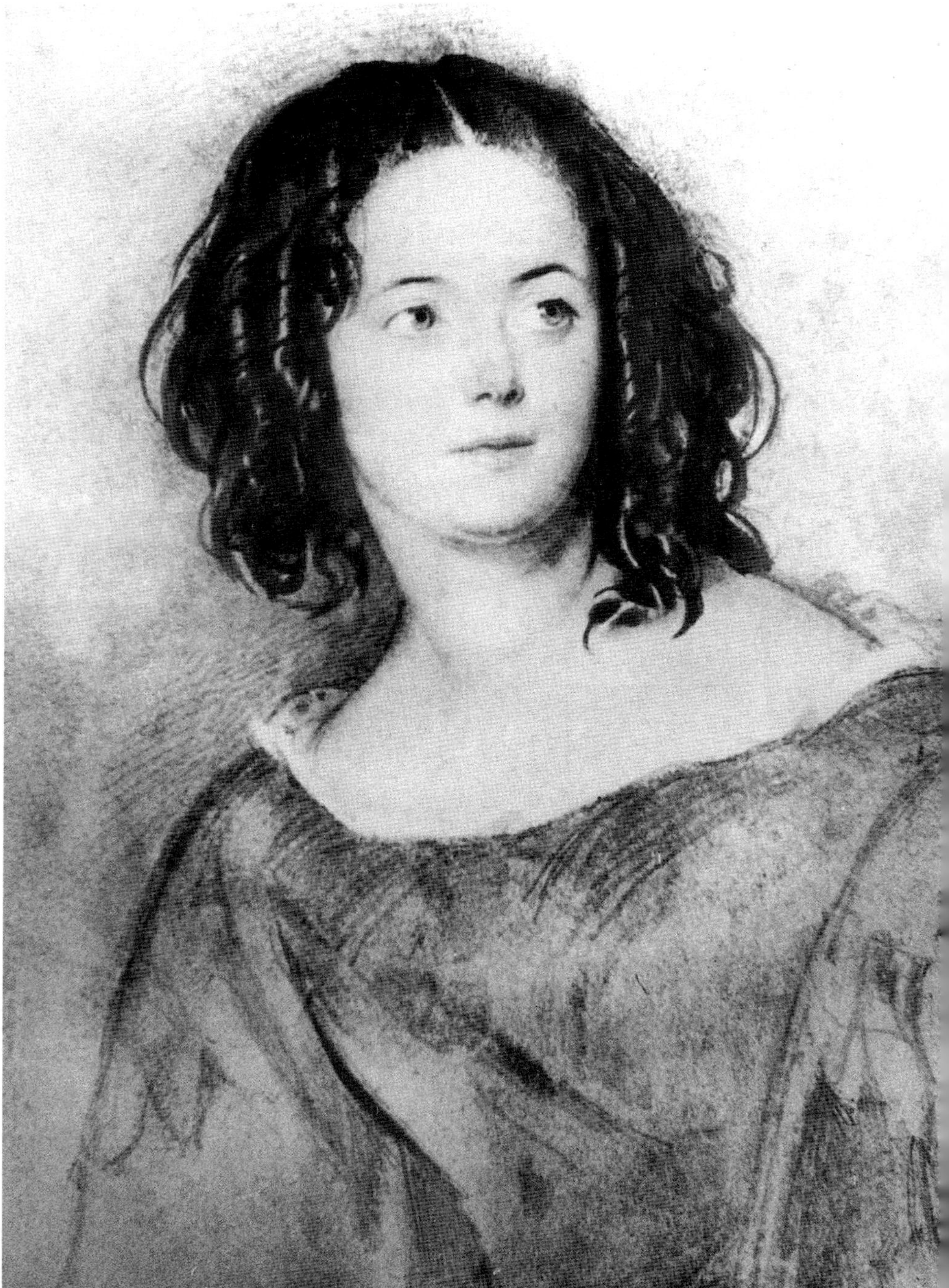

Daniel Maclise, *Anna Maria Hall*, pencil and watercolour, 1833, Chertsey Museum, Surrey

17
Retrospect of a Long Life

Anna Maria died suddenly on 30 January 1881. Only three weeks earlier the Halls had given a large party for her birthday when she sang for her friends. They were then living in East Molesey in a house to which they had just moved.

As far as one can tell, theirs had been a happy marriage. Carter's life in London may have been different before he met Anna Maria; as a young man, coming to London from a quiet Irish district where everyone knew each other in a small Protestant population, he probably enjoyed this new freedom. On the other hand, he must have found the bizarre household of Ugo Foscolo very strange. It is not surprising that Carter and Anna Maria, both with nostalgic memories of an Irish childhood, should have been drawn together when they met in the busy London scene. Daniel Maclise's water-colour drawing shows how pretty Anna Maria was.[1] The sketch is of a young girl (though Anna Maria was then thirty-three years old) with delicate features and fine eyes, wearing a simple dress with no adornments, her hair falling loosely on her bare neck. The mood is highly romantic, reminiscent of Lady Morgan's *Wild Irish Girl*.

Carter always wrote a letter to Anna Maria on her birthday, and on this her last he wrote about their marriage. 'You have been to me a guide, a counsellor, a comfort, a companion, a friend, a wife from that day to this', and calls her 'the love of my youth, the love of my age'. A comfort to him she certainly was when his moods of optimism gave place to despondency and gloom. Probably, too, she saved him from some foolish actions, though one wonders at her reticence when he made himself slightly ridiculous with fulsome speeches and trite literary quotations. His pride in her was immense, verging on vanity; his intellectual pleasures were the richer because he shared them with an intelligent wife. He was justly proud of this accomplished kindly woman who welcomed the struggling writer as well as the celebrity to her drawing room. 'In that drawing room', wrote Goss, 'met all the wit and genius which … made the world laugh and weep.'[2]

Anna Maria was the most eminent woman writer on Ireland in the latter part of the nineteenth century, Maria Edgeworth having died in 1849 and with Lady Morgan, who never returned to Ireland after she left in 1839, dismissively referring to 'wretched Dublin, the capital of wretched Ireland'. Anna Maria's descriptions of rural life were simple and sympathetic, but it must be said that her stage-Irish dialogue, whether or not it amused English readers then, is quite unreadable today. That she really did go to such lengths to show impartiality in political and religious matters by wearing green and orange ribbons in her cap is borne out by a story told by William Goss. Dining with the Earl of Carlisle at the Vice-Regal Lodge, Anna Maria wore just such a cap. 'Ah,' said His Excellency, 'I have been long striving to mingle these colours, as you do, and not yet succeeded.'

In 1876 Carter had reprinted a letter of 1863 entitled 'The Use of Spiritualism?'[3] Spiritualism at this time was a resource of many people whose faith in revealed religion had declined. This, however, was not the reason for the interest which Carter, a firm believer in Christian teaching, had in spiritualism. In his memoirs Carter refers to Anna Maria's 'natural body' being buried in the graveyard of St Paul's Church at Addlestone, where the happiest years of their lives had been spent. His firm belief in the progress of the soul after it has left its earthly life, and the possibility of communication between the dead and the living now sustained him in his grief.

Unfortunately, Carter's retirement came in the same year as Anna Maria's death. Late in 1880 he had written 'Some words of Farewell' in *The Art Journal*.[4]

> It seemed a visionary scheme to issue a periodical that should be *only* a representative of Art, depending for success on the support of artists, Art patrons and Art lovers. But that such a publication was needed, there could be no question … I had to create a Public for Art … I had many obstacles to encounter, and serious difficulties to surmount. There was literally no patronage for British Art. Collectors – wealthy merchants and manufacturers – did indeed buy pictures … but they were 'old

masters' with familiar names; canvases that had never been seen by the artists to whom they had been attributed.

I convinced those who desired to purchase pictures. I destroyed by conclusive evidence and continual disclosure, the extensive and nefarious trade in 'old masters'. I have lived to see such old masters valued accordingly, and a thorough transfer of patronage to Modern Art.

The article goes on to claim the influence that *The Art Journal* had on art manufactures when he began to associate the industrial arts with the fine arts proper. (Carter believed that *The Art Journal* would not have succeeded as a publication for artists only and that, in the early days, it only survived by representing art manufactures.)

Carter's editorship of such a prestigious journal was clearly of personal advantage to the Halls. Few authors have been provided with the means of advertising and publishing their own works as they were. Wide coverage was given to *Ireland: Its Scenery, Character, etc.* and their other topographical books. Anna Maria's novels were announced in the *Journal* and some of Carter's works such as *The Royal Gallery of Art* appeared in monthly series.

Carter's services to art and literature were officially recognised when, in 1880, he was granted a civil pension. It seems from a letter of thanks from Carter that Bennock had yet again been a loyal friend and used his influence on his behalf.[5]

It is not difficult to imagine what the loss of his wife, coming at the same time as retirement, must have meant to Carter. One admires his courage and energy in that he now set about writing his *Retrospect of a Long Life*. Though rather given to platitudinous comments, as an account of a life of intellectual satisfaction and of achievement in both the art and literary worlds it has many points of interest and genuine appeal. Carter, an Englishman by descent, was an Irishman both by his place of birth and by his inclination. It is not surprising, therefore, that in *Retrospect* he dwells on life as it had been in Ireland at the beginning of the century. He describes the difficulties of travel before the days of the steamship companies, the system of tithes, the grand juries, the hardships of the peasants, the importance of 'the bit of land', the iniquities of the middle-man, the drunkenness and the prevalence of smuggling (sometimes even taking place from country houses in which he stayed).

Given that Carter was such a strong churchman, his lack of feeling about the disestablishment of the Irish Church is curious. Completely ignoring the full implications of the measure and the fears of various Protestant groups, he merely wrote, 'I for one do not consider the abolition of the Irish Church by any means *entirely* a good for Ireland', pointing out the benefit of the Protestant clergy in rural districts to people of all faiths.

Politics was another matter. Carter was born the year of the Union and, firmly believing in its benefits, deplored the unrest caused by those in opposition to it. 'It was true in 1831,' he said, 'it is true in 1883, that the agitation for Repeal has frightfully retarded the progress of the country. The vain pursuit of a shadow, while the substance of national prosperity is neglected, has been a blight to Ireland even more disastrous than the potato famine of 1847.' Now, however, there was the possibility of the shadow becoming a reality because of Gladstone's change of heart with regard to Ireland. In his first premiership the keynote of his policy was his mission to pacify Ireland, but this he hoped to do under the Union. By the time Carter was writing, Gladstone was gradually becoming convinced the Union was 'Pitt's gigantic but excusable mistake' and that Home Rule was the best policy for the country. He rejected the idea that the Irish were incapable of governing themselves, a view held by Carter and many Englishmen. Gladstone also thought it untrue that they thought little of prosperity, and that violence was a way of life which outweighed the pursuit of justice. Carter refers with derision to the governments before the Union:

> Both houses of parliament were hotbeds of corruption. The few really sincere and honest politicians in them were lost among a crowd of venal upholders of the government of the day, and of equally venal opponents to it, whose noisy pretences of patriotism could always be silenced when necessary by similar arguments to those that converted so many patriots on the occasion of the Union.[6]

Carter had not visited Ireland as regularly in the 1860s and 1870s as he had in the past and was no doubt somewhat out of touch. This (and perhaps the concessions granted to tenants under the recent land acts) may account for his apparent complacency that Ireland's grievances had been redressed, and that all was well at a time when agrarian crime was rampant and the activities of secret societies increasing. The Phoenix Park Murders, however, disillusioned him.

He now made several journeys to Devon, and visited the Manor House at Topsham where his parents had lived. He discovered that the colours of his father's regiment, the Devon and Cornwall Fencibles, were no longer in the parish church of St Margaret, but had been sold to a Major Keating to help in the church restoration. Major Keating generously gave them back provided they were returned to the church, where they still remain.[7]

In August 1882 Carter was in Plymouth making arrangements for the ultimate bequest of several hundreds of his books to the free public library.[8] He gave a talk at the library lasting for two and a half hours (without notes) with the title 'Gossip about People I Have Known'. One marvels at his stamina in his eighty third year – and also at that of his audience.

Carter was again short of money and, as the following letter shows, was worried about debts. We have no idea as to the nature of these debts. Writing to Francis Bennock he says:

> I want money – grievously to pay debts – debts which are no more ... mine than they are yours. To pay them I am selling some of my art treasures. There is no one I would care to leave them to and I shall then relieve myself of fearful depression and oppression. Enough! Now among specimens of beautiful china there are two vases which ought to be yours. I gave you two many years ago ... These two something like them are of Miss Landon and the other one of S. C. Hall. They are paintings of the rarest order – painted by the famous artist (Bott) of the Worcester works whose productions are of the scarcest and best of the English school and bring any price when on the market. I ask you to give me £25 for them; they will always bring and be worth more.
>
> God be with and bless you both Amen.
>
> Ever your friend of the present and the long ago.[9]

Presumably Bennock bought the vases – he would have had little option but to do so. Possibly this is when Carter sold some of his pictures. None is listed in his will apart from some engravings, and a portrait of himself and one of Anna Maria bequeathed to the Portrait Gallery in Dublin.[10] In fact he left very little. Fanny, his adopted daughter, inherited some jewellery that had belonged to Anna Maria, and his goddaughter, Diana Croke, was left all the Halls' published and unpublished manuscripts.

In 1885 Carter was living at 24, Stanford Road, Kensington. He wrote to Francis Bennock on Christmas Day sending greetings. He was well, he said, but yearned to believe that he might soon join Anna Maria. He was to live into his ninetieth year.

Carter's works fall broadly into two categories. There are his major topographical books such as *Ireland: Its Scenery, Character, etc.*, *The Baronial Halls and Picturesque Edifices of England* and the works dealing purely with pictures. It is the illustrations in the first category, however, which provide information about British art in the nineteenth century.

Apart from Thomas Creswick and Samuel Prout, Carter chose mainly Irish artists for the illustrations of *Ireland*, artists familiar with the Irish countryside. Most of these were now living in London for, Carter said, the Royal Hibernian Academy (chartered in 1823) 'appears to have effected very little for the fine arts in Ireland; the state of which, until lately was a reproach to the country'. Many of the illustrations are by Andrew Nicholl whose early sharp-edged style was eminently suitable for engravings of buildings of antiquarian interest. These he set in romantic landscapes, often lit by moonlight, as in his *Shane's Castle, Co. Antrim* for volume III. He is said to have been influenced by Turner, especially by Turner's technique. In his later watercolours the moonlight has been replaced by blue skies, and the buildings and landscapes are used as a background for his exquisite treatment of wild flowers in the foreground.

J. H. Burgess was another Irish landscape painter, well known for his romantic antiquarianism, and his watercolour *Pilgrims at the High Cross at Clonmacnois* was then immensely popular. The pyramidal shape of this painting is noticeable in many of his illustrations for *Ireland*. For the third volume Burgess drew the ruins of Castle Caulfield, built by Sir Toby Caulfield (afterwards Lord Charlemont),

Carter calling it a 'fair house', quoting from a seventeenth-century *Survey of Ulster*.[11]

Henry Gastineau, one of the last artists to draw in the picturesque style in topographical works, drew many of the scenes in the North of Ireland. Thomas Crofton Croker contributed nineteen illustrations and Samuel Prout, whom Ruskin praised above all others for the vitality of his architectural drawings, drew for volumes I and II. Frederick Fairholt went with the Halls on several of their journeys and contributed much antiquarian knowledge as well as drawings. The landscapes by Thomas Creswick, by then a popular artist though painting a rather narrow variety of scenery, were pre-eminently suitable for a romantic work, and the engravings are indeed very beautiful.

The Halls' *Ireland* is an exceptionally good example of the Victorian delight in romantic antiquarianism. There are none of Ireland's great eighteenth-century houses, and Carter did not even record the fine squares in Dublin. He only gives a few lines to James Gandon's superb Four Courts and Custom House – though they are drawn by Creswick. Considerable space, on the other hand, is given to places like Kilmallock in County Limerick, which the Halls called 'the Balbec of Ireland' with its thirteenth/fifteenth century Abbey of SS Peter and Paul and the Dominican friary, drawn by Prout.

These topographical works, together with some of the books on art, also tell us much about their author. Carter was a man of the Romantic Movement, which in its diversity is so difficult to define. Baudelaire said, 'Properly speaking, romanticism lies neither in the subject an artist chooses nor in his exact copying of truth, but in the way he feels.'[12] It was because Carter had this way of feeling that he recognised, and encouraged, young British artists whose genuine emotional impetus gave a validity to their work. One senses that he derived little pleasure from the so-called Realist Movement which followed this romanticism.

Apart from their literary merit, Carter's works were of considerable benefit to British artists. *The Stately Homes* of *England*, *The Book of the Thames*, *The Book of British Ballads*, *The Book of Gems* and several guide books were all illustrated by British artists. As has been seen, Carter was out of pocket in paying artists to copy the royal pictures for engraving. The series *Selected Pictures* and *British Artists: Their Style and Character* published in *The Art Journal* from 1855 to 1864 and from 1869 until Carter's retirement, provided the public with information about contemporary artists, and influenced wealthy patrons in the buying of British art. William Goss, who had known Carter for more than forty years, said of him: 'During a much longer period than that he was the wielder of great power in the literary and artistic world – a far greater power than any man has wielded before or since.' This may be a piece of Victorian hyperbole, but though Carter had some detractors from amongst editors of the literary periodicals, he was certainly a highly respected figure in the art world. When so many connoisseurs, despite the help of modern technology, are still continually deceived by fakes, it is hardly surprising that the dealers in the nineteenth century were able to foist their dark canvases on to the more gullible of the public. Goss was in no doubt about the importance of Carter's campaign against forgery and his encouragement of patrons to buy contemporary British art, the authenticity of which was not in question. The production of fakes continued, but at least by the 1860s and 1870s the public was more aware of them. The number of Titians in England had become such a joke that *Punch* published its famous cartoon *Sic Vos Non Vobis*. In it a young artist watching the auction of a 'Titian' says to the friend with him, 'Downright dishonest, I call it! Old Aaron's got thirty for that Titian and he only gave me three for painting it.'[13]

Approaching his ninetieth year, Carter was still to be seen at the London exhibitions, a venerable figure with aquiline features and a shock of white hair. For sixty years he had not missed a Spring Exhibition at the Academy. Though *The Art Journal* had been among the critics of the Academy from time to time, Carter had always respected the society. These were the days before entrepreneurs and the art market could influence the promotion of exhibitions, and even dictate what art should be valued. He had been fortunate that he had lived most of his working life in a period of wealthy patronage and artistic achievement. He died on 16 March 1889 when this artistic epoch was at its zenith. Nevertheless, he had had to face changing theories in art which he can never have found acceptable. He had known High Art in the mid-nineteenth century when Old

Testament subjects, pointing a moral lesson, could be explained in cultural terms and historical reference. He had seen the Classical Revival leading to the new aestheticism where painters sought beauty in subjective experiences and fleeting sensations. The frank discussion of sexuality in poetry and painting by Rossetti and his friends must have seemed to Carter a deliberate threat to undermine conventional morality. Like many another, Walter Pater hoped that art would fill a void hitherto filled by religious beliefs. Pater saw life as an interval, after which we cease to be; he saw art as bringing quality to this brief moment. For Carter, art was an enrichment to a transitory existence, an existence leading to eternal life.

Carter undoubtedly appeared as a quaint figure to his contemporaries; though inclined to be pompous and talkative, he was also cultured and hospitable, capable of considerable kindness and a faithful friend. He was a man who invited ridicule, but also affection. Some people laughed gently at his foibles while appreciating his goodness. Contemporary opinions differed as to his knowledge and appreciation of art, and he certainly had no formal education in the subject. If he had to create a public for art, it followed that the public required guidance as to taste. There were those who questioned his taste, which was for moral art, a type of art preferred by many intellectual middle-class Victorians, but under Carter's editorship *The Art Journal* never restricted contributors to one viewpoint. It respected changes in taste, though it is unlikely that Carter himself was influenced by fashion. In the quality of articles in the *Journal*, in the quality of the woodcuts and of the steel engravings his aesthetic taste would be hard to fault. Some of the engravers whom he employed had such delicacy of touch that the prints they produced lost little of the quality of the original painting.[14] The art critic of *The Athenaeum*, for one, had doubts whether this high standard would be maintained when, three years after Carter's retirement, he remarked that the new series of *The Art Journal* was improving though,

> At the same time it has parted with some solid qualities, and in becoming brilliant has ceased to be quite so useful as before. It is more strictly aesthetical and critical, and the contributors are mostly competent to produce 'clever' articles on the refined

> subjects of their pens ... In general there seems disproportion between the importance of the subjects treated and the space allotted to them.

Of the illustrations he went on to say, 'The subjects of most of the elaborate steel plates from pictures and sculptures are scarcely worthy of publication.'[15]

This assessment by *The Athenaeum* seems as valid today as when it was written. Many of the valuable qualities of *The Art Journal* under Carter's editorship had been lost. From 1839 to 1881 it provided an authoritative record of Victorian art, and for this, if for no other reason, the name of Samuel Carter Hall should never be forgotten.

Notes

CHAPTER ONE

1 Samuel Carter Hall, *Retrospect of a Long Life*, 1883, p. 343.
2 F. W. Hilles, *The Literary Career of Sir Joshua Reynolds*, 1936, p. 38.
3 Over the years *The Athenaeum* was to acquire a reputation for its somewhat inimical reviews, which may well have originated with Hervey.
4 Hall, *op. cit.* p. 341.
5 It was said that such was the press around *The Sleeping Children* that it was almost impossible to get near to the sculpture and that mothers, with tears in their eyes, ignored Canova's famous figures Hebe and Terpsichore exhibited alongside. The monument is in Lichfield Cathedral and commemorates the daughters of Mrs Robinson whose father was the Dean of the Cathedral.
6 *The Distressed Mother*, seen at the R.A. Exhibition, was acquired by the Marquess of Lansdowne and placed in Bowood, Wilts. A duplicate was made for Mrs Warren's monument, and a third for Mrs Ferguson of Beal near Reith, Scotland. *Art Journal*, 1849, p. 376.
7 Henry Curwen, *A History of Booksellers*, 1873, p. 376.

CHAPTER TWO

1 *Retrospect of a Long Life*, vol. II, 1883, p. 479, although the obituary in *The Times* states that he was born in Devon in 1801. The parish records of St Margaret's, Topsham state that he was born and baptised in Geneva Barracks.
2 For further information about Geneva Barracks see *The Journal of the Waterford and S.E. of Ireland Archaeological Society*, vol. IX, 1906, pp. 26 and 27; vol. XV, 1912, pp. 181–94; vol. XVI, 1913, pp. 1–17, 86–92; vol. XVII, 1914, pp. 164–69; vol. XVIII, 1915, pp. 108–12.
3 S. C. Hall, *op. cit.*, p. 486.
4 For a description of the reception of the casts see *Dublin University Magazine*, no. XLV, 1847. Some of the casts can be seen at the Crawford Gallery of Art, Cork, and at the Cork School of Art.
5 'The Athens of Ireland', *Fraserian Papers*, vol. 5, 'Miscellaneous Writings of Dr Maginn', ed. Dr Shelton Mackenzie, p. xix.

6 William Makepeace Thackeray, *The Irish Sketch Book,* 1875, p. 324.

7 William Jerden, *Autobiography,* vol. III, p. 82.

8 E. V. Kenealy to S. C. Hall, n.d. This item is reproduced by kind permission of the Huntington Library, San Marino, California, *1832–82 Guide to Literary MSS*, 1979, no MS numbers.

9 *The Maclise Portrait Gallery*, vol. I, p. 40, ed. William Bates, 1883, 'William Maginn "The Doctor"'.

10 Hall presented *The Talents* to the Cork Library in 1876. It is now in the Boole Library, University College, Cork, and I am grateful for permission to quote from it.

11 Sydney Lady Morgan, *Memoirs*, ed. W. Hepworth Dixon (to whom she left her papers and journal), assisted by Miss Jewsberg, 1862.

CHAPTER THREE

1 Originally the same family in the seventeenth century, Thomas Crofton Croker was the great-grandson of John Croker of Dublin. John Wilson belonged to the Waterford Croker family. See 'The Family of Croker', *Herald and Genealogist*, vol. VIII, 1874.

2 Thomas Crofton Croker Correspondence, vol. I, letter 128, Cork Central Library.

3 I have found no entries in parish records of Spitalfields churches of this name. William Goss in *Life and Death of Llewellynn Jewitt* thought that the name in France might have been Jouet.

4 According to Samuel Lewis – *Topographical Dictionary of Ireland*, 1st ed., 1837 – Graige was still inhabited. Thomas Moore visited Graige when Richard Boyse was building a new house and dismantling the old one. *Thomas Moore's Diary*, 1935 edition, ed. J. B. Priestley.

5 Charlotte Elizabeth Tonna, miscellaneous writer, author of *No Surrender* for the Orange cause.

6 Croker Correspondence, *op. cit.*, vol. IV (no letter piece), 24 August 1837.

7 Carter sold his collection of autographs to a Philadelphia publisher, George W. Childs, and it now forms part of a large collection of autographs held by the Historical Society of Pennsylvania in Philadelphia.

8 For example, *The British Schools of Art*, n.d., but published before 1850 by J. S. Virtue, 2 vols. of engravings with descriptions, Anon.

9 William Hazlitt, *The Spirit of the Age*, vol. 2, pp. 131 & 135.

10 This may seem surprising today when Lytton Bulwer is generally only remembered for two of his novels, *The Last Days of Pompeii* and *The Last of the Barons*. He was highly regarded by Victorian literary critics who were influenced by his view of the novel as a serious art

form aiming at the idealistic. See Lytton Bulwer's *On Art in Fiction* (1838). Anna Maria, therefore, would have been very grateful for his criticism of *The Buccaneer* and of her other works.

11 *Fraser's Magazine*, December 1831, p. 522.

12 Lytton Bulwer went out of his way to establish this fact. He sent a card to Hall stating that his editorship was from January 1832 to August 1833. Hertfordshire County Archives DE/KC 28/9 7 November 1833.

13 E. V. Kenealy with D. Moir wrote a Memoir for the *Dublin University Magazine*, January 1844.

14 S. C. Hall to E. V. Kenealy, 6 October (1842), HM 38625. This item is produced by kind permission of The Huntington Library, San Marino, California.

15 For further information about wood-engravings in the nineteenth century see Paul Goldman, *Victorian Illustrated Books: the Heyday of Wood Engraving*, London, 1994.

CHAPTER FOUR

1 *Ireland: Its Scenery, Character, etc.*, vol. I, p. 153.

2 Samuel Carter Hall to Lytton Bulwer, Hertfordshire County Archives, DEXC2, item 45.

3 In a letter to Thomas Crofton Croker of 24 August 1837: 'I am sure if you read from the first to the last of Lights and Shadows of Irish Life you would not find a bitter remark upon religious matters. I cannot say I have avoided this because I can say I have never felt it.' Thomas Crofton Croker Correspondence, vol.4, no letterpiece, Cork Central Library.

4 *Irish Melodies from 1807–1828*, 'Prefatory letter on Music'.

5 *Quarterly Review*, vol. 85, 1849, p. 491.

CHAPTER FIVE

1 *The Art Union*, November 1842, p. 263.

2 *Ibid.*, 1850, p. 265.

3 'Jendwine v Slade 2 Espinasse's Nisi Prius Reports' 572, *The Art Journal*, 1854, p. 344.

4 *Fine Arts Quarterly Review*, May 1863, p. 15.

5 *The Art Journal*, 1855, p. 161.

6 *Ibid.*, 1 April 1855, p. 126.

7 *Ibid.*, July 1855, p. 167.

8 Francis Greenacre, *Catalogue of Francis Danby, an Exhibition at the Tate Gallery in association with the City of Bristol Museum and Art Gallery*, no. 142, *Fairies*, c. 1840, p. 162.

9 Daniel Maclise to Crofton Croker, Crofton Croker Correspondence,

vol. 3, piece 134. Carter probably felt a certain affinity with Maclise. Like Carter, Maclise's father served in a corps (the Elgin Fencibles) raised in 1794 by Lady Drummond in Perthshire, which went to Ireland during the Rebellion of 1798 and was stationed in Cork where Daniel was born. *Autobiography of Daniel Maclise*, 1846, by kind permission of the Royal Academy.

CHAPTER SIX

1 *Dublin University Magazine*, 1849, p. 694.
2 William Makepeace Thackeray, *Irish Sketches*, 1875 ed., p. 312.
3 Mrs Carlyle, *Letters and Memorials of Jane Welsh*, p. 220.
4 *Punch*, 1843, vol. 5, p. 218.
5 S. C. Hall, *A Letter to Irish Temperance Societies*, The Rosery, Old Brompton, London, 6 November 1843, Price 3d.
6 W. J. FitzPatrick, *Life of Charles Lever*, 1879, p. 218.
7 John O'Neill, *Fifty Years' Experience of an Irish Shoemaker in London*, published posthumously in weekly instalments in *St Crispin*, a weekly boot and shoe magazine 1869–70. I am most grateful to Mr John Egan for all the information that he has kindly given me on this subject.
8 Quoted in David Borowitz, *George Cruikshank: Mirror of an Age*, Los Angeles, William Andrew Clark Memorial Library, 1871.
9 *The Art Journal*, 1854, vol. VI, pp. 214 & 215.
10 In 1828 a small party of Fellows of the Society of Antiquaries excavated a site at Holywood, Keston, Kent, supposed to be the Roman station of Noviomagus, mentioned in the itinerary of Antoninus. They discovered the foundations of a temple and other Roman remains. The Society of Noviomagus was formed with officers having names such as 'The Lord High President' (Carter in 1867), 'the Architect' (George Godwin) and the 'Public Orator'. They met for supper every Thursday evening after meetings of the Society of Antiquaries.
11 *Autobiographical Notes of the Life of William Bell Scott 1830–1882*, ed. W. Minto, vol. I, 1892, p. 108.
12 Quoted in Colm Kerrigan, *Father Mathew and the Irish Temperance Movement*, p. 184.

CHAPTER SEVEN

1 John Forster, *Life of Charles Dickens*, 1911 ed., vol. I, p. 308.
2 *Letters of Charles Dickens*, ed. Madeline House and Graham Storey (Pilgrim ed.), Clarendon Press, 1965–88, vol. I, p. 483.
3 J. Comyns Carr, *Some Eminent Victorians*, ch. 12, p. 146.

4 Nathaniel Hawthorne, *The English Notebooks*, ed. Randall Stewart, pp. 310 & 313. Douglas Jerrold (1803–57), author and wit. Dr Charles Mackay, poet and journalist, editor of the *Illustrated London News* 1852–59.

5 Wackford Squeers and Pecksniff: an unpublished letter by Charles Dickens (with foreword by Clement Shorter for publication amongst his friends), 1915 (one of 25). Shorter says the letter was in the catalogue of Maggs Bros. of the Strand in London at 100 gns.

6 Chertsey Reference Library, Library Card Index 93, 053 dated 26 March 1870, CFB/CA N Ch 921 (Hal).

7 George Carr's sister married Simon Osborne. Their son, Richard Boyse Osborne, inherited the lands of Graige.

8 *The Independent Review*, September 1906, p. 325. Charles Churchill Osborne, 'Mr Pecksniff and His Prototype'.

9 Henry Vizetelly, *Glances Back through Seventy Years*, 1893.

10 S. C. Hall, *A Book of Memories of Great Men and Women of the Age*, p. 457.

11 Walter Bagehot, *Literary Studies*, vol. II, 1878, p. 197.

CHAPTER EIGHT

1 Joseph Nash, *Mansions of England in the Olden Times*, 1839, 1840, 1841 and 1849.

2 Sir Uvedale Price, *An Essay on the Picturesque as Compared with the Sublime and the Beautiful*, 1796.

3 John Ruskin, *Modern Painters*, Book I, pt. II, sec. 1, ch. 7, para. 24.

4 John Barrell, *Dark Side of Landscape*, paperback ed., Cambridge, 1983.

5 John Ruskin, *ibid*., paras. 33 & 34.

6 John Ruskin, *ibid*., para. 24.

7 I am indebted to Clive Paine for this information, which can be found in his book *The Culford Estate*, p. 120, researched by the Ingram Local History Group. Mary Tudor was buried in the Abbey at Bury St Edmunds. Her remains were later removed to St Mary's Church and a monument was inscribed to her.

8 S.H.A.H., *Suffolk Green Books*, 1905, Record Office, Bury St Edmunds.

9 John Ruskin, *op. cit*., Book I, pt. II, sec. 1, ch. 7, para. 31.

CHAPTER NINE

1 Nathaniel Hawthorne, *The English Notebooks*, ed. Randall Stewart, 1941, p. 317.

2 *The Autobiography and Letters of Mrs Oliphant*, arr. and ed. Mrs Harry Coghill, 1899.

3 An infant daughter is buried at Kensal Green.

4 Letters of Anna Maria Hall to Francis Bennock, Iowa MSL, HI74be. By kind permission of the University of Iowa Libraries, Iowa City, Iowa.

5 *A Short History of* The Art Journal, published by George Virtue's grandson 1905.

6 J. C. Horsley, *Recollections of a Royal Academician*, 1903.

7 Unpublished letter of John Roberts Herbert to Francis McCracken, 3 December 1845. By kind permission of the Ulster Museum, Belfast.

8 Herbert told Francis McCracken that he had painted this picture in consequence of a wager between himself and Carter that he could not paint a picture (in nine days) in time for the Royal Academy Exhibition. The loser was to pay a sum to charity. Herbert painted a smaller version, intended for engraving purposes, and partly intended for Carter. It seems, however, that Carter (who lost the wager) forgot to pay his debt, and Herbert refused to send him the small picture and sold it to McCracken. J. R. Herbert letters, Ulster Museum, Belfast.

9 S. C. Hall, *The Acquittal of the Seven Bishops. A Descriptive History ... Designed to Illustrate and Explain a Picture Commemorating an Event ... Painted by J. R. Herbert.* A copy of this in the British Library was a bombing casualty in the 1939–45 war, and I have been unable to trace another copy. There is an engraving of the picture in the V and A Museum.

10 Richard and Samuel Redgrave, *A Century of British Painters,* 1946 ed., p. 286.

11 S. C. Hall, *Memories of Great Men and Women of the Age,* 2nd ed., 1877, p. 481.

12 *The Art Journal*, 1851, p. 116.

13 Allan Cunningham, in his *Life of Sir David Wilkie*, says that when Maria Edgeworth saw the sketch of The Peep O'Day Boys' cabin, she thought neither the dress nor the expression characteristically Hibernian, but 'too neat, too nice, too orderly for the Irish and Ireland'. On the other hand, she thought the girl keeping watch was Irish all over. Cunningham goes on to say that Wilkie tried to improve on this in the finished picture.

14 Anna Maria to Francis Bennock, 28 November n. y., University of Iowa MSL H 174be.

15 Hawthorne, *op. cit.*, p. 317.

16 William Buckland (1784–1856), famous geologist and President of the Royal Geographical Society, suffered from a mental disease after 1840 which debarred him from attempting further work. *D.N.B.*, p. 246.

17 Anna Maria Hall (no date, but Ingram became MP 1856) to Francis Bennock. University of Iowa MSL H 174be.
18 Hawthorne, *op. cit.*, p. 398.
19 Unpublished diary of Richard Boyce Osborne 1834–35 with some account of the family of Boyse and Carr, his immediate descendants. National Library of Ireland MSS 7888 –7895.

CHAPTER TEN

1 Thomas Moore, *Irish Melodies*, Prefatory Letter on music, 1807.
2 *Dublin University Magazine*, 'Recollections of Moore', vol. XXXIX, April 1852, p. 485.
3 Thomas Moore, *Travels of an Irish Gentleman in Search of a Religion*, April 1829.
4 Sydney Smith, quoted by Charles Kent in *Memoir: Centenary Edition of Moore's Poetical Works.*
5 Moore's principal works:
1800 *Odes of Anacreon*
1806 *Odes and Epistles*
1807–34 *Irish Melodies*
1808 *Corruption*
1808 *Intolerance*
1814 *The Twopenny Post-bag*
1816 *Sacred Songs*
1817 *Lalla Rookh*
1818 *The Fudge Family in Paris*
1819–28 *National Airs*
1823 *The Loves of the Angels*
1823 *Humorous and Satirical Poems*
1830 *Life of Lord Byron*
1840 *A History of Ireland*
6 S. C. Hall, *Retrospect of a Long Life*, vol. 11, 1883, p. 83.
7 Quoted by John Wilson Croker in the *Quarterly Review*, vol. XCIII, 1853, p. 245.
8 John Wilson Croker (originally the same family as Thomas Crofton Croker in the seventeenth century), politician and essayist. Secretary to the Admiralty.
9 *Quarterly Review, op. cit.*, p. 246.
10 S. C. Hall, *Memories of Great Men and Women of the Age*, 1871, p. 16.
11 S. C. Hall, *ibid.*, p. 17.
12 Walter G. Strickland, *Dictionary of Irish Artists*, 1913.
13 Visiting Aungier Street some years later, Carter found that the then

owner of the house had taken down the stone when painting his house. There is a stone there today which has the following inscription: '1794 The Birthplace of Thomas Moore. Ireland's Lyric Poet Reconstructed in 1963.'

14 Thomas Moore, *Irish Melodies*, 'On Music'.

CHAPTER ELEVEN

1 I am grateful to the authorities of the State Art Collection, Dresden for permission to reproduce this drawing.

2 John Eagles, 'The Fine Arts and Public Taste', *Blackwood's Edinburgh Magazine*, July 1853, pp. 89–104.

3 Owen Jones, *Grammar of Ornament*, Proposition 36.

4 S. C. Hall, *Retrospect of a Long Life*, vol. II, p. 388.

5 S. C. Hall, National Library of Scotland MS. 9813 ff 18.

6 Anna Maria Hall to Francis Bennock, Firfield, 27 August n.y. MSL H 174be, by permission of the University of Iowa Libraries, Iowa City, Iowa. The number of deaths in England in 1854 from cholera was 20,000. There was an epidemic centred round Broad Street, Golden Square that year which the epidemiologist John Snow described as 'the most terrible outbreak of cholera which ever occurred in this kingdom'. Snow suspected a street pump in Broad Street was supplying an affected area and tells a story of a lady who had once lived there but had not visited the district in months. She was so fond of the water that 'a carter brought daily to her home in Hampstead a bottle filled from the Broadstreet pump, and on August 31st she came down with the disease. A niece who was visiting the old lady also drank the water at Hampstead and returned to her home in Islington to die of cholera. There were no cases of the disease in either of these communities.' (Extract from Charles Edward Amory Winslow, *The Conquest of Epidemic Disease*, p. 274.)

7 Anna Maria Hall to Francis Bennock, Firfield, 8 September n.y., Iowa University Library MSL H 174be (16).

8 S. C. Hall to Francis Bennock 7 November n.y., Iowa University Library MSL H 179be.

9 Anna Maria Hall to Francis Bennock Sunday night n.d., Iowa University Library MSL H 174be.

10 & 11 Anna Maria Hall to Francis Bennock 1 December 1854, Iowa University Library MSL H 174be.

12 S. C. Hall to Francis Bennock 17 February n.y., Iowa University Library MSL H 179be.

13 My thanks are due to the County Archivist, Surrey County Council who checked these entries for me in the Register of Baptism for St

Paul's, Addlestone: 25 June 1856 John St Vincent, son of John and Agnes Eliza Crowder of Firfield. Father's profession Gentleman. 23 February 1859 Emily Jane, daughter of John and Susannah Watson of Firfield. Father's profession Esquire.

14 Paper from J. C. Deane and P. Cunningham printed in the *Art Treasures Examiner*, Tuesday 5 May 1857, published by the *Manchester Examiner and Times.*

15 Letter from Prince Albert to Lord Ellesmere dated 3 July 1856, quoted in Sir Theodore Martin, *Life of HRH The Prince Consort*, vol. 4, p. 35.

16 John Ruskin, afterwards published as *A Joy for Ever*, 1880.

17 *The Art Journal*, 1857, p. 185.

18 Anna Maria Hall to Sir Bulwer Lytton, Saturday n.d. Hertfordshire County Archives 125/146.

CHAPTER TWELVE

1 *The Art Journal*, 1857, p. 361.

2 Diane Sachko Macleod, 'Mid-Victorian Patronage of the Arts; F. G. Stephens: 'The Private Collections of England', *Burlington Magazine*, August 1986, p. 597.

3 Frederick George Stephens was one of the original members of the Pre-Raphaelite Brotherhood. He gave up painting and became an art critic. He wrote for *The Germ*, the short-lived journal of the Pre-Raphaelites. He called Dr Waagen 'a wretched fool', probably because of Waagen's derogatory letter on the P.R.s to *The Times*. Stephens was supplementing and correcting Waagen's *Treasures of Art in Great Britain* (1854–7), when he wrote his 90-part series on the private collections of England. He was art critic of *The Athenaeum* 1861–1901, and wrote many catalogues and monographs of artists.

4 John Ruskin, *Modern Painters*, 2nd ed., Book I, pt. II, sect. 6, ch.3, p. 458.

5 *The Art Journal*, 1849, p. 171.

6 *Ibid.*, 1853, p. 145.

7 *Ibid.*, 1856, p. 161.

8 *Ibid.*, 1856, p. 166.

9 F. G. Stephens, *The Athenaeum*, September 1873, p. 373.

10 *Op. cit.*, 1868, p. 156.

11 Pliny, *Natural History*, XXXVI, 4, 20–21.

12 *Op. cit.*, September 1859, p 277. Lord Haddo's motion in the House of Commons was in fact defeated. See Alison Smith, *The Victorian Nude: Sexuality, Morality and Art*, 1996.

13 *Op. cit.*, 1867, p. 141.

14 *Op. cit.*, 1857, p. 5.
15 *Op. cit.*, 1857, p. 7.
16 S. C. Hall, *Social Notes*, no. 40, 7 December 1878, 'The Nude in Art'.
17 S. C. Hall, *Memories of Great Men and Women of the Age*, 1871, 3rd ed., p. 463.
18 Anthony Trollope, *Autobiography*, ch. 10, p. 191.

CHAPTER THIRTEEN

1 *Addlestone Historical Society News*, July 1987, no. 12. This house must have been Bannow Lodge (named no doubt nostalgically by Anna Maria) which they had built and had an offer for. See letter to 'Miss Catherine', n.d., Iowa University MSL H174c.
2 W. Goss, *Life and Death of Llewellynn Jewitt*, p. 192, quotation from Jewitt's diary 7 October.
3 *The Autobiography and Letters of Mrs Oliphant*, ed. Harry Coghill, 1899, p. 37.
4 *Lyrics of Ireland*, ed. and ann. Samuel Lover, 1858.
5 Henry Vizetelly, *Glances Back through Seventy Years*, 1893, p. 305.
6 John O'Neill, *Fifty Years' Experiences of an Irish Shoe-maker in London*, published posthumously in weekly instalments in *St Crispin*, a weekly boot and shoe magazine, 1869–70.
7 *Royal Literary Fund Archives World Microfilms Publication*, 1984, 361 7 632 0941 HV 244 Reel 141. A11 catalogues of sponsors give names and dates of those whom Anna Maria sponsored.
8 Anthony Trollope, *Miss Mackenzie*, ch. 27, 'The Negro Soldiers' Orphan Bazaar'.
9 Anna Maria Hall, Ashley Place, to Francis Bennock, Iowa University Library MSL H. 174be (18).
10 Anna Maria Hall to Joseph Durham, n.d., Iowa University MSL H 174du.
11 W. Goss, *op. cit.*, p. 368.

CHAPTER FOURTEEN

1 Hall, Anna Maria Fielding, ch.H 10, 22, Boston Public Library/Rare Books Department. Courtesy of the Trustees.
2 Maria Edgeworth, 'Thoughts on Bores', 1833.
3 S. C. Hall, *Retrospect of a Long Life*, vol. I, 1883, p. 94.
4 S. C. Hall, *ibid.*, vol. II, 'Recollections of Mrs Hall', p. 426.
5 Anne Ritchie, An Introduction to *Ormond* by Maria Edgeworth.
6 Anna Maria Hall to Edward Lytton Bulwer, Hereford Street, 59 Sloane Street Monday n.d. Hertford County Archives DEK C 23/50.

7 Perhaps this was the basis for a plot which was to be used many times later, but most effectively in Evelyn Waugh's 'Bella Fleece Gave a Party' in which Bella finally tells the butler to dismiss the band in the empty ballroom; only four uninvited guests had arrived. Evelyn Waugh, *Work Suspended and Other Stories*, 'written before the Second World War', London, 1948.

8 John Wilson, Professor of Moral Philosophy at Edinburgh University, was the main support of *Blackwood's Edinburgh Magazine*. As 'Christopher North', his series 'Noctes Ambrosianae' ran from 1822 to 1835. Mrs Oliphant asserted, contrary to general belief, that he never became editor.

9 Dr Charles Mackay, poet and journalist, editor of the *Illustrated London News* 1852–59. Quoted in Nathaniel Hawthorne's *The English Notebooks*, 1941 ed., p. 315.

10 S. C. Hall, *op. cit.*, vol. II, p. 113.

11 Schools in Bristol today which were in operation in the first quarter of the nineteenth century have no record of S. C. Hall in their archives.

12 *A Week in Killarney* is of course a joint work with Anna Maria. However, it seems that most of the text was written by Carter (as was *Ireland: Its Scenery, Character, etc.*) with Anna Maria supplying little anecdotes. Moreover, the style in these works is very different from Anna Maria's own work.

13 Joseph Comyns Carr, *Some Eminent Victorians*, ch. 12, p. 146.

14 Anthony Trollope, *Autobiography*, ch. 14, p. 263.

15 S. C. Hall, *op. cit.*, vol. I, p. 313.

16 Anthony Trollope, *Later Short Stories*, 'Mrs Brumby'.

17 *The Standard*, 19 March 1889.

CHAPTER FIFTEEN

1 *The Art Journal*, 1855, p. 229.

2 John Ruskin, *Lectures on Architecture and Painting*, Lecture III, Edinburgh, November 1853.

3 *The Art Journal*, 1856, p. 161 footnote.

4 *Ibid.*, 1861, p. 13.

5 Revd R. St John Tyrwhitt, *The Contemporary Review*, vol. II, May 1869, p. 101. Richard St John Tyrwhitt (1827–95), vicar of St Mary Magdalen, Oxford; exhibited Royal Academy and Suffolk Street. Fervent admirer of John Ruskin. Publications include *A Handbook of Pictorial Art* (1866) and *Christian Art and Symbolism* (1872).

6 Leslie Steven, 'Art and Morality', *Cornhill Magazine*, 1875, p. 91.

7 Tom Taylor, *The Times*, 3 May 1862, p. 14.

8 *The Spectator*, 1869, p. 847.
9 F. G. Stephens, *The Athenaeum*, 4 May 1867.
10 *The Art Journal*, 1867, p. 141.
11 *Ibid.*, 1856, p. 164.
12 Elizabeth Prettejohn, *Burlington Magazine*, February 1996, p. 82.
13 *The Art Journal*, 1864, p. 158.
14 *The Spectator*, May 1866, p. 523.
15 P. G. Hamerton, 'Art Criticism', *Cornhill Magazine*, 8 September 1863, pp. 334–43.
16 Sidney Colvin, knighted 1911, Slade Professor of Fine Art at Cambridge 1883–1912, Keeper of Prints and Drawings at the British Museum. His preference was for the Italian School not later than the sixteenth century. He did much to assist the growth of collections and to increase the appreciation of them by his scholarship. I am indebted to Edward Miller for this information from his book *That Noble Cabinet*.
17 Revd R. St John Tyrwhitt, *op. cit.*, vol. II, May 1869, p. 108.
18 *Discourses Delivered to the Students of the Royal Academy by Sir Joshua Reynolds KT. 15th Discourse*, 1790, p. 405, in the 1905 edition with an Introduction and Notes by Roger Fry, published by Seeley & Co, Great Russell Street, London.
19 *The Art Journal*, 1877, p. 244.
20 I am indebted to Linda Merrill for information about the trial in her book *A Pot of Paint*, published by the Smithsonian Institution Press. She says that her reconstruction of the trial is based on fragmentary testimony preserved in the press, and is not a word-for-word transcription of Victorian newspaper reports.
21 J. McNeill Whistler, *Whistler v Ruskin: Art and Art Critics*, Chatto and Windus, 24 December 1878. 'Peter Parley' was the pseudonym of Samuel Griswold Goodrich (1793–1860), who wrote a series of books for the young – historical, geographical, scientific etc. In England William Martin published several children's books in imitation, and under the name of Peter Parley. *Universal History*, for example, is elementary and factual, and included a list of discoveries and inventions with dates ranging from such items as 'First Pyramid begun' to 'Stockings of silk first worn by Henry II of France'.
22 Letter from W. M. Rossetti to James Whistler from Somerset House, 27 January n.y. By kind permission of Glasgow University Library, Department of Special Collections, ref. R.144 GUL.
23 Letter from Comyns Carr to J. M. Whistler from the Clarendon Hotel, Brighton, n.d., Glasgow University Library, ref. C.43 GUL.
24 D. C. Thompson, *The Art Journal*, 1879, p. 225.

CHAPTER SIXTEEN

1 S. C. Hall, *Retrospect of a Long Life*, vol. I, p. 335.
2 *The Art Journal*, 1878, 'Minor Topics', p. 234.
3 Anna Maria Hall to Francis Bennock Christmas Day 1878, Iowa University Library MSL H174be.
4 *The Times*, 14 June 1879.
5 *Social Notes*, no. 49, 8 February 1879, p. 780.

CHAPTER SEVENTEEN

1 Daniel Maclise, pen and watercolour signed with initials and dated 1833, 8 by 6½ ins. By kind permission of the Chertsey Museum.
2 W. H. Goss, *Life and Death of Llewellynn Jewitt*, p. 363.
3 S. C. Hall, *The Use of Spiritualism?*, 1876, printed for private circulation by Hay and Nisbet, 219 George Street, Glasgow.
4 *The Art Journal*, 1880, p. 353.
5 S. C. Hall to Francis Bennock, Avenue Villa, 50 Holland Road, Kensington, 14 April n.y. Iowa University Library MSL H 179be.
6 S. C. Hall, *Retrospect of a Long Life*, vol. II, p. 397.
7 The colours hung in St Margaret's Church until quite recently. I am indebted to the Rector, the Revd Roy Wheeler, for information about the Hall family. He tells me that the flags are now in such a sorry state of repair that they can no longer be hung, and have been placed in the vestry.
8 *The Western Figaro*, 25 August 1882.
9 S. C. Hall to Francis Bennock 12 July 1885, Stanfield Road, St Albans Road, Victoria Road, Kensington. Iowa University Library MSL H 179be.
10 The portrait of S. C. Hall by Paul Delaroche bequeathed in his will to the National Gallery of Ireland does not appear to be there, and I have been unable to trace its whereabouts.
11 S. C. and A. M. Hall, *Ireland: Its Scenery, Character, etc.*, vol. III, p. 42. Hall is quoting from Pynnar's *Survey of Ulster 1816–1819*.
12 Charles Baudelaire, *Art in Paris 1845–1862*, 'The Salon of 1846, II: Romanticism', p. 46 in the 1965 edition, trans. and ed. Jonathan Mayne.
13 *Punch*, Fig. 67, 18 November 1871.
14 For example, see William Millar's engraving of *Vietri* by C. Stanfield, RA, *The Art Journal*, 1859, p. 112.
15 *The Athenaeum*, 20 January 1883, p. 93.

Appendices

APPENDIX A

Engravings from the Royal Pictures

The Art Journal, 1856

W. E. Frost, ARA, *L'Allegro*; engr. T. Garner. Osborne House. p. 4.
W. Callow, *The Bay of Naples*; engr. R. Wallis. Osborne House. p. 16.
W. Mulready, RA, *The Wolf and the Lamb*; engr. C. W. Sharpe. Buckingham Palace. p. 36.
Thomas Gainsborough, RA, *The Walk at Kew*; engr. C. H. Jeens. Windsor Castle. p. 48.
A. Cuyp, *The Troupers*; engr. E. Hacker. Buckingham Palace. p. 68.
W. Hensel, *Miriam*; engr. H. Bourne. Osborne House. p. 92
D. Roberts, *The Fountain at Madrid*; engr. J. Cousen. Osborne House. p. 100.
Baron Wappers, *Genevieve of Brabant*; engr. J. C. Armytage. Windsor Castle. p. 124.
J. T. Peele, *The Children in the Wood*; engr. H. Bourne. Osborne House. p. 136.
G. E. Hering, *Amalfi, Gulf of Salerno*; engr. E. Goodall. Osborne House. p. 140.
Sir C. L. Eastlake, PRA, *The Visit to the Nun*; engr. S. Smith. Osborne House. p. 174.
J. F. Herring, *The Queen's Horses*; engr. C. Cousen. Osborne House. p. 192.
P. Potter, *Milking Time*; engr. J. Godfrey. Buckingham Palace. p. 200.
E. Courbould, *'Go, and Sin No More'*; engr. C. H. Jeens. Osborne House. p. 232.
H. Warren, *The Star in the East*; engr. R. Brandard. Osborne House. p. 248.
J. Jacobs, *Constantinople: The Golden Horn*; engr. T. A. Prior. Osborne House. p. 264.
Guido, *St Catherine*; engr. J. M. St Eve. Windsor Castle. p. 288.
J. D. Harding, *Hyde Park in 1851*; engr. J. B. Allen. Buckingham Palace. p. 302.
Carlo Dolci, *The Madonna*; engr. F. Bal. Windsor Castle. p. 312.
J. B. Pater, *Fête Champêtre*; engr. Pelée. Buckingham Palace. p. 340.
E. Steinle, *St Luke Painting the Virgin*; engr. L. Stocks. Osborne House. p. 344.
van Dyck, *Children of Charles I*; engr. J. Burnet. Windsor Castle. p. 360.
G. E. Hering, *Capri*; engr. R. Brandard. Osborne House. p. 372.

The Art Journal, 1857

Canaletto, *Venice: the Bucentaur*; engr. J. B. Allen. Windsor Castle. p. 20.
J. van Eycken, *Charity*; engr. P. Lightfoot. Osborne House. p. 32.
D. Maclise, RA, *A Scene from 'Midas'*; engr. S. Sangster. Osborne House. p. 40.
W. Collins, *The Young Shrimpers*; engr. A Willmore. Windsor Castle. p. 44.
van Dyck, *Queen Henrietta Maria*; engr. F. Joubert. Windsor Castle. p. 72.
Vander Heyde, *The River Bank*; engr. J. Outhwaite. Buckingham Palace. p. 88.
Tscheggeny, *The Harvest Field*; engr. J. Cousen. Osborne House. p. 120.
Rembrandt, *Noli Me Tangere*; engr. G. Levy. Buckingham Palace. p. 140.
F. Winterhalter, *The Amazon, Portrait of Princess Helena*; engr. T. Vernon. Osborne House. p. 144.
F. van Mieris, *Blowing Bubbles*; engr. J. Bein. Buckingham Palace. p. 176.
W. A. Knell, *Dover: the Landing of Prince Albert*; engr. W. Miller. Osborne House. p. 188.
W. Wyld, *Manchester from Kersal Moor*; engr. E. Goodall. Windsor Castle. p. 204.
F. Winterhalter, *The Princess of Belgium*; engr. D. Devachez. Osborne House. p. 226.
F. van Mieris, *Teasing the Pet*; engr. R. C. Bell. Buckingham Palace. p. 244.
J. Tennant, *Rest at Eve*; engr. C. Cousen. Osborne House. p. 252.
Mourenhout, *Preparing for the Chase*; engr. T. Sherratt. Osborne House. p. 278.
F. Winterhalter, *The Princess Victoria Gouramma of Coorg*; engr. R. Graves, ARA. Buckingham Palace. p. 293.
F. Bouvy, *The Prison Group*; engr. D. Devachez. Osborne House. p. 304.
W. L. Leitch, *The Birth of Belphoebe and Amorett*; engr. C. Cousen. Osborne House. p. 312.
F. Danby, ARA, *Gate of the Seraglio: Constantinople*; engr. J. T. Willmore, ARA. Osborne House. p. 344.
A. Riedel, *The Beauty of Albano*; engr. L. Stocks. Osborne House. p. 356.
T. M. Richardson, *Evening in Italy*; engr. E. Goodall. Osborne House. p. 364.
F. Foltz, *The Jager*; engr. C. H. Jeens. Osborne House. p. 384.

The Art Journal, 1858

W. E. Frost, ARA, *The Disarming of Cupid*; engr. P. Lightfoot. Osborne House. p. 4.
C. Stanfield, RA, *The Opening of the New London Bridge*; engr. T. A. Prior. Windsor Castle. p. 16.

J. Phillip, ARA, *The Spanish Letter Writer*; engr. L. Stocks. Osborne House. p. 36.
G. A. Fripp, *Kilchurn Castle*; engr. R. Wallis. Osborne House. p. 56.
Sir D. Wilkie, *The King at Holyrood*; engr. W. Greatbach. Windsor Castle. p. 68.
H. Jutsum, *The Noon Day Walk*; engr. R. Brandard. Osborne House. p. 92.
F. Zuccherelli, *The Spring Head*; engr. R. Brandard. Windsor Castle. p. 108.
F. Taylor, *The Young Falconer*; engr. C. W. Sharpe. Osborne House. p. 120.
Sir Charles Eastlake, PRA, *The Good Samaritan*; engr. S. Smith. Osborne House. p. 131.
Sir T. Lawrence, PRA, *Sir Walter Scott*; engr. J. Horsburgh. Windsor Castle. p. 144.
Cuyp, *The Negro Page*; engr. J. Godfrey. Buckingham Palace. p. 172.
van Dyck, *Family of Charles I*; engr. H. Bourne. Windsor Castle. p. 180.
C. Stanfield, RA, *Ischia*; engr. R. Brandard. Osborne House. p. 197.
Carlo Maratti, *The Infant Christ*; engr. Le Comte. Windsor Castle. p. 212.
J. C. Horsley, ARA, *Il Penseroso*; engr. T. Garner. Osborne House. p. 230.
W. Van De Velde, *The Storm*; engr. W. Miller. Buckingham Palace. p. 240.
van Dyck, *Marriage of St Catherine*; engr. W. Ridgway. Buckingham Palace. p. 260.
Rubens, *Farm at Lacken*; engr. A. Wilmore. Buckingham Palace. p. 272.
M. Hobbema, *The Old Mill*; engr. J. Cousen. Buckingham Palace. p. 292.
A. E. Plassan, *The Foot Bath*; engr. P. Pelée. Buckingham Palace. p. 300.
P. Foltz, *The Jager's Wife*; engr. C. H. Jeens. Osborne House. p. 324.
N. Berghem, *Crossing the Ford*; engr. J. Cousen. Buckingham Palace. p. 336.
G. Metzu, *The Bunch of Grapes*; engr. G. Levy. Buckingham Palace. p. 336.
F. Zuccherelli, *The Waterfall*; engr. E. Radcliffe. Windsor Castle. p. 364.

The Art Journal, 1859

Sir E. Landseer, RA, *The Mamozettes*; engr. T. Landseer. Osborne House. p. 4.
D. Maclise, *Gilblas at Pennaflor*; engr. J. C. Armytage. Osborne House. p. 20.
Claude, *A Sea Port*; engr. W. Floyd. Windsor Castle. p. 52.
Guercino, *The Woman of Samaria*; engr. B. Meunier. Windsor Castle. p. 56.
J. B. van Eycken, *Abundance*; engr. T. Vernon. Osborne House. p. 68.

O. Achenbach, *The Monastery*; engr. E. Goodall. Osborne House. p. 80.
W. Mulready, RA, *The Home Expected*; engr. J. Cousen. Buckingham Palace. p. 100.
C Stanfield, RA, *Vietri*; engr. W. Miller. Osborne House. p. 112.
J. Phillip, ARA, *The Spanish Sisters*; engr. D. Devachez. Osborne House. p. 130.
J. Jacobs, *Morning on the Nile*; engr. T. A. Prior. Osborne House. p. 144.
Sir Charles Eastlake, PRA, *The Sisters*; engr. R. Graves, ARA. Osborne House. p. 172.
N. Berghem, *The Herdsman*; engr. J. B. Allen. Windsor Castle. p. 184.
P. Folz, *Prayer in the Tyrol*; engr. P. Lightfoot. Osborne House. p. 200.
W. C. T. Dobson, *The Alms Deeds of Dorcas*; engr. H. Bourne. Osborne House. p. 212.
J. G. Schaeffer, *The Nun*; engr. N. Lecomte. Osborne House. p. 232.
J. A. Hammersley, *Drachenfels from Bonn*; engr. R. Brandard. Buckingham Palace. p. 236.
C. W. Cope, *Wolsey at Leicester Abbey*; engr. W. Greatbach. Osborne House. p. 264.
Rubens, *Summer Time*; engr. A. Willmore. Windsor Castle. p. 276.
Claude, *Europa*; engr. E. Radclyffe. Windsor Castle. p. 296.
Domenichino, *St Agnes*, engr. S. Smith. Osborne House. p. 308.
G. Chambers, *Greenwich Hospital*; engr. J. B. Allen. Osborne House. p. 332.
Sir T. Lawrence, PRA, *The Princess Charlotte* engr. T. Garner. Windsor Castle. p. 336.
Sir D. Wilkie, *A Guerilla Council of War*; engr. J. C. Armytage. Buckingham Palace. p. 368.
Greuze, *Childhood*; engr. A. J. Annedouche. Buckingham Palace. p. 376.

The Art Journal, 1860

W. E. Frost, ARA, *Una*; engr. P. Lightfoot. Osborne House. p. 4.
F. X. Winterhalter, *The Lady Constance*; engr. T. Vernon. Osborne House. p. 20.
H. Le Jeune, *Liberation of the Slaves*; engr. C. H. Jeens. Osborne House. p. 36.
Carlo Maratti, *The Virgin and Child*; engr. J. Tourny. Windsor Castle. p. 48.
Q. Massys, *The Misers*; engr. H. Bourne. Windsor Castle. p. 68.
C. Tscheggeny, *The Cow Doctor*; engr. C. Cousen. Osborne House. p. 88.
Domenichino, *St Catherine*; engr. F. Knolle. Windsor Castle. p. 100.
Sir David Wilkie, *Blindman's Buff*, engr. W. Greatbach. Buckingham Palace. p. 108.

Baron Wappers, *The Ommeganck at Antwerp*; engr. W. M. Lizars. Osborne House. p. 142.
van Dyck, *The Lady Digby*; engr. A. J. Annedouche. Windsor Castle. p. 172.
Sir David Wilkie, *The Penny Wedding*; engr. W. Greatbach. Buckingham Palace. p. 184.
J. Drummond, RSA, *Peace*; engr. P. Lightfoot. Osborne House. p. 196.
Rubens, *The Wife of Rubens*; engr. de Mare. Windsor Castle. p. 236.
J. S. Copley, *The Royal Princesses: Children of George III*; engr. R. Graves, ARA. Buckingham Palace. p. 260.
Mignard, *Henrietta of Orleans*; engr. H. Bourne. Windsor Castle. p. 292.
M. Anthony, *Killarney, the Lower Lake*; engr. R. Wallis. Osborne House. p. 332.
P. Delaroche, *The Rock at St Helena*; engr. C. W. Sharpe. Osborne House. p. 360.
Raffaelle, *Bearing the Cross*; engr. W. Holl. Osborne House. p. 16.
Raffaelle, *Madonna Di San Sisto*; engr. W. Holl. Osborne House. p. 76.
J. B. Greuze, *Simplicity*; engr. F. Joubert. p. 134.
J. C. Ibbetson, *Going to Labour*; engr. W. Hullard. p. 248.

The Art Journal, 1861

J. Drummond, RSA, *War*; engr. P. Lightfoot. Osborne House. p. 4.
G. S. Newton, RA, *The Duenna*; engr. C. H. Jeens. Buckingham Palace. p. 38.
H. Leys, *The Armourer*; engr. T. Godfrey. Windsor Castle. p. 68.
Sir David Wilkie, *The Wounded Guerilla*; engr. J. C. Armytage. Buckingham Palace. p. 100.
J. Sant, *The Royal Sisters*; engr. D. Devachez. Buckingham Palace. p. 136.
Sir David Wilkie, *The Guerilla's Departure*; engr. J. C. Armytage. Buckingham Palace. p. 172.
Claude, *The Beacon Tower*; engr. E. Radcliffe. Windsor Castle. p. 182.
G. Chambers, *Dover*; engr. T. Prior. Osborne House. p. 204.
J. V. Gibson, *The Cottage Home*; engr. S. Smith. Osborne House. p. 228.
Guido, *Death of Cleopatra*; engr. Shenton and Bourne. Windsor Castle,. p. 260.
Sir David Wilkie, *The Maid of Saragossa*; engr. W. Greatbach. Buckingham Palace. p. 292.
J. Phillip, RA, *The Gipsy*; engr. T. Sherratt, Jun. Osborne House. p. 328.
M. Weigmann, *The Two Grandmothers*; engr. C. H. Jeens. Osborne House. p. 374.

APPENDIX B

British Artists: Their Style and Character

Absolon, John, 1862, pp. 201–3.
Alma-Tadema, Lawrence, 1875, pp. 9–11.
Ansdell, Richard, 1860, pp. 233–5.
Archer, James, RSA, 1871, pp. 97–9.
Armitage, Edward, 1863, pp. 177–80.
Barker, Thomas Jones, 1878, pp. 69–72.
Baxter, Charles, 1864, pp. 145–7.
Beavis, Richard, 1877, pp. 65–8.
Bonington, Richard Parkes, 1858, pp. 137–9.
Boughton, George Henry, 1873, pp. 41–4.
Brooks, Thomas, 1872, pp. 197–9.
Burgess, John Bagnold, ARA, 1880, pp. 297–300.
Burr, Alexander Hohenloe, 1870, pp. 309–11.
Burr, John P., 1869, pp. 337–9.
Calderon, Philip Hermogenes, RA, 1870, pp. 9–11.
Callcott, Sir Augustus Wall, RA, 1856, pp. 9–11.
Cattermole, George, 1857, pp. 209–11.
Chalon, Alfred Edward, RA, 1862, pp. 9–11.
Chevalier, Nicholas, 1879, pp. 121–4.
Clark, Joseph, 1863, pp. 49–51.
Cole, George Vicat, ARA, 1870, pp. 177–9.
Collins, William, RA, 1855, pp. 141–4.
Constable, John, RA, 1855, pp. 9–12.
Cooke, Edward William, RA, FRS, 1869, pp. 253–5.
Cooper, Abraham, RA, 1863, pp. 89–91.
Cooper, Thomas Sidney, RA, 1861, pp. 133–5.
Cope, Charles West, RA, 1869, pp. 177–9.
Cox, David, 1860, pp. 41–4.
Creswick, Thomas, RA, 1856, pp. 141–4.
Cross, John, 1862, pp. 117–19.
Crowe, Eyre, 1864, pp. 205–7.
Danby, Francis, ARA, 1855, pp.77–80.
Desanges, Louis William, 1864, pp. 41–3.
Dicksee, Thomas Francis, 1872, pp. 5–7.
Dobson, William Charles Thomas, ARA, 1860, pp. 137–9.
Douglas, William, RSA, 1869, pp. 137–9.

Dyce, William, RA, 1860, pp. 293–6.
Eastlake, Sir Charles Lock, KB, PRA, 1855, pp. 277–80.
Elmore, Alfred, RA, 1857, pp. 113–15.
Etty, William, RA, 1858, pp. 233–5.
Faed, John, RSA, 1871, pp. 237–9.
Faed, Thomas, RA, 1871, pp. 1–3 and p. 62.
Flaxman, John, RA, 1855, pp. 205–9.
Ford, Ford Madox, 1873, pp. 105–8.
Foster, Myles Birkett, 1871, pp. 157–9.
Frith, William Powell, RA, 1856, pp. 237–40.
Frost, William Edward, ARA, 1857, pp. 5–7.
Fuseli, Henry, RA, 1861, pp. 325–7.
Gale, William, 1869, pp. 373–5.
Gibson, John, RA, 1857, pp. 273–5.
Gilbert, John, 1857, pp. 241–3.
Gill, Edmund, 1874, pp. 41–3.
Goodall, Frederick, ARA, 1855, pp. 109–12.
Grant, William James, 1864, pp. 233–5.
Hague, Louis, 1859, pp. 13–15.
Halswelle, Keeley, ARSA, 1879, pp. 49–52.
Harding, James Duffield, OWS, 1856, pp. 269–72.
Hardy, Frederick Daniel, 1875, pp. 73–6.
Harvey, George, RSA, 1858, pp. 73–5.
Haydon, Benjamin Robert, 1856, pp. 181–3.
Hering, George Edward, 1861, pp. 73–5.
Herkomer, Hubert, ARA, 1880, pp. 109–12.
Hicks, George Elgar, 1872, pp. 97–9.
Hill, David Octavius, RSA, 1869, pp. 317–9.
Hillingford, Robert Alexander, RA, 1871, pp. 213–15.
Hilton, William, RA, 1855, pp.253–5.
Holl, Frank, 1876, pp. 9–12.
Hook, James Clarke, ARA, 1856, pp. 41–4
Horsley, John Callcott, ARA, 1857, pp. 181–4.
Houston, John Adam, RSA, 1869, pp. 69–71.
Hulme, Frederick William, 1958, pp. 101–3.
Johnston, Alexander, 1857, pp. 57–60.
Jutsum, Henry, 1859, pp. 269–71.
Knight, William Henry, 1863, pp. 133–5.
Lance, George, 1857, pp. 305–9.
Lawrence, Sir Thomas, PRA, 1859, pp. 325–8.
Le Jeune, Henry, 1858, pp. 265–7.
Leader, Benjamin William, 1871, pp. 45–7.
Lehmann, Rudolf, 1874, pp. 169–72.

Leslie, Charles Robert, RA, 1856, pp. 73–5; 105–7.
Lewis, John Frederick, 1858, pp. 41–3.
Linnell, James Thomas, 1872, pp. 250–1.
Linnell, John, 1859, pp. 105–7.
Linton, William, 1858, pp. 9–11.
Macallum, John Thomas Hamilton, 1880, pp. 149–51.
McCallum, Andrew, 1877, pp. 321–4.
MacWhirter, John, ARSA, 1879, pp. 9–11.
Marks, Henry Stacy, 1870, pp. 361–3.
Morris, Philip Richard, 1872, pp. 161–3.
Muller, William James, 1864, pp. 293–5.
Mulready, William, RA, 1864, pp. 65–7.
Naish, John George, 1875, pp. 329–32.
Newton, Gilbert Stuart, RA, 1864, pp. 13–15.
Nichol, Edwin, RSA, ARA, 1870, pp. 65–7.
Niemann, Edmund John, 1877, pp. 201–4.
Oakes, John Wright, ARA, 1879, pp. 193–6.
Orchardson, William Quiller, ARA, 1870, pp. 233–5.
Osborn, Emily Mary, 1864, pp. 261–3.
Paton, Sir Joseph Noel, RSA, 1869, pp. 1–3.
Peele, John Thomas, 1876, pp. 109–12
Pettie, John, ARA, 1869, pp. 265–7.
Pickersgill, F. R., ARA, 1855, pp. 233–6.
Poole, Paul Falconer, ARA, 1859, pp. 41–3.
Pott, Laslett John, 1877, pp. 257–60.
Poynter, Edward John, RA, 1877, pp. 17–19.
Prout, Samuel, FSA, 1857, pp. 337–9.
Pyne, James Baker, 1856, pp. 205–8.
Redgrave, Richard, RA, 1859, pp. 205–7.
Reynolds, Sir Joshua, PRA, 1860, pp. 357–9.
Riviere, Briton, 1878, pp. 5–9.
Roberts, David, RA, 1858, pp. 201–3.
Ross, Robert Thorburn, 1871, pp. 281–3.
Solomon, Abraham, 1862, pp. 73–5.
Stanfield, Clarkson, RA, 1857, pp. 137–9.
Stone, Frank, ARA, 1856, pp. 333–6.
Stone, Marcus, 1869, pp. 33–5.
Storey, George Adolphus, 1875, pp. 173–6.
Taylor, Frederick, 1858, pp. 329–31.
Thomas, William Cave, 1869, pp. 217–19.
Thompson, Jacob, 1861, pp. 9–11.
Tidey, Henry, 1869, pp. 109–11.
Topham, Francis William, 1880, pp. 21–3.

Walker, Frederick, ARA, 1876, pp. 297–300.
Ward, Edward Matthew, ARA, 1855, pp. 45–8.
Ward, Mrs E. M., 1864, pp. 373–9.
Ward, James, RA, 1862, pp. 169–71.
Warren, Henry, 1861, pp. 265–8.
Webster, Thomas, RA, 1855, pp. 293–6.
West, Benjamin, PRA, 1863, pp. 218–20.
Wilkie, Sir David, RA, 1858, pp. 265–7.
Williams, Penry, 1864, pp. 101–3.
Willis, Henry Brittan, 1879, pp. 93–6.
Witherington, William Frederick, RA, 1859, pp. 73–5.
Wyburd, Francis John, 1877, pp. 137–40

In 1869 the *Art Journal* explained: 'Four years have elapsed since the publication of the last of a long series of biographical sketches bearing the above title. Several members of the Royal Academy and others of almost equal reputation were from various causes omitted in the first series, while, with two or three exceptions, the principal painters of Scotland were altogether excluded, solely on the ground of our inability at that time to gain access to their works for the purpose of engraving.'

APPENDIX C

Selected Pictures from the Galleries and Private Collections of England

The Art Journal, 1862

Sir E. Landseer, RA, *The Chieftain's Friend*; engr. J. C. Armytage. From the Collection of His Grace the Duke of Devonshire at Chatsworth. p. 6.

F. Goodall, ARA, *The Swing*; engr. E. Goodall. From the Collection of James Fallow Esq., Sunnybank, Manchester. p. 46.

W. Mulready, RA, *Brother and Sister*; engr. R. C. Bell. From the Vernon Collection, National Gallery. p. 69.

Alexander Johnston, *The Sabbath Eve*; engr. P. Lightfoot. From the Collection of William Renshaw Esq., Salford. p. 108.

T. Faed, ARA, *The First Sunbeam*; engr. L. Stocks, ARA. From the Collection of James Fallow Esq., Sunnybank, Manchester. p. 116.

T. Webster, RA, *Going to School*; engr. W. Ridgway. From the Collection of James Dugdale Esq, Wroxall Abbey, Warwickshire. p. 138.

J. Sant, ARA, *The Duet*; engr. F. Holl. From the Collection of William Renshaw Esq., Salford. p.156.

F. Goodall, RA, *The Post Office*; engr. C. W. Sharpe. From the Collection of Thomas Greenwood Esq., Sandford Lodge, Hampstead. p. 172.

Jacob Thompson, *The Signal*; engr. C. Cousen. From the Collection of William Preston Esq., Ellel Grange, Lancashire. p. 184.

W. C. T. Dobson, *The Prosperous Days of Job*; engr. H. Bourne. From the Collection of Henry Holdsworth Esq., Coltness, Lanarkshire. p. 204.

J. Linnell, *Rest*; engr. J. Cousen. From the Collection of James Fallow Esq., Sunnybank, Manchester. p. 216.

D. Maclise, RA, *The Origin of the Harp*; engr. R. Graves, ARA. From the Collection of Alan Potter Esq., Liverpool. p. 236.

Engravings from Selected Pictures

The Art Journal, 1863

C. R. Leslie, RA, *Olivia*; engr. T. Vernon. From the Collection of J. Bickerstaff Esq., Preston. p. 4.

F. Goodall, RA, *Fellice Ballarin Reciting Tasso to the People of Chioggia*; engr. E. Goodall. Exhibited at the Royal Academy, 1859. p. 28.

J. Clark, *Hagar and Ishmael*; engr. J. C. Armitage. In the possession of Mrs Clark. p. 52.

J. N. Paton, RSA, *Bathran's Dirge*; engr. D. Devachez. From the Collection of John Pender Esq., Crumpsall House, Manchester. p. 64.

W. Etty, RA, *Cupid and Psyche*; engr. F. Joubert. From the picture in the Sheepshank Collection. p. 92.

G. Smith, *First Day of Oysters*; engr. G. Greatbach. From the Collection of William Bashall Esq., Farington Lodge, Preston. p. 126.

Sir David Wilkie, RA, *John Knox Preaching before the Lords of the Congregation June 10 1558*; engr. G. Greatbach. From the Collection of Sir Robert Peel, Bart, MP. p. 132.

F. R. Pickersgill, *A Rest on the Hill*; engr. W. Ridgeway. From the Collection of Frederick Somes Esq., Beech Hill Park, Waltham, Essex. p. 152.

F. Taylor, *A Hawking Party*; engr. C. Cousen. From the Collection of John Mitchell Esq., Preston. p. 174.

J. C. Horsley, ARA, *The Pet of the Common*; engr. H. Lemon. From the Collection of James Eden Lytham. p. 196.

H. Warren, *Joseph's Coat Brought to Jacob*; engr. S. Smith. In the possession of the Publishers. p. 217.

A. Johnston, *The Visit to Melancthon*; engr. C. W. Sharpe. From the Collection of Francis Bennock Esq., FSA, Blackheath. p. 236.

The Art Journal, 1864

E. M. Ward, RA, *Alice Lisle*; engr. F. Heath. From the Collection of D. Price Esq., Regent's Park. p. 4.

H. O'Neil, ARA, *Purity*; engr. H. Bourne. From the Collection of T. Birchall Esq., Ribbleton Hall, Preston. p. 40.

W. P. Frith, RA, *The Crossing Sweeper*; engr. C. W. Sharpe. From the Collection of W. Holdsworth Esq., Halifax. p. 64.

E. H. Corbould, *The Lesson of the Passover*; engr. F. Heath. In the possession of the Publishers. p. 98.

R. Dadd, *Puck and the Fairies*; engr. G. Lizars. From the Collection of Major Birchall, Ribbleton Hall, Preston. p. 130.

F. R. Pickersgill, RA, *Christian in the Valley of Humiliation*; engr. G. Greatbach. From the Collection of the late T. E. Plint Esq., Leeds. p. 184.

J. Dyckmans, *The Blind Beggar*; engr. D. Devachez. From the picture in the National Gallery. p. 198.

C. Landseer, RA, *Temptation of Andrew Marvell*; engr. J. Stancliffe. From the picture in the Sheepshank Gallery. p. 232.

G. P. O'Neill, *The Foundling*; engr. P. Lightfoot. From the picture in the Bell Collection, National Gallery. p. 260.

C. R. Leslie, RA, *Le Bourgeois Gentilhomme*; engr. C. Sharpe. From the picture in the Sheepshank Collection. p. 290.

P. F. Poole, RA, *The Gleaner*; engr. J. C. Armytage. From the Collection of J. Bickerstaff Esq., Preston. p. 320.

F. Goodall, RA, *Hunt the Slipper*; engr. E. Goodall. Exhibited at the Royal Academy in 1849. p. 352.

The Art Journal, 1865

Sir E. Landseer, RA, *Rout of Comus and His Band*; engr. J. C. Armytage. From the picture in the National Gallery. p. 6.

J. Phillip, RA, *Gipsy Musicians of Spain*; engr. Professor Knolle. From the Collection of T. Robinson Esq., Lingdale, Birkenhead. p. 60.

A. Elmore, RA, *The Novice*; engr. T. Vernon. From the Collection of W. Bashall Esq., Faringdon Lodge, Preston. p. 68.

F. Goodall, *Arrest of a Peasant Royalist, Brittany 1793*; engr. E. Goodall. In the possession of the Publishers. p. 104.

D. Maclise, RA, *The Ballad Singer*; engr. J. Stevenson. From the Collection of John Mitchell Esq., Bradford. p. 140.

J. F. Herring, *Mazeppa*; engr. C. Cousen. From the Collection of Alderman Copeland, MP, Stoke on Trent. p. 172.

F. W. Topham, *The Zouave's Story*; engr. C. W. Sharpe. In the possession of the Publishers. p. 184.

T. Faed, RA, *Words of Comfort*; engr. R. C. Bell. From the Collection of W. Holdsworth Esq., Halifax. p. 200.

J. Linnell, *Labour*; engr. J. Cousen. From the Collection of James Fallows Esq., Sunnybank, Manchester. p. 208.

W. Collins, RA, *Rustic Civility*; engr. C. Cousen. From the picture in the Sheepshank Collection. p. 234.

W. H. Knight, *The Broken Window*; engr. H. Lemon. From the Collection of B. Gibbons Esq., Athol House, Edgbaston. p. 240.

J. M. W. Turner, *The Vale of Ashburnham*; engr. W. B. Cooke. p. 250.

Baron Wappers, *The Death of Columbus*; engr. D. Devachez. In the possession of the Artist. p. 268.

J. C. Hook, RA, *A Passing Cloud*; engr. R. Wallis. From the Collection of D. Bruce Esq., Regent's Park. p. 276.

A. L. Egg, RA, *Life of Buckingham*; engr. W. Greatbach. From the Collection of James Dugdale Esq., Wroxall Abbey, Lancs. p. 296.

A. L. Egg, RA, *Death of Buckingham*; engr. W. Greatbach. From the Collection of James Dugdale Esq., Wroxall Abbey, Lancs. p. 304.

A. Hughes, *Ophelia*; engr. C. Cousen. From the Collection of the late T. E. Plint Esq., Leeds. p. 332.

A. Johnston, *Suspense*; engr. A. Bourne. From the Collection of Francis Bennock Esq., Blackheath. p. 336.

Frith, Creswick and Ansdell, *A Dream of the Future*; engr. J. Cousen. From the Collection of S. Gurney Esq, MP, Princes Gate. p. 360.

P. F. Poole, RA, *The Gipsy Queen*; engr. F. Joubert. From the Collection of T. Birchall, Ribbleton Hall, Preston. p. 364.

The Art Journal, 1866

T. Faed, RA, *The Orphan*; engr. P. Lightfoot. From the Collection of John W. Leather Esq., Newton Green, Leeds. p. 4.

R. Gavin, ARSA, *Phoebe Mayflower*; engr. C. H. Jeens. From the Collection of Ralph Brocklebank Esq., Liverpool. p. 12.

T. Webster, RA, *Spring*; engr. Pelée. From the Collection of James Eden Esq., Lytham. p. 40.

J. R. Herbert, RA, *Susannah*; engr. H. Bourne. From the Collection of James H. Macrae Esq., Liverpool. p. 48.

Herring, Bright and Baxter, *The Cavalier*; engr. J. C. Armytage. From the Collection of Frederick Chapple Esq., Huyton Hall, Liverpool. p. 72.

W. E. Frost, *Chastity*; engr. T. Garner. From the Collection of Thomas Birchall Esq., Ribbleton Hall, Preston. p. 76.

Herring, Bright and Baxter, *The Trooper*; engr. C. Cousen. From the Collection of Frederick Chapple Esq., Huyton Hall, Liverpool. p. 100.

W. P. Frith, RA, *New Shoes*; engr. H. Bourne. p. 116.

J. N. Paton, RSA, *Paulo and Francesca Da Rimini*; engr. R. Graves, ARA. From the Collection of the late T. E. Plint Esq., Leeds. p. 140.

J. Nash, *The May-Pole*; engr. C. Cousen. In the possession of the Publishers. p. 148.

A. Elmore, RA, *The Countess Isabelle of Croye (Quentin Durward)*; engr. J. Stancliffe. From the Collection of John Rhodes Esq., Potternewton House, Leeds. p. 172.

W. Hemsley, *The Bird Catchers*; engr. R. Brandard. From the Collection of David Price Esq., Regent's Park. p. 178.

Elmore, RA, *The Wife's Portrait*; engr. S. S. Smith. From the Collection of John Dillon Esq., Craven Hill. p. 204.

P. F. Poole, RA, *The Parting*; engr. F. Bacon. From the Collection of Charles Hargitt Esq., Liverpool. p. 212.

J. H. Mann, *Hush Asleep!*; engr. J. Franck. From the Collection of J. Knowles Esq., Manchester. p. 232.

C. L. Muller, *The Fountain*; engr. C. Cousen. In the possession of the Publishers. p. 240.
J. M. W. Turner, RA, *Wreck off Hastings*; engr. W. Miller. p. 272.
J. Phillip, RA, *Spanish Contrabandistas*; engr. W. Ridgway. From the Collection of Her Most Gracious Majesty the Queen at Osborne. p. 288.
R. F. Lee, RA, and T. S. Cooper, ARA, *Evening in the Meadows*; engr. J. Cousen. From the picture in the National Collection. p. 298.
J. Meissonier, *The Student*; engr. E. Gervais. p. 298.
T. Webster, RA, *The Breakfast Table*; engr. G. Greatbach. From the Collection of John Graham Esq., Skelmorie Castle, Largs, near Greenock. p. 330.
D. Cox, *Hay-Time*; engr. E. Radcliffe. p. 344.
Rembrandt, *Weary Travellers*; engr. Mauduit. p. 352.
Sir David Wilkie, RA, *The Confessional*; engr. T. W. Knight. p. 365.
F. Goodall, RA, *The Postboy*; engr. E. Goodall. p. 380.

The Art Journal, 1867

C. R. Leslie, RA, *Florizel and Perdita*; engr. L. Stocks, ARA. From the picture in the Sheepshank Collection. p. 4.
J. Phillip, RA, *The Signal*; engr. J. Frank. p. 16.
E. M. Ward, RA, *James Receiving News of the Landing of the Prince of Orange*; engr. F. A. Heath. From the Bell Collection in the National Gallery. p. 38.
H. Le Jeune., ARA, *The Eft*; engr. L. Stocks, ARA. From the Collection of George Simpson Esq., Wray Park, Reigate. p. 60.
C. R. Leslie, RA, *Autolycus*; engr. L. Stocks, ARA. From the picture in the Sheepshank Collection. p. 76.
A. Solomon, *Art Critics in Brittany*; engr. H. Bourne. p. 84.
R. P. Bonington, *The Fish Market*; engr. C. Lewis. p. 90.
T. Webster, RA, *The Village Choir*; engr. H. Bourne. From the Collection of John Tyson Esq., Waterloo, Liverpool. p. 100.
G. Smith, *The Sisters*; engr. C. Cousen. From the Collection of John Robinson Esq., Linydale, Birkenhead. p. 112.
J. Gilbert, *Christiana in the House of Gaius*; engr. J. C. Armytage. From the Collection of Charles Fraser Esq. p. 120.
J. Phillip, RA, *Scottish Lassies*; engr. Professor Knole. In the possession of Mr F. W. Cosens. p. 128.
J. C. Hook, RA, *Arming the Knight*; engr. W. Ridgway. From the Collection of the late T. E. Plint Esq., Leeds. p. 148.
J. C. Horsley, RA, *Lady Jane Grey and Roger Ascham*; engr. L. Stocks, ARA. From the Collection of John Hick Esq., Bolton. p. 154.
P. H. Calderon, ARA, *After the Battle*; engr. F. A. Heath. p. 164.

W. P. Frith, RA, *The Rejected Poet*; engr. C. W. Sharpe. From the Collection of John Hick Esq., Bolton. p. 172.
J. C. Horsley, RA, *The Novice*; engr. H. Bourne. From the Collection of John Rhodes Esq., Leeds. p. 184.
H. O'Neil, ARA, *Scribes Reading to Ahasuerus*; engr. W. M. Lizars. From the Collection of James Spence Esq., Liverpool. p. 192.
J. Sant, ARA, *The Fair Correspondent*; engr. H. Bourne. From the Collection of the late T. E. Plint Esq., Leeds. p. 206.
W. Q. Orchardson, *Chistopher Sly*; engr. C. W. Sharpe. From the Collection of C. P. Matthews Esq., Havering. p. 212.
A. H. Burr, *Playmates*; engr. L. Stocks, ARA. In the possession of the Publishers. p. 218.
C. R. Leslie, RA, *Les Femmes Savantes*; engr. P. Lightfoot. From the picture in the Sheepshank Collection. p. 230.
Sir C. R. Eastlake, PRA, *An Italian Family*; engr. S. Smith. From the Collection of Thomas Birchall Esq., Preston. p. 244.
J. Thompson, *The Height of Ambition*; engr. C. Cousen. In the possession of the Publishers. p. 256.
H. O'Neil, ARA, *L'inamorata*; engr. H. Bourne. From the Collection of Josiah Evens Esq., St Helens. p. 266.
J. C. Hook, RA, *The Brook*; engr. A Willmore. From the Collection of Charles Prater Esq., Notting Hill. p. 272.

The Art Journal, 1868

Daniel Maclise, RA, *Orlando the Wrestler*, engr. C. W. Sharpe. From the Collection of H. L. Betts Esq., Preston Hall, Kent. p. 4.
E. M. Ward, RA, *A King's Daughter*; engr. C. W. Sharpe. In the possession of the Publishers. p. 10.
E. Crowe, *Dr Foe in the Pillory*; engr. J. C. Armytage. From the Collection of J. L. Newall Esq., Ongar. p. 28.
T. Creswick, RA, and F. Goodall, RA, *The Wayfarers*; engr. C. Cousen. From the Collection of J. C. Northcote Esq. p. 36.
J. Faed, RSA, *The Justice of the King*; engr. C. H. Jeens. From the Collection of John Pender, Esq., Manchester. p. 48.
C. R. Leslie, *Sancho Panza*; engr. R. C. Bell. From the picture in the Sheepshank Collection. p. 56.
T. Faed, RA, *Going Home*; engr. F. A. Heath. From the Collection of Ralph Brocklebank Esq., Annesley, Liverpool. p. 66.
J. L. Hamon, *The Skein Winder*; engr. J. C. Thevenin. In the possession of the Publishers. p. 72.
C. R. Leslie, *Falstaff and His Friends*; engr. W. Greatbach. From the picture in the Sheepshank Collection. p. 84.

A. Clint, *Sunset – St Heliers, Jersey*; engr. J. Saddler. p. 92.
J. Phillip, RA, and R. Ansell, RA, *The Wayside in Andalusia*; engr. C. Cousen. From the Collection of Robert Rawlinson Esq, CB. p. 112.
Mrs E. M. Ward, *Palissy the Potter*; engr. C. W. Sharpe. From the Collection of Andrew Holtz Esq. p. 120.
M. Stone, *Watt's First Experiment*; engr. H. Bourne. From the Collection of George Virtue Esq., Oatlands Park. p. 140.
A. Elmore, *The Controversy*; engr. C. H. Jeens. From the Collection of John Knowles Esq., Manchester. p. 156.
W. F. Yeames, ARA, *Arming the Young Knight*; engr. P. Lightfoot. From the picture in the possession of Mr Morby. p. 168.
D. Cox, *Carreg-Cennen Castle, Llandilo*; engr. W. Chapman. From the Collection of Tom Taylor. p. 174.
P. R. Morris, *Where They Crucified Him*; engr. J. C. Armytage. From the Collection of Robert Rawlinson Esq., CB. p. 200.
E. W. Cooke, RA, *Venice – the Arrival*; engr. C. Cousen. From the Collection of J. C. Northcote Esq. p. 208.
Sir E. Landseer, RA, *The Friend in Suspense*; engr. C. Lewis. p. 232.
T. Webster, RA, *The Christmas Pudding*; engr. W. Ridgway. From the Collection of David Price Esq., London. p. 244.
A. Cuyp, *A Sunny Day*; engr. J. C. Bentley. From the picture in the Dulwich Gallery. p. 256.
W. Mulready, RA, *The Negligent Boy*; engr. J. de Mare. In the Collection of W. Holdsworth Esq., Halifax. p. 268.
C. S. Lidderdale, *Courtship by the Sea-Side*; engr. G. Greatbach. From the picture in the possession of Mr Morby. p. 278.
C. Stanfield, *Entrance to Portsmouth Harbour*; engr. W. Chapman. p. 284.

The Art Journal, 1869

W. Mulready, RA, *Choosing the Wedding Gown*; engr. F. A. Heath. From the picture in the Sheepshank Collection. p. 4.
J. Constable, RA, *The Corn-field*; engr. C. Cousen. From the picture in the National Gallery. p. 10.
E. Ward, RA, *The Last Toilet of Charlotte Corday*; engr. L. Stocks. From the Collection of Thomas Williams Esq. p. 36.
Ary Scheffer, *Christ and St John*; engr. E. Rousseau. p. 52.
L. J. Pott, *The Defence*; engr. W. Greatbach. In the possession of the Publishers. p. 68.
Ary Scheffer, *The Kiss of Judas*; engr. Chevron. p. 76.
H. Dawson, *A Stormy Sunset*; engr. W. Chapman. In the possession of James Orrocks Esq., Leicester. p. 112.

D. Maclise, RA, *The Warrior's Cradle*; engr. J. Franck. From the Collection of R. C. May, Clapham Park. p. 120.

W. Mulready, RA, *The Butt – Shooting a Cherry*; engr. H. Bourne. From the picture in the Sheepshanks Collection. p. 144.

W. F. Yeames, ARA, *The Peril of the Queen, Henrietta Maria*; engr. P. Lightfoot. From the Collection of H. T. Hall Esq., Cambridge. p. 158.

R. Ansdell, ARA, *In the Pasture*; engr. C. Cousen. In the possession of the Publishers. p. 172.

Miss R. Solomon, *The Claim for Shelter*; engr. W. Greatbach. In the possession of the Publishers. p. 184.

M. Stone, *A Young Painter's First Work*; engr. H. Bourne. p. 212.

C. Stanfield, RA, *Wreck off Dover*; engr. A. Willmore. From the Collection of C. J. Northcote Esq. p. 220.

P. Delaroche, *L'Ange Gabriel*; engr. A. Blanchard. p. 238.

C. J. Lewis, *The Mill-Door*; engr. J. C. Armytage. In the possession of the Publishers. p. 244.

F. Goodall, RA, *The School of Sooltan Hassan*; engr. E. Goodall. p. 268.

J. Burr, *Domestic Troubles*; engr. W. Greatbach. From the Collection of C. C. Grimes Esq., Stonehouse, Glos. p. 272.

J. Clark, *The Return of the Runaway*; engr. L. Stocks, ARA. In the possession of the Publishers. p. 296.

R. Carrick, *In the Highlands*; engr. E. Brandford. In the possession of the Publishers. p. 302.

Sir E. Landseer, RA, *Jack in Office*; engr. C. J. Lewis. From the picture in the Sheepshank Collection. p. 334.

F. R. Pickersgill, RA, *Pirates of the Mediterranean Playing at Dice for Prisoners*; engr. W. Ridgway. From the Collection of C. J. Northcote Esq. p. 344.

M. Claxton, *In the Sepulchre*; engr. S. Smith. From the picture presented by the artist to the Museum S. Kensington. p. 368.

H. Marks, *The Lady's Tailor*; engr. C. W. Sharpe. p. 372.

The Art Journal, 1870

Birket Foster, *Primrose Gatherers*; engr. C. Cousens. From the Collection of Giles Redmayne Esq. p. 6.

Mrs E. M. Ward, *The Maid of Orleans*; engr. T. Ballin. In the possession of the Publishers. p. 12.

P. R. Morris, *Drift-Wreck from the Armada*; engr. C. H. Jeens. In the possession of the Publishers. p. 36.

G. Bellini, *Procession of the Virgin*; engr. J. L. Raab. From the picture in the church of St Giovani & St Paulo, Venice. p. 56.

H. S. Marks, *My Lady's Page in Disgrace*; engr. F. A. Heath. From the Collection of George Fox Esq., Harefield, Alderley. p. 68.
J. M. W. Turner, RA, *Norham Castle*; engr. W. Chapman. From the picture in the National Collection. p. 80.
J. F. Portaels, *A Daughter of the East*; engr. J. Demannez. p. 108.
Titian, *St Peter Martyr*; engr. C. Geyer. p. 112.
E. H. Corbould, *The Eve of the Flight*; engr. F. Goutière. In the possession of the Publishers. p. 132.
Sir E. Landseer, *The Stag at Bay*; engr. Charles Mottram. p. 144.
Jacob Thompson, *Drawing the Net at Haweswater*; engr. J. C. Armytage. In the possession of the Hon. Sir W. Baliol Brett. p. 172.
Palma Il Veccio, *Sta Barbara*; engr. Erskine Merze. p. 188.
E. Nicol, ARA, RSA, *Renewal of the Lease Refused*; engr. R. C. Bell. From the Collection of Alfred Harris Esq., Ashfield, Bingley, Yorks. p. 200.
G. Da Murano, *The Virgin Enthroned*; engr. J. L. Appold. p. 220.
J. B. Pyne, *On the Yorkshire Coast*; engr. W. Chapman. p. 224.
F. Madox Brown, *The Last of England*; engr. H. Bourne. From the Collection of John Crossley Esq., Halifax. p. 236.
P. Veronese, *The Martyr St Sebastian and His Companions*; engr. C. Ceyer. p. 248.
G. D. Leslie, ARA, *The Defence of Latham House 1644*; engr. J. Godfrey. From the Collection of Edward Salt Esq., Ferniehurst, Yorks. p. 266.
Sir E. Landseer, *The Twa Dogs*; engr. Chas. G. Lewis. From the picture in the Sheepshank Collection. p. 276.
W. Hemsley, *Left in Charge*; engr. H. Lemon. From the Collection of Thomas Williams Esq. p. 296.
Titian, *St Mark and the Saints*; engr. G. Geyer and G. Pommer. p. 312.
Edward Davies, *On the Way to School*; engr. W. Ridgway. In the possession of James Jardine Esq., Brookdale, Alderley Edge. p. 328.
van Dyck, *Children of Charles I*; engr. C. J. Thevenin. From the picture in the Royal Collection, Turin. p. 336.
T. Creswick, *The Church at Bettws-y-coed*; engr. A. Willmore. From the Collection of George Fox Esq., Harefield, Alderley Edge. p. 364.
Tintoretto, *The Miracle of St Mark*; engr. A. Fleischmann. From the picture in the Academy of Fine Arts, Venice. p. 372.

The Art Journal, 1871

M. Stone, *The Duel Interrupted*; engr. H. Bourne. In the possession of the Publishers. p. 4.
G. B. O'Neill, *A Visit to the Armourer*; engr. P. Lightfoot. From the Collection of William Webster Esq., Blackheath. p. 20.

P. J. Castan, *Our Pets*; engr. T. Brown. From the Collection of W. Cottrill Esq., Singleton House, Higher Boughton. p. 36.

S. Bough, RSA, *Borrowdale*; engr. W. Richardson. From the Collection of Robert Clark Esq., Edinburgh. p. 56.

J. F. Portaels, *The Daughter of Zion*; engr. W. Greatbach. From the Collection of W. Cottrill Esq., Singleton House, Higher Boughton. p. 72.

H. Campotosto, *The Spring of Life*; engr. J. C. Armytage. From the Collection of W. Cottrill, Singleton House, Higher Boughton. p. 80.

Louisa Starr, *David Brought before Saul*; engr. S. S. Smith. p. 100.

H. T. Dawson, *Men of War at Sheerness*; engr. A. Willmore. In the possession of the Publishers. p. 112.

A. Solomon, *Le Malade Imaginaire*; engr. H. Bourne. From the Collection of R. P. Harding Esq., Wood Hall, East Dulwich. p. 136.

F. W. Popham, *A Baby Was Sleeping*; engr. C. W. Sharpe. From the Collection of Frederick Craven Esq., Hope Lodge, Manchester. p. 140.

W. Q. Orchardson, ARA, *Talbot and the Countess of Auvergne*; engr. C. W. Sharpe. In the possession of the Publishers. p. 154.

Gabe, *The Children's Offering*; engr. S. S. Smith. In the possession of the Publishers. p. 164.

E. Nichol, ARA, *Kept In*; engr. J. Stephenson. p. 180.

R. A. Hillingford, *The White Cockade*; engr. W. Greatbach. From the Collection of Frederick Wilkinson Esq. p. 184.

R. Ansdell, RA, *The Highland Keeper's Daughter*; engr. C. Cousen. From the picture in the possession of Robert Rawlinson, CB, Boltons, West Brompton. p. 196.

C. Stanfield, RA, *The Market Boat*; engr. J. C. Armytage. From the picture in the Sheepshank Gallery. p. 200.

J. L. Gérôme, *Dante*; engr. C. H. Jeens. From the Collection of H. J. Turner Esq., Hamilton Terrace, St John's Wood. p. 216.

J. Coomans, *The Reproof*; engr. J. Demannez. In the possession of the Publishers. p. 220.

H. Le Jeune, ARA, *The Hindoo Maiden*; engr. D. Devachez. From the Collection of Joshua Satterfield Esq., Alderley Edge. p. 236.

Sir E. Landseer, RA, *The Sleeping Bloodhound*; engr. C. G. Lewis. From the picture in the National Collection. p. 244.

J. Phillip, RA, *The Fortune Teller*; engr. Professor Knolle. p. 260.

J. W. Inchbold, RA, *A Bypath to Chamouni*; engr. T. A. Prior. In the possession of the Publishers. p. 264.

G. Da Udine, *The Coronation of the Virgin*; engr. K. Mayr. p. 272.

H. Cameron, RSA, *Going to the Hayfield*; engr. G. Burton. p. 280.

H. Dawson, Sen., *The Hamoaze, Devonport*; engr. E. Brandard. In the possession of the Publishers. p. 288.

The Art Journal, 1872

E. M. Ward, RA, *Marie Antoinette Listening to the Act of Accusation*; engr. L. Stocks, ARA. From the Collection of Thomas Williams Esq., St John's Wood. p. 4.

J. Linnell, *The Mountain Shepherd*; engr. C. Cousen. From the Collection of R. Brooks Esq. p. 20.

P. De Coninck, *The Tambourine*; engr. H. Bourne. From the Collection of Lt. Col. Radcliff Wyddrington, Edgbaston. p. 40.

H. Tidey, *The Woman of Samaria*; engr T. Sherratt. From the Collection of Francis Fuller Esq. p. 48.

J. Faed, RSA, *Within a Mile of Edinbro Town*; engr. R. C. Bell. From the Collection of W. Cottrill Esq., Singleton House, Higher Boughton, Manchester. p. 68.

Raffaelle, *The Madonna*; engr. P. Lutz. From the picture in the Royal Collection, Dresden. P. 84.

Th. Gerard, *A Triumphant Procession*; engr. W. Ridgway. From the Collection of W. Cottrill Esq., Singleton House, Manchester. p. 92.

Metzacher, *Cherries Ripe!*; engr. P. Lightfoot. In the possession of the Publishers. p. 104.

G. Pope, *Accident or Design?*; engr. G. Greatbach. In the possession of the Publishers. p. 112.

Sir J. Reynolds, PRA, *The Robin*; engr. L. Stocks. From the picture in the National Gallery. p. 132.

G. H. Boughton, *The March of Miles Standish*; engr. G. C. Finden. From the Collection of George B. Whitney Esq., Philadelphia. p. 140.

H. Campotosto, *The Dead Lamb*; engr. T. Brown. From the Collection of George Fox Esq., Harefield, Alderley. p. 156.

F. Stone, ARA, *The First Voyage*; engr. F. A. Heath. From the Collection of Arthur Burnand Esq., Hyde Park Gate. p. 164.

Raffaelle, *The Angels of the Madonna di San Sisto*; engr. P. Lutz. From the picture in the Royal Collection, Dresden. p. 168.

E. M. Ward, RA, *Goldsmith on His Travels*; engr. W. Greatbach. From the Collection of T. Williams, St John's Wood. p. 180.

Birket Foster, *The Rustic Bridge*; engr. C. Cousen. In the possession of the Publishers. p. 192.

J. Pettie, ARA, '*What D'Ye Lack, Madam? What D'Ye Lack?*'; engr. F. A. Heath. In the possession of the Publishers. p. 200.

A. Bellows, *The Christening Party*; engr. J. Saddler. In the possession of S. C. Hall Esq., Upper Norwood. p. 216.

Henrietta Browne, *The Critics*; engr. C. W. Sharpe. From the Collection of Henry McConnell Esq., Cressbrook, Derbyshire. p. 224.

C. W. Nicholls, *Tomb of Grace Darling*; engr. J. Godfrey. From the Collection of Mr Wellington E. Groves, Blandford. p. 240.

C. W. Cope, RA, *Othello Relating His Adventures*; engr. T. Vernon. p. 252.

A. van Ostade, *The Alchemist*; engr. J. C. Bentley. From the picture in the National Gallery. p. 256.

R. Rothwell, RHA, *Novitiate Mendicants*; engr. H. Bourne. From the picture in the Sheepshank Collection. p. 271.

W. Q. Orchardson, ARA, *Prince Henry, Poins and Falstaff*; engr. J. C. Armytage. From the Collection of H. Moxon Esq., Kensington. p. 280.

J. Pettie, ARA, *Touchstone and Audrey*; engr. C. Cousen. From the Collection of H. Moxon Esq., Kensington. p. 296.

Sir Joshua Reynolds, PRA, *The Snake in the Grass*; engr. H. Robinson. From the picture in the National Gallery. p. 300.

Tintoretto, *The Crucifixion*; engr. Schultheis. From the picture in the Scuola di San Rocco, Venice. p. 312.

The Art Journal, 1873

J. C. Horsley, RA, *Detected*; engr. L. Stocks, RA. From the picture in the Collection of Henry Brassey Esq., MP. p. 4.

G. J. Pinwell, *Strolling Players*; engr. C. Cousen. p. 8.

E. M. Ward, *Juliet in the Cell of Friar Lawrence*; engr. H. Bourne. From the picture in the possession of Andrew Holts Esq. p. 40.

J. Linnell, *The Nest*; engr. C. Cousen. From the Collection of Sir Daniel Cooper, Bart, Prince's Garden, Kensington. p. 56.

Paul Veronese, *Venice Triumphant*; engr. J. L. Raab. p. 60.

A. Yvon, *A Shrine in Russia*; engr. G. Finden. In the possession of the Publishers. p. 72.

Sir J. Gilbert, ARA, *Shylock after the Trial*; engr. G. Greatbach. From the Collection of Lynch White Esq., The Grange, Clapham Common. p. 76.

S. A. Hart, RA, *The Quarrel of Wolsey and Buckingham*; engr. W. Greatbach. From the Collection of Joseph Lovegrove Esq., Elton House, Gloucester. p. 104.

Sebastian del Piombo, *Venetian Painters' Sta Magdalene*; engr. H. Mertz. p. 122.

A. Johnston, *Il Penseroso*; engr. J. Demannez. In the possession of the Publishers. p. 132.

C. Green, *The Letter Bag*; engr. S. S. Smith. In the possession of the Publishers. p. 140.

J. M. W. Turner, *Scarborough*; engr. W. Chapman. p. 148.

R. Ansdell, RA, *The Goatherd of Granada*; engr. C. Cousen, From the Collection of Robert Rawlinson, CB, Boltons, West Brompton. p. 165.

Venetian Painters. G. Bellini, *The Madonna with SS Paul and George*; engr. C. Geyer. p. 179.

C. R. Leslie, *Queen Catherine*; engr. C. W. Sharpe. From the picture in the Sheepshank Collection. p. 204.

T. Graham, *The Wayfarers*; engr. J. Stephenson. In the possession of the Publishers. p. 208.

Baron Wappers, *Louis VII*; engr. J. B Meunier. From the Collection of H. M. the King of the Belgians. p. 241.

Venetian Painters. Giorgione, *Dead Christ Supported by Cherubs*; engr. G. Goldberg. p. 242.

L. J. Pott, *Prince Arthur and Hubert*; engr. D. Devachez. In the possession of the Publishers. p. 264.

Birket Foster, *The Convalescent*; engr. C. Cousen. In the possession of the Publishers. p. 268.

N. Chevalier, *Mallee Scrub Victoria*; engr. W. Forest. From *Australia* by Edwin C. Booth: illustrated. p. 272.

J. F. Portaels, *Coming from Church*; engr. A. Danse. p. 296.

Venetian Painters. Bonifazio, *Adoration of the Magi*; engr. C. Geyer. p. 305.

J. A. Houston, RSA, *Death of the Earl of Warwick*; engr. T. Brown. In the possession of the Publishers. p. 328.

J. B. Madou, *The Arquebusier*; engr. S. Meunier. p. 336.

V. W. Bromley, *Troilus and Cressida*; engr. J. C. Armytage. In the possession of the Publishers. p. 358.

Venetian Painters. Paris Bordone, *The Fisherman of St Mark*; engr. C. Geyer. p. 362.

R. Herdman, RSA, *A Fern Gatherer*; engr. E. Burton. p. 376.

The Art Journal, 1874

A. Anker, *The Toy Rattle*; engr. A. and E. Varin. p. 8.

E. J. Poynter, ARA, *Feeding the Sacred Ibis in the Halls of Karnac*; engr. F. Joubert. From the Collection of Thomas Wardell Esq., Rathgar, Dublin. p. 26.

G. F. Watts, RA, *The Poet Laureate*; engr. J. Stephenson. p. 27.

H. Le Jeune, ARA, *Spring Flowers*; engr. E. Mohn. From the Collection of Theophilus Burnard Esq., Lowndes Square. p. 40.

T. Lobrichon, *Bubbles*; engr. A. and E. Varin. p. 54.

J. L. Gérôme, *Death of Caesar*; engr. J. C. Armytage. p. 68.

Titian, *Assumption of the Virgin*; engr. E. Schuler. p. 76.

L. Alma-Tadema, *Pastime in Ancient Egypt*; engr. C. W. Sharpe. In the possession of the Publishers. p. 100.

A. Anker, *The Reading Lesson*; engr. A. and E. Varin. p.108.

J. Pettie, RA, *The Rival Roses*; engr. F. A. Heath. p. 132.

A. Anker, *The Little Architect*; engr. A. and E. Varin. p. 148.

A. Yvon, *A Russian Peasant's Home*; engr. R. C. Bell. In the possession of the Publishers. p. 168.

Venetian Painters. Veronese, *Marriage of St Catherine*; engr. J. L. Raab. p. 184.

W. Mulready, RA, *The Seven Ages of Man*; engr. H. Bourne. From the picture in the Sheepshank Collection. p. 204.

J. S. Raven, *Twilight in the Woods*; engr. C. Cousen. From the Collection of J. H. Trist Esq., Brighton. p. 212.

G. J. Vibert, *The Tithe Collectors Return*; engr. S. Cucinotta. p. 232.

Marcus Stone, *Lear and Cordelia*; engr. W. Ridgway. In the possession of the Publishers. p. 244.

J. C. Thom, *The Grandfather's Grave*; engr. P. Lightfoot. In the possession of the Publishers. p. 248.

G. H. Boughton, *Queen Isabella and Her Ladies*; engr. T. Sherratt. In the possession of the Publishers. p. 268.

Venetian Painters. Padovanino, *The Musicians – Marriage at Cana*; engr. J. L. Raab. p. 293.

W. Hunt, *The Attack*; engr. F. Heath. From the Collection of William Barfoot Esq., Leicestershire. p. 296.

R. W. Buss, *The Ghost Story*; engr. R. Graves. p. 300.

Gustave Jundt, *Reed Gathering*; engr. J. F. Bracquemond. p. 308.

Sir E. Landseer, RA, *Waiting*; engr. J. C. Webb. p. 324.

P. F. Poole, RA, *Rest by the Way*; engr. C. Cousen. From the Collection of David Price Esq., Queen Anne Street, London. p. 328.

E. Hédouin, *An Arab Café at Constantine*; engr. C. Courtry. p. 348.

T. Graham, *Imogen in the Cave*; engr. D. J. Devachez. In the possession of the Publishers. p. 356.

Venetian Painters. Bassano, *Pastoral with Animals*; engr. F. Sonnenleiter. p. 368.

APPENDIX D

Visits to Private Galleries of the British School

The Art Journal, 1857

The Collection of Joseph Arden Esq., Cavendish Square, pp. 309, 385.

The Collection of William Bashel Esq. of Farington, Lancashire, p. 206.

The Collection of Elkanah Bicknell Esq. at Herne Hill, p. 8.

The Collection of Henry Cooke Esq. of Manchester, p. 42.

The Collection of Chas. Fredk. Huth Esq., Upper Harley Street, p. 90.

The Collection of J. H. Mann Esq. of Old Chapel House, Kentish Town, p. 283.

The Collection of Thomas Miller Esq. of Preston, p. 41.

The Collection of Hugh Munro Esq., Hamilton Place, Piccadilly, p. 133.

The Art Journal, 1858

The Collection of W. A. Joyce Esq, Tulse Hill; selected by Mr Bates, the landscape and marine painter, p. 13.

Visits to Private Galleries of Modern Art

The pictures of John Chapman Esq. of Hill-end, near Mottram, Cheshire, p. 39.

Visits to Private Galleries of the British School

The pictures of Richard Newsham Esq. of Preston, p. 322.

Visits to Private Galleries

The Art Journal, 1870

The Collection of Arthur C. Burnand Esq., Hyde Park Gate, p. 366.
The Collection of W. Cottrill Esq., Singleton House, Higher Broughton, Manchester, p. 68
The collection of Frederick Craven Esq., Hope Lodge, Manchester, p. 16; Addenda, p. 41.
The Collection of Charles Kurtz Esq., Springwell House, Orwell, Liverpool, p. 355.
The Collection of Henry McConnel Esq., Crewsbrook, Derbyshire, p. 286.
The Gallery of S. Mendel Esq., Manley Hall, Manchester, pp. 106, 153.

The Art Journal, 1871

The Collection of W. M. Quilter Esq., Lower Norwood, p. 110.
The Collection of C. H. Rickards Esq., The Beeches, Old Trafford, Manchester, p. 256.
The Collection of H. J. Turner Esq., Hamilton Terrace, St John's Wood, p. 18.

The Art Journal, 1872

The Collection of Henry Bicknell Esq., Cavendish House, Clapham Common, p. 90.
The Collection of Frederick William Cosens Esq., 27 Queens Gate, p. 224.
The Collection of George Fox Esq., Harefield, Alderley, p. 117.
The Collection of John Pender, Esq., MP, Arlington Street, p. 8.
The Collection of David Price Esq., 4 Queen Anne Atreet, p. 281.
The Collection of D. Roberts Esq., Old Kent Road, p. 53.

The Art Journal, 1873

Visits to Private Galleries (p. 319): A number of these visits were published in earlier issues of the *Art Journal*, but 'recently we have been compelled to let the series "stand over", a result of the absorption of space by the several International Exhibitions. We gave but two last year, and none this; we shall, however, resume.'
[No visits are recorded in 1874, and none appears before Hall retired.]

Select Bibliography

UNPUBLISHED SOURCES

Boston Public Library, English Literary Manuscripts, Hall, Anna Maria Fielding. MSI L1.

Cork Central Library, Thomas Crofton Croker Correspondence, vols. I & II.

Hertfordshire County Archives, Catalogue C 2/45 Index 1, Edward Bulwer Lytton General Letters Received.

University of Iowa Libraries, S. C. Hall Letters MSL H 179be, A. M. Hall Letters MSL H 174be.

National Library of Scotland, Catalogue of Manuscripts acquired since 1925 (vol. I), S. C. Hall Correspondence.

The Royal Academy Library, London, Daniel Maclise Autobiography.

Ulster Museum, Belfast, J. R. Herbert Letters.

Wolverhampton Public Library, S. C. Hall Correspondence, 1873. No MSS numbers.

PRINTED SOURCES

The Art Union/The Art Journal during Hall's editorship 1839–81 have been a most important source for my research, and nearly every issue during the period has something of relevance to offer.

Bagehot, Walter, *Literary Studies*, London, 1879.

Barrell, John, *Dark Side of Landscape*, Cambridge, 1980.

Bates, William, *George Cruikshank*, Birmingham, 1878.

Bryon, Michael, *Dictionary of Painters and Engravers*, ed. Robert Edmund Graves, London, 1886.

Bulwer, Edward George Earle Lytton, *On Art in Literature*, London, 1838.

Burke, Edmund, *Enquiries into the Origin of Our Ideas of the Sublime and the Beautiful*, London, 1775.

Carr, J. W. Comyns, *Some Eminent Victorians*, London, 1908.

Colvin, Sidney, 'Art and Criticism', *Fortnightly Review*, August 1879.

Croker, Thomas Crofton, *Fairy Legends and Traditions of the South of Ireland*, London, 1825 & 1826; with plates, 1828.

Dickens, Charles, *Letters*, ed. Madeline House and Graham Storey (Pilgrim Edition), Clarendon Press, Oxford, 1965–88.

——, *Martin Chuzzlewit*, with illustrations by Phiz, London, 1844.

Eagles, John, 'The Fine Arts and the Public Taste', *Blackwood's Edinburgh Magazine*, July 1853.

Edgeworth, Maria, *Popular Tales*, London, 1804.

Foster, R. F., *Modern Ireland 1600–1972*, London, 1988, parts II & III.

Goss, William, *Life and Death of Llewellynn Jewitt with Fragmentary Memoirs of His Friends especially of S. C. Hall*, 1887.

Hall, Samuel Carter, *The Acquittal of the Seven Bishops... Designed to Illustrate and Explain the Picture Commemorating the Event...Painted by J. R. Herbert*, London and Manchester, 1846.

——, *The Baronial Halls and Picturesque Edifices of England*, London, 1848.

—— (ed.), *The Book of British Ballads*, London, 1842, 1853, 1879 & 1881.

——, *The Book of Gems: The Poets and Artists of Great Britain*, London, 1836.

——, *A Book of Memories of Great Men and Women of the Age*, London, 1871 & 1877.

—— (ed.), *The Gallery of Modern Sculpture*, London, 1849–54.

——, *A Letter to Irish Temperance Societies*, London, 1843.

——, *A Memory of Thomas Moore*, London, 1879.

——, *An Old Story. A Temperance Tale in Verse*, London, 1875.

——, *Retrospect of a Long Life, 1815–1883*, London, 1883.

—— (ed.), *The Royal Gallery of Art Ancient and Modern*, 4 vols., London, 1858–59.

——, *Selected Pictures from Galleries and Private Collections of England*, 4 vols., London, 1862.

——, *The Stately Homes of England*, London, 1874.

——, *The Talents, A Dramatic Sketch*, Cork, 1820.

——, *The Trial of Sir Jasper, A Temperance Tale in Verse*, London, 1875.

——, *The Use of Spiritualism?*, Glasgow, 1876, and London, 1884.

—— (ed.), *The Vernon Gallery of British Art; a descriptive catalogue with plates*, 3 vols., London, 1854.

——, and Hall, Anna Maria, *The Book of the Thames*, 1859 & 1877.

——, ——, *Handbooks for Ireland*, 4 vols., London, 1853.

——, ——, *Ireland: Its Scenery, Character, etc.*, 3 vols., London, 1841–43; Berlin, 1850.

——, ——, *A Week in Killarney*, 1843, 1850, 1858 & 1865.

——, ——, *A Companion to Killarney*, London, 1878.

Hall, Anna Maria, *Boons and Blessings*, London, 1875.

——, *The Buccaneer*, London, 1831, 1832 & 1847.

——, *Chertsey and Its Neighbourhood*, London 1853 & 1858.
——, *The Governess; A Tale*, London, 1858.
——, *The Groves of Blarney*, London, ?1836; 3 vols., London, 1838.
——, *Lights and Shadows of Irish Life*, 3 vols., London, 1838.
——, *Midsummer Eve*, London, 1848 & 1870.
——, *Pilgrimages to English Shrines*, 1850; 2nd series, 1853.
——, *Popular Tales and Sketches*, London, 1856.
——, *Sketches of Irish Character*, London, 1829, 1831, 1841 & 1855.
——, *Stories of Irish Peasantry*, Chambers's Instructive and Entertaining Library, 1848.
——, *Tales of Women's Trials*, London, 1835 & 1847.
——, *The Whiteboy: A Story of Ireland in 1822*, London, 1845.
Hamerton, P. G., 'Art and Criticism', *Cornhill Magazine*, 1863.
Hawthorne, Nathaniel, *The English Notebooks*, ed. Randall Stewart, New York & London, 1941.
Kenealy, E. V., with D. Moir, 'A Memoir of William Maginn', *Dublin University Magazine*, January 1844.
Kibble, Thomas, *Illustrations of Modern Sculpture*, London, 1834.
Lewis, Samuel, *Topographical Dictionary of Ireland*, London, 1839.
Maginn, William, *Miscellaneous Writings of the Late Dr William Maginn*, ed. Dr Shelton Mackenzie, New York, 1855–57.
——, 'Epistles to the Literati', *Fraser's Magazine for Town and Country*, December 1831.
Mathew, Father, 'Portrait Gallery no. LIX', *Dublin University Magazine*, June 1849.
Merrill, Linda, *A Pot of Paint: Aesthetics on Trial in Whistler v. Ruskin*, The Smithsonian Institution, Washington, 1992.
Moore, Thomas, *Diary*, ed. J. B. Priestley, Cambridge, 1925.
——, *The Poetical Works*, Centenary Edition with Memoir and Notes by C. Kent, London, 1879.
——, *Travels of an Irish Gentleman in Search of a Religion*, London, 1833 & 1853.
——, *Letters between Thomas Moore and His Music Publisher, James Power, with an Introductory Letter by Thomas Crofton Croker*, New York, 1854.
——, *Memoirs, Journals and Correspondence*, ed. Lord John Russell, 8 vols., London, 1853–56.
Morgan, Sydney (Lady, née Owenson), *Memoirs*, ed. W. Hepworth Dixon, London, 1862. (*See also* Owenson.)
Nash, Joseph, *Mansions of England in the Olden Times*, London, 1839, 1840, 1841 & 1849.
Oliphant, Margaret, *Biography and Letters*, ed. Mrs H. Coghill, Edinburgh and London, 1899.

Olmstead, J. C., *Victorian Painting, Essays and Reviews*, Garland Publishing, New York and London, 1983.

O'Neill, John, *The Drunkard*, London, 1840; 2nd ed. illustrated by George Cruikshank, London, 1842.

——, *Handerahan the Fairy Man and Legends of Carrick with an Introduction by Mrs S. C. Hall*, London, 1854.

Osborne, Charles, 'Mr. Pecksniff and His Prototype', *The Independent Review*, London, September 1906.

Owenson, Sydney, *The Wild Irish Girl*, London, 1806. (*See also* Morgan.)

Prettejohn, Elizabeth, 'Morality versus Aesthetics in Critical Interpretations of Frederic Leighton', *Burlington Magazine*, February 1996.

Price, Sir Uvedale, *An Essay on the Picturesque as Compared with the Sublime and the Beautiful*, London and Hereford, 1796.

——, *A Dialogue on the Distinct Character of the Picturesque and the Beautiful*, Hereford, 1801.

Ritchie, Anne (Lady), *An Introduction to* Ormond *by Maria Edgeworth* [1817], London, 1895.

Royal Literary Fund Archives Catalogue of Sponsors, World Microfilm Publications, British Museum.

Ruskin, John, *Modern Painters*, 5 vols., London, 1843–60.

——, *Notes on Some of the Principal Pictures Exhibited in the Rooms of the Royal Academy*, London, 1855, 1856, 1857, 1858, 1859, & 1875.

——, *A Joy for Ever*, London, 1880.

Stephens, F. G., 'Series on the Private Collections of England', *The Athenaeum*, 1873–84.

Steven, Leslie, 'Art and Morality', *Cornhill Magazine*, 1875.

Strickland, W. G., *Dictionary of Irish Artists*, 2 vols., Dublin, 1913.

Thackeray, William Makepeace, *The Irish Sketch Book of 1842*, London, 1875.

Tyrwhitt, Revd R. St John, 'Skilled and Literary Art Criticism', *The Contemporary Review*, May 1869.

Vernon, Robert, *Robert Vernon's Gift; British Art for the Nation 1847*, Tate Gallery Catalogue, London, 1993.

Vizetelly, Henry, *Glances Back Through Seventy Years*, London, 1893.

Waagen, Dr G. F., *Treasures of Art in Great Britain*, 4 vols., London, 1854–57.

Whistler, J. McNeill, *Whistler v. Ruskin: Art and Art Critics*, London, 1878.

Wood, Christopher, *The Dictionary of Victorian Painters*, London, 1971.

Index